JOAN OF ARC

JOAN OF ARC

MAID, MYTH AND HISTORY

TIMOTHY WILSON-SMITH

SUTTON PUBLISHING

First published in the United Kingdom in 2006 by
Sutton Publishing Limited · Phoenix Mill
Thrupp · Stroud · Gloucestershire · GL5 2BU

British Library Cataloguing in Publication Data
A catalogue record for this book is available from the British Library.

ISBN 0-7509-4341-6

Typeset in 11/14.5pt Sabon.
Typesetting and origination by
Sutton Publishing Limited.
Printed and bound in England by
J.H. Haynes & Co. Ltd, Sparkford.

Contents

Illustrations

(Between pages 110 and 111)

A clock tower at Chinon Castle, now a small museum dedicated to
  Joan of Arc
Portrait of Charles VII by Jean Fouquet
An early French medal struck to commemorate Charles's victory
  over the English
A fifteenth-century illumination from the *Chronique de Charles VII*,
  illustrating the battle of Patay
Joan of Arc on horseback removing prostitutes from camp
Here Joan is compared to Judith, who vanquished Holofernes
Joan portrayed, inaccurately, with long hair
Joan in prison, with Cardinal Beaufort, by Paul Delaroche
Jean-Auguste-Dominique Ingres shows Joan at the coronation of
  Charles VII
An 1874 sculpture of Joan by Emmanuel Fremiet
A magnificent Joan on horseback in an 1893 action statue by Jules-
  Pierre Rouleau
A procession to celebrate the canonisation of St Joan
Maria Falconetti, who played Joan in a silent film of 1928
Flags in honour of France's patron saint flutter over the rue Jeanne
  d'Arc in Orléans
The bronze copy of Marie d'Orléans' charming statue of Joan, also
  in Orléans

Preface

In 1428 a young girl, almost a woman, in a remote part of eastern France, believes that she is called by God, His angels and saints to revive the cause of the true King of France. She convinces the king and his theologians that she should be given a chance to prove her worth. She gives hope to dispirited soldiers, leads them to relieve a key city and recapture several fortified towns, then takes the king across enemy country to be crowned. She tries to take his capital city, fails and is sent away to campaign in an area of the country that is strategically unimportant. Without authorisation she rushes to defend a city her master had promised to give up, is captured and imprisoned. Wounded trying to jump from a castle, she is sold to the highest bidder, who is determined that she must die after a trial that will be technically independent of secular authority. On trial she shows a degree of composure that amazes some of her learned judges, but then she falters, admits she was deceived, abjures her abjuration, is condemned to death and is burnt as a sorceress and heretic – yet her last act is to call on the name of Jesus.

Joan of Arc, the girl-woman of this story, was so unusual a person that she has been the subject of many biographies, the protagonist of many plays and films, the theme of many statues and paintings. Of those who took part in what is called the Hundred Years War she has proved to be by far the most fascinating participant. Joan comes into history for a brief moment, was the centre of attention for a few months, and then disappears. She had a remarkable effect on those who fought with her before she was taken into captivity and ultimately killed, but the manner of her death, as a sorceress and heretic, must have left those who believed in her disillusioned and confirmed the suspicions of the doubters. She had been a comet in the sky, exciting to observe, quick to evaporate.

In the fifteenth century the Church knew what it considered to be a saint. There was a long tradition of writing hagiography and yet nobody wrote about Joan in a way that conformed to the stereotypes. There was a time when priests had told the story of holy men and sometimes of holy women in predictable ways. Signs alerted a pious mother to the imminent birth of a remarkable child. In childhood a boy was self-sacrificing and wise, he learnt to read early and preferred reading lives of the saints to tales of romance, he looked for an austere order to join, he prayed for long hours, fasted often, was outstandingly submissive until raised to the role as abbot for which his gifts suited him. A fearless critic of powerful men, his eloquent preaching converted the weak and captivated the strong, he encouraged knights to go crusading, kings to rule justly, rich merchants to share their wealth, theologians to abandon their comfortable lives in a cathedral close, to meditate on his sermons in a secluded cell. Such a man was Bernard, Abbot of Clairvaux. An alternative scenario was that of the repentant sinner. Francesco Bernardone found the world attractive and was attractive to the world, a charmer whom it was easy to spoil. His renunciation was correspondingly drastic. He wanted not just to be poor but to have nothing; instead of the beautiful clothes his father had given him he wanted to be naked and to find beauty only in the natural world. He welcomed repulsive lepers and at the end of his life was the first man said to experience the stigmata, the five wounds of Christ, on his hands and feet and at his side. Nobody who wrote about St Bernard or St Francis had any difficulty in accepting that the men were saints. In each case their lives were marvellous in a remarkable and convincing way; at some stage such a saint performed miracles that demonstrated his sanctity to the sceptics – and so they did. Within a few years of their edifying deaths each had a feast day in the Church's calendar. None doubted their status.

Joan of Arc fits into neither category, and not just because she failed to perform any miracles. She showed some ability to predict events and to know what had happened without having had any obvious means to know it, but there were few such instances. Most of the evidence of her religious character comes from trials whose verdicts were contradictory – one in 1431 that led to her conviction, others in 1452–6 that led to that conviction being declared unsafe. It took almost five hundred years after an English soldier had declared 'we have burnt a saint' for the Catholic Church to conclude that she was indeed a saint.

This book is not merely an account of a life that was cut short in 1431. Its focus is also on Joan's history, which in 1431 had just begun. That history ranges over many centuries and involves the work of writers, artists and *cinéastes* as well as of cautious scholars, Church or canon lawyers, theologians and the simply devout. It is a history that has involved passionate controversy, that has been disfigured by distortion and prejudice, but that has also been illuminated by honest attempts to understand a young woman, still a teenager, who came from an unimportant area of Europe to transform the military and political situation of a great country. The manner of her imprisonment, trial and execution dealt a blow to the high reputation of the inquisitions as an instrument of justice; it gave the French additional reasons to quarrel among themselves and to unite in their opposition to the English. Her rehabilitation produced new views on the relationship between the private revelations of individual Christians and the public revelation of Christ's Church. Her claims for her voices still fascinate students of human psychology, but then her martial skills also distinguish her from all other women of her times. Most of those who wrote about her in the fifteenth century knew her only for a brief period or not at all, but her words at her hostile trial and the memory of her preserved by her friends give her an immediacy found in few figures from the distant past. With every year, as more and more research is under-taken, she becomes easier to know now than when she was alive; and it is this quality in her that justifies the writing of a book that sets out to explore the ways in which she matters as a person, as a cultural, a national and a spiritual phenomenon. The last time an English author made such an attempt was more than twenty years ago. Marina Warner, a formidably erudite feminist, categorises the various ways in which Joan has been understood and for those attracted to conceptual analysis her book must remain essential reading. This book has a different aim: to tell a saga that has taken almost six hundred years to unfold and is still unfolding. It is the latest in a series of attempts by an English Francophile to comprehend Anglo-French relations. It is also an attempt by a Catholic writer to come to terms with the grim fact that a political trial masqueraded as a religious one and with the encouraging fact that Joan's unjust trial and condemnation soon forced Catholic theologians to rethink the value of private religious experience. Even in the early twentieth century those who thought she might be a saint were worried by her independence of mind: she was not one of them, for she was ill educated and she was not a nun. Above all, this book aims to explain how an extraordinary woman with flaws may be a saint or a heroine, yet accessible to all.

Acknowledgements

Research for this book was facilitated by the use of libraries at Eton College and above all by the resources of Cambridge University Library. That research has involved reading texts in English, French and Latin, but not alas in German. Anyone hoping for an adequate literary discussion of the styles of Schiller and Brecht must look elsewhere, as too must anyone in search of a subtle analysis of the relevance of Joan of Arc to Franco-German tensions over Alsace-Lorraine after France's defeat in the Franco-Prussian War.

Like all English writers on French history, I have pursued an inconsistent policy in the forms I have given to French names. Names of prominent people, such as kings, dukes and counts, are usually anglicised; it would be pedantic to say 'Bourgogne' instead of Burgundy, but in an age when Reims is familiar as a centre of the manufacture of champagne rather than as home to a certain jackdaw, I have spelt the city without an 'h'. In a household where Franglais is common, I have kept the acute accent in Orléans, but not in Domremy (as in the latter the word was originally spelt without one). In some cases it seems natural to write 'Jean', in others 'John', and my protagonist is not Jehanne, nor Jeanne, but Joan – I am sure somebody will disagree with me.

It is a pleasure to recall the genesis of a book. Thanks to my late parents a family holiday in 1957 ended with a meal in the Vieux-Marché in Rouen, the square where Joan was burnt to death; and I found and still have a picture book, *Dans les pas de Jeanne d'Arc*, by the late Régine Pernoud, later doyenne of Johannic studies. Forty years on I began to revisit Rouen in my imagination. A generous grant by the Authors' Foundation, through the good offices of the Society of Authors, has helped me to trace some of Joan's footsteps as Régine Pernoud recommended. I thank Ben Glazebrook and Christopher Foley of Lane Fine Art for their helpfulness respectively at the beginning and the end of this project. One or two key pieces of information I owe to the tireless Virginia Frohlick. In technical matters concerning Joan's various 'trials' I have relied on articles by Emeritus Professor Andy Kelly of the University of California, and little of this book could have been written without the labours of many other distinguished scholars. Among these people I must single out people at the Centre Jeanne d'Arc in Orléans both for help in the centre and for help received by e-mail. My special contribution has been my references to the ideas of certain Catholic philosophers and theologians, especially when their works have not been translated into English. For technical expertise in the art of computing I have relied on Nick Kulkarni of Home & Business Computing and I owe a continuing debt to the perceptiveness and encouragement of Laura Longrigg, my agent, and to the incisive comments of Jaqueline Mitchell, my editor at Sutton Publishing, and Anne Bennett. I thank Bow Watkinson, too, who has drawn the maps. Navigating in the unfamiliar world of picture research has been much facilitated by Jane Entrican at Sutton and several friendly voices at various picture libraries. All mistakes, naturally, are my own.

Looking through my late mother-in-law's possessions after her death, I discovered pages of a liturgy of Joan of Arc that must date from the early 1920s. To my late mother-in-law, Odette Starrett, and my wife Pam a mere Englishman owes insights into France and Anglo-French relations he would not otherwise have. I dedicate this book to them both.

Timothy Wilson-Smith

Chronology

1415   Henry V wins battle of Agincourt and captures Charles,
          Duke of Orléans
1417–19   Henry V conquers Normandy
1420   Treaty of Troyes: the Dauphin Charles disinherited in
          favour of Henry V (soon married to Charles's sister
          Catherine) and of Henry's heirs
1422   Deaths of Henry V and Charles VI: Henry VI, as King of
          England, and Henry II, as King of France, succeeds his
          father and grandfather
1428   Joan of Arc's first journey to Vaucouleurs; the Earl of
          Salisbury in command at Orléans

1429–31: THE PUBLIC CAREER OF JOAN OF ARC
1429   Joan returns to Vaucouleurs
          6 February: Joan visits Nancy and meets Charles II of
          Lorraine
          12 February: battle of Rouvray ('Battle of the Herrings')
          23 February: Joan leaves for Chinon
          4–5 March: Joan at Ste-Catherine-de-Fierbois
          6 March: Joan arrives at Chinon
          c. 9 March: Joan meets Charles VII
          21 March: Joan in Poitiers
          29 April: Joan enters Orléans
          4 May: Bastard of Orléans returns to Orléans; fall of St-Loup
          6 May: the French capture Les Augustins
          7 May: the French capture Les Tourelles
          8 May: the English fall back on Meung
          11–12 June: the French capture Jargeau
          15 June: Joan at Meung-sur-Loire
          16–17 June: the French capture Beaugency
          18 June: battle of Patay
          30 June: Joan travels towards Reims
          Early July: Joan near Auxerre
          5–11 July: Joan near Troyes
          17 July: coronation of Charles VII at Reims
          8 September: Joan leads attack on Paris
          10–13 September: Joan at St-Denis
          October and early November: Joan at St-Pierre-le-Moûtier
          24 November: Joan leads attack on La Charité-sur-Loire

29 *December:* Joan and her family are ennobled

1430   23 *May:* Joan is captured at Compiègne

Late *May–July:* Joan held prisoner at Beaulieu

Mid-July–mid-November: Joan at Beaurevoir

1431   3 *January:* Joan transferred to the custody of Bishop Cauchon

9 *January:* beginning of the first trial

21 *February:* first public session of the trial

10–17 *March:* closed sessions of the trial

18 *April:* Joan admonished to recant

19 *May:* reading of the condemnation of the University of Paris

30 *May:* Joan executed

AFTER 1431: THE CAUSE OF JOAN OF ARC

1435   Treaty of Arras between Charles VII and Philip, Duke of Burgundy

1436   Paris surrenders to the French

1440   Release of Charles, Duke of Orléans, from prison in England

1449   French invasion of Normandy; capture of Rouen

1450   Charles VII authorises investigation into trial of Joan of Arc

1452   Pope Nicholas V authorises Joan of Arc's retrial process; Cardinal d'Estouteville and the Inquisitor Jean Bréhal preside

1453   English finally driven out of Guyenne

1455   Pope Calixtus III authorises Joan's mother, Isabelle, to appeal; 7 *November:* opening session of the retrial held at Notre-Dame, Paris

1456   7 *July:* public announcement of the judgment of the court: the original verdict is nullified

1589   End of the Valois line: Henry IV becomes first Bourbon King of France by reason of the Salic Law of inheritance

1789   Outbreak of the French Revolution

1793   Suspension of the feast of Joan of Arc in Orléans

1801   Napoleon concludes the Concordat with Pope Pius VII

1803   Napoleon allows revival of festival of Joan in Orléans

1804   Napoleon crowned Emperor of the French in Notre-Dame

1825   Charles X consecrated and crowned at Reims: the last king of France to be so

1869   Dupanloup, Bishop of Orléans, begins process of canonising Joan

1870–1	Franco-Prussian War leads to loss of part of Lorraine and creation of the Third Republic
1878–1903	Papacy of Leo XII
1894	Joan declared Venerable; Alfred Dreyfus court-martialled for forgery
1898	Founding of Action Française
1903	Formal proposal for canonisation of Joan
1909	*11 April:* Joan beatified by Pius X (Pope 1903–14)
1920	*16 May:* Joan canonised by Pope Benedict XV; Joan given a national feast day
1922–39	Papacy of Pius XI
1926	Action Française placed on the Index
1931	*30 May:* five hundredth anniversary of the death of Joan
1939	Pius XII (1939–58) lifts ban on Action Française
1940–4	Vichy France and Free French dispute devotion to Joan
1945	*6 February:* execution of Robert Brasillach
	8 May: Feast of St Joan of Arc; VE Day
1959	As First President of the Fifth Republic, de Gaulle presides over the ceremonies at Orléans
1974	The Centre Jeanne d'Arc in Orléans founded by Régine Pernoud, with the encouragement of de Gaulle's former minister of culture, André Malraux
1980	*1 May:* the first meeting of the Front National to celebrate its feast of St Joan
1989	In the bicentenary year of the French Revolution, President Mitterrand presides over the ceremonies at Orléans for the second time.

Prologue: *the Limits of History*

In the Middle Ages the principal sources of abnormal psychology are found in the archives of the Catholic Church. The Church maintained that in and through Christ it revealed God to man, but the Church was also a human institution, with all the faults that institutions have, and above all a concern with self-preservation and self-aggrandisement. Its rulers were ordained clerics, who by accidents of history were at one stage almost the only educated people in Western Europe, conscious that few kings, dukes and counts could read any language, let alone the Latin in which the clergy thought, wrote and prayed. Literacy spread slowly, but as it did so a spirit of criticism and independent thought evolved. There also emerged professional lay lawyers, lay merchants and eventually a large element of the lay upper class, all of whom felt that their voices should be heard. But most of the population, even in northern Italy or the Netherlands, homes to many prosperous towns, were peasants whose only education came from local folk customs and Latin prayers learnt by rote and whose acquaintance with the world hardly reached beyond the next village. A sophisticated celibate male cleric found such people virtually incomprehensible, especially if the person were a woman and one who claimed to have had unusual religious experiences beyond their ken.

Joan first heard a voice, she said, while aged thirteen as she was running with her friends in the fields near her home in Domremy. In the next few years she came to hear voices several times a day and slowly she came to identify them. One was St Margaret of Antioch and one St Catherine of Alexandria, both revered as virgin martyrs, and the third St Michael, archangel patron of France, whose famous shrine *au péril de la mer*, better known now as Mont-St-Michel, lay off the country's northern coast.

A few details of her early days give Joan's life a context. She was born in a sizeable farmhouse, which still stands, in Domremy on the River Meuse. Domremy was situated in the marches or border lands of Lorraine; and Joan had from childhood a sense of identity that, paradoxically, comes naturally to someone born at the point of intersection between various worlds. Geographically, linguistically and politically, she lived her childhood on the edge.

North-eastern France, a land of undulating plains, is criss-crossed by rivers. To the west of Domremy the Marne moves northwards through champagne country just south of Reims, where French kings were crowned, before turning east to join the Seine near Paris. East of Domremy the Moselle snakes its way along another valley of vineyards, past Nancy, capital of the duchy of Lorraine, into Germany, where it becomes the Mosel. The Meuse, the river of Domremy, also flows through rich agricultural land, past a fortress, at Verdun, into the lands of the powerful bishopric of Liège before it turns into the Maas and, like the Mosel, empties into the Rhine.

Domremy lies near one of the great linguistic divides in Europe. To the north of Domremy people spoke low German, Flemish or Dutch or Frisian; to the east people spoke high German, what we call German and the Germans *hoch Deutsch*. Even if the dialect Joan spoke was regarded as a peasant patois, without the cultural prestige of what Chaucer, with his Anglo-Norman, called 'Frenssh of Paris', she was clear that her own tongue was French. And she was conscious that most French speakers lived west of Domremy.

Joan was acutely aware that she lived on the edge of various political systems. Domremy was close to Champagne, just in Lorraine, but most of Lorraine was outside France. Its duke was a subject of the Holy Roman Emperor, who was also King of Germany and King of Bohemia; and yet, though the Duke of Lorraine was, through the Duke of Bar, the overlord of most of Domremy, Joan knew that the overlord of her part of the village was the King of France. Much more powerful locally was the Duke of Burgundy, a French royal prince soon to be allied to the King of England. Just south of Lorraine, the duchy of Burgundy lay in eastern France, but the adjoining county of Burgundy (Franche-Comté) lay in the empire. A series of family alliances gradually gave the duke control of three wealthy provinces of the lands between France and Germany: of Flanders, where French was spoken in Lille and Flemish in Ghent (or Gand) and Brugge (or Bruges); of Brabant; and of Holland. Merchants had every reason to be grateful for the power of their duke, which opened to them the trade routes of northern Europe. Joan, who was not from that class, hated being thought a Burgundian. She knew the neighbouring village of Maxey was 'Burgundian'; and the paths along which she rode were cleared by the success of Vaucouleurs's castellan in keeping his fort, a little to the north of Maxey, loyal to France. And yet, if Joan was sure she was 'French' too, when she travelled west to see her king, she said she was going into 'France'. It was the very confusion of her environment that accounts for her distinct political loyalties.

Joan was a peasant. Her parents were Jacques or Jacquot d'Arc and Isabelle Romée, and she had three brothers and a sister: the eldest, Jacquemin, who went away from home while she was a child; next Catherine, who married and died young; and lastly Jean and Pierre. She was never Joan 'of Arc', since in her part of the country children took their mothers' names. She was born in January 1412 or 1413 and baptised by master Jean Minet. She had many godparents and could identify five of them. Her childhood was unremarkable. From her mother she learnt simple prayers, the 'Our Father', the 'Hail Mary' and the Apostles' Creed. She helped in the fields, she was useful around the house. She experienced the results of taking sides in political matters when the boys of Maxey and Domremy indulged in a brawl, in which the Domremy boys got the worse bruises.

When questioning her about life in Domremy, her judges tried to find out whether she had taken part in superstitious rituals connected with a tree associated with fairies. She admitted that she had danced round the tree but supposedly superstitious practices bored her and she did not conceal her lack of interest. If she was unusual, she was unusually pious, but religious needs could have been satisfied, as her mother's were, by going on pilgrimages to famous shrines. Her mother had gone to Le Puy-en-Velay, perched high on a rock, from which pilgrims set out en route to Santiago de Compostela or to Rome; and perhaps the surname Romée referred to a journey to Rome made either by her mother or by some maternal ancestor. In the last years of her short life Joan travelled far, but she might have gone nowhere but for her voices. Her voices changed her life for ever.

The account of them must be taken from a transcript of her trial in Rouen, by which time it was well known that she claimed to be directed by 'voices'. Whatever she had told those sympathetic to her before, the most complete record is the one drawn out of her by hostile interrogators trying her for heresy. The inner thoughts of this illiterate peasant girl are known largely by means of the constructions put on her words by lawyers. At Rouen, lawyers of the inquisition gave one version: in pretending to have revelations and apparitions she was 'pernicious, seductive, presumptuous, of light belief, rash, superstitious, a diviner, a blasphemer of God and His saints, a despiser of Him in His sacraments, a prevaricator of the divine teaching . . . therefore of right excommunicate and heretic'.[1] A generation later, lawyers nominated by the king and lawyers nominated by the pope published the conclusions of successive inquiries into her 1431 trial, and after many, many years the Church pronounced its own final sentence: Joan was a saintly virgin. No judgement on her person or her role in history can avoid references to her 'voices'. In all the investigations into her case, however, only at her trial were the judges obsessed with them.

When the Rouen judges asked when she was first aware of them, Joan replied that at the age of thirteen she had a voice from God to help her and guide her. On the first occasion she was very afraid. It was about midday, in summer, in her father's garden and she recalled that she had not fasted the previous day. The voice came from her right side, from the direction of the church; and she seldom heard it without a light. This light came from the same side as the voice, and generally there was a great light. She added that when she had come to 'France', she heard the voice often. The judges were not satisfied. How could she see the light she spoke of, if it was at the side? She did not reply. She said that if she was in a wood she easily heard the voices come to her – changing to the singular, she thought 'it' was a worthy voice, and believed it was sent from God; the third time she heard it, she was certain that it was an angel's voice and that the voice always took good care of her and that she understood it well. What did it tell her to do for her soul's salvation? She replied that it told her to be good and to go to church often; it also told her she ought to go to 'France'. And, she added, this time Beaupère, one of the judges, would not learn from her in what form that voice appeared to her. Once or twice a week it told her to go to France, her father knew nothing about her plans, and she felt unable to stay where she was; and the voice told her too that she would raise the siege of the city of Orléans. It also ordered her to see Robert de Baudricourt, the town's captain, at Vaucouleurs, and assured her that he would provide an escort for her. She was, she told them a little naively, a poor maid, who knew nothing about riding or fighting. She had gone to one of her uncles, stayed with him about eight days, and, when she told him she must go to the town of Vaucouleurs, he had taken her.

They asked her whether the voice that spoke to her was that of an angel, or of a saint, male or female, or straight from God. She answered that 'the' voice was the voice of St Catherine and of St Margaret. Their heads, she explained, were crowned in a rich and precious fashion with beautiful crowns. 'I have God's permission to tell this. If you doubt it, send to Poitiers where I was examined before.' Soon after her arrival at the French court at Chinon, she had been interrogated by churchmen in Poitiers.

She had seen their faces. Asked if the saints who appeared to her had hair, she answered: 'It is well to know that they have.' Was there anything between their crowns and their hair? No. Was their hair long, did it hang down? 'I do not know.' She did not know if they had arms or legs, but they spoke very well and beautifully and she understood them very well. Did they have other limbs? 'I leave that to God.' The voice she heard was gentle, soft and low, and French. Asked if St Margaret spoke in English, she answered: 'Why should she speak English when she is not on the English side?' She did not know if their crowns had rings of gold or any other substance. When asked if she had rings, she was tart: 'You have one of mine; give it back to me.' She said the Burgundians have another ring; and she said that if they had her ring, could they show it to her. It was a ring, she said, given her by her father or her mother; she thought the names Jhesus Maria were written on it; she did not know who had them written; she did not think there was any stone in it; she was given the ring at Domremy. Her brother had given her the other ring they had and she charged them to give it to the Church. She had never cured anyone with any of her rings. She knew well enough they were trying to accuse her of using enchantment. This was obvious from the line of questioning that followed.

Had St Catherine and St Margaret spoken to her under the fairies' tree? She did not know. Had they spoken to her at the fountain by the tree? Yes, but she did not know what they said. Asked what the saints promised her, there or elsewhere, she replied that they made no promises to her, except by God's leave. The questioning was relentless. What had they promised? Had the angel failed her when she was taken (by the English)? Did she summon them? Did St Denis, patron of France come too? No, he did not. Did she speak to Our Lord about keeping her virginity? It was quite enough to speak about that to those he sent, namely St Catherine and St Margaret. Had she spoken to anyone about her visions? Only to Robert de Baudricourt and to her king. How did she greet St Michael and the angels, when she saw them? She reverenced them and kissed the ground where they had stood after they had gone. Did they not call her 'daughter of God, daughter of the Church, daughter great-hearted?' Before the raising of the siege of Orléans, and every day since, when they have spoken to her they have often called her Joan the Maid, daughter of God. In what form had St Michael appeared? She did not see his crown, and knew nothing about his clothes. Was he naked? 'Do you think God has nothing to clothe him with?'

These were not idle questions, for the questioners had to convince themselves. They claimed:

> The said Joan, though from her youth up she has spoken, done, and perpetrated many sins, crimes, errors and faults, that are shameful, cruel, scandalous, dishonourable and unsuitable to her sex, all the same proclaims and asserts that everything she has done is at God's command and in accordance with His will, that she has never done anything that does not come from Him, through the revelations of His holy saints and blessed virgins Catherine and Margaret.

She was irritating, though they did not say so, because she seemed on easy terms with her voices, of whom she begged three things, her own freedom, God's support for the French and her own salvation. She had claimed that St Michael went with her into the castle of Chinon, where she first met her king, yet 'to say this of archangels and of holy angels must be held presumptuous, rash, deceitful; especially seeing that it is not written that any man, however upright, nor even Our Lady, Mother of God, received such reverence or greetings'. Often she said that the Archangel Gabriel, St Michael, and sometimes a million angels came to her. Joan boasted that at her prayer the said angel brought with him, in this company of angels, a most precious crown for her king, to put upon his head, and that it is now put into the king's treasury; with it, according to Joan, the king would have been crowned at Reims had he waited a few days, but because of the speed with which the coronation was carried out he used another crown. These, it was asserted, were less divine revelations than lies invented by Joan, suggested to her or shown to her by the demon in illusions, in order to mock at her imagination while she meddled in things beyond her ability to comprehend.

The sense of the court was clear: Joan was not mad, she was bad.

The clergy of the University of Paris and others have considered the manner and end of these revelations, the content of the things revealed, and the quality of your person and having considered everything relevant they declare that it is all false, seductive, pernicious, that such revelations and apparitions are superstitions and proceed from evil and diabolical spirits. You have declared that you know well that God loves certain living persons better than you, and that you learned this by revelation from St Catherine and St Margaret; also that those saints speak French, not English, as they are not on the side of the English. And since you knew that your voices were for your king, you began to dislike the Burgundians.

This idea, said the clergy (who were either Burgundians or their allies), was 'a foolish, presumptuous assertion, a superstitious guess, a blasphemy against St Catherine and St Margaret, and a failure to observe the commandment to love our neighbours . . . If you [Joan] had the revelations and saw the apparitions of which you boast in such a manner as you say, then you are an idolatress, an invoker of demons, an apostate from the faith, a maker of rash statements, a swearer of an unlawful oath.' Finally, they admonished her:

You have believed these apparitions lightly, instead of turning to God in devout prayer to give you certainty; and you have not consulted prelates or learned clerics to enlighten you [this wounded them deeply] though, because of your status and the simplicity of your knowledge, you should have done so. Take this example: suppose your king had appointed you to defend a fortress, forbidding you to let any one enter. Would you not refuse to admit anyone who claimed to come in his name but brought no letters or authentic sign? So too Our Lord Jesus Christ, when He ascended into Heaven, committed the government of His Church to the apostle St Peter and his successors, forbidding them to receive in future those who claimed to come in His name but brought no other sign than their own words. So you should not have put faith in those which you say came to you, nor ought we to believe in you, as God commands the opposite.

Sadly for her, she did not agree with her accusers.

Her voices made Joan a test case. What her case tested was, first, the discernment of spirits, and, secondly, the nature and the validity of private visions. In fact the two matters were related, for if someone was a saint, his or her visions were probably authentic. Joan's accusers were sure that she was evil, so they knew that when she claimed to be a visionary, she was a liar.

In modern clinical experience, schizophrenics are often deluded and hallucinate: they see, hear, touch, smell people present only in their imaginations. Joan may or may not have hallucinated, but in no other way did she behave like a schizophrenic. The evidence of her behaviour provided by the records of her original trial and the accounts of her given twenty-five years later when that trial's verdict was nullified suggest that she was a young woman who was remarkably sane. She could think clearly, express herself coherently, act decisively.

There is an older view of her, that she may have been an hysteric. Germaine Greer has pointed out in *The Female Eunuch* that hysteria is a condition that had often been regarded as peculiarly feminine; and at a time when the Church was considering Joan's possible canonisation and secular writers like her biographer Anatole France thought that she was deluded, it was natural to wonder if she showed the symptoms of hysteria. Both the clerics and a secular doctor consulted by France agreed, however, she did not.[2]

Another possible explanation is offered by Edward Lucie-Smith, in his scholarly, elegant and modern biography of Joan. He seems to apply a principle derived from a late medieval philosopher – Occam's razor. According to William of Occam, an English philosophical theologian of the early fourteenth century, if a simple explanation for a phenomenon will do, there is no need to look for a more complex one. Lucie-Smith applies this idea by preferring a natural to a supernatural explanation of events: Joan's visions operated, he believes, as a means of helping her to resolve conflicts in her family by leaving home. This is comforting for one who believes in a Freudian view of human life – and Lucie-Smith also talks about her unconscious incestuous desires for her father and younger brother – but it will not do because it misuses Occam's razor. On the existing evidence the visions involved religion, not sex, and there is no reason to say they must have had a sexual meaning, unless, which cannot be proved, all experience is ultimately sexual. Lucie-Smith assumes what he tries to demonstrate.

Medieval theologians were more subtle. They began with the Bible, knowing that the Bible mentions certain rare experiences, such as St Paul's conversion on the way to Damascus, when he was blinded and talked to a voice nobody could see, and his tale of being rapt into the third heaven where he was told mysteries that the soul cannot relate. Various accounts in the gospels of the risen Jesus, whom Paul also 'saw' (but much later) imply that a 'risen' body has properties that before death it does not have: it appears or disappears suddenly, it can be recognised or not be recognised by those who know the person. Belief in the risen Christ was what the Christians preached, and Christians, according to St Paul, look forward to their own resurrection. Along with certain distinctive views, Christians inherited much then current in Jewish thinking. Pharisees too believed in a form of life after death and many Jews believed in the activity of angels. In St Matthew's Gospel angels give Joseph and the wise men good advice in sleep. In St Luke's Gospel the angel Gabriel 'appears' to Mary while she is awake. The early texts puzzled the theologians. They tried to understand how such events could happen. They assumed that visions could occur, they assumed that the dead in heaven could contact the living, they assumed that angels could act in human lives. To deny the possibility of such events would be to deny the faith, but that a particular vision was God-given, that a particular saint in heaven had visited a particular man or woman on earth, that a particular angel had helped a particular man or woman, that was a different matter. Each case should be examined on its merits. If an event is possible but rare, then the sensible habit is a sceptical habit.

The greatest of the Latin church 'fathers' or early theologians, St Augustine, Bishop of Hippo, distinguished certain kinds of vision: they could be corporeal, imaginative or intellectual. The seer can 'see' a person, as Bernadette seemed to see the Virgin Mary, in much the way in which the Apostles 'saw' Jesus after he had risen from the dead. The seer can 'imagine' the presence of a saint; and it may be in this way that Joan 'saw' her voices. Finally, the seer can 'see' a truth. St Thomas Aquinas is said to have stopped composing his summary of theology, or *Summa Theologica*, on 6 December 1273, when after a long ecstasy during Mass he confessed, 'I can do no more. Such secrets have been revealed to me that all I have written now appears to be of little value.' In heaven, mercifully, there will be no theological textbooks; the truth will be apparent.

It does not follow from this that people claiming to have had visions have had them. Claimants may be bogus, may be self-deceiving, even evil; indeed it is reasonable to assume that a vision is incredible if it is not perverse to deny it. The men who judged Joan harshly at Rouen in 1431 were confident that they knew a fraud when they came across one; and such a fraud, they thought, was the young lady in front of them. As lawyers who were also theologically trained, they had learnt to make certain distinctions that Joan, with no equivalent education, would have made with difficulty. They had repeatedly asked her to describe the look of her voices – their faces, hair, limbs, clothes, crowns – and the sound of the voices (low, gentle and French speaking) and their smell (she mentioned their perfume). They also asked whether she saw St Michael with his scales, the way in which he was normally depicted in a scene of the Last Judgement. They were seeking to confirm the shrewd guess that she must have envisaged her voices in ways in which it was easy to imagine them. St Michael, being by definition incorporeal, could not hold an actual pair of scales, but that was a naturally human way to imagine him, for how else could there be religious art?

The judges could have made a point of trying to find out why she was singled out by Sts Margaret of Antioch and Catherine of Alexandria and why among the angels the one who mattered to her was St Michael. Her visions merely transfigured her ordinary experience, for how could a devout girl in Domremy not know of the two female saints and a patriotic girl from Domremy not know of St Michael? The style of the statue of St Margaret still in

Domremy today suggests that it had only recently been placed in the church. Just across the river at Maxey, St Catherine, the patroness of her older sister, was patroness of the village. Both saints were celebrated in the church's martyrology as virgin martyrs, noble young women who had died to remain pure. As such they evidently appealed to a young woman who was sure that she had a similar vocation. Joan had refused to accept her parents' plans that she should marry, and when she had been sued by the disappointed suitor for breach of promise of marriage, she won her case.

Her chief counsellor was St Michael. In the late Old Testament Book of Daniel, St Michael is 'Michael the prince' who will overcome Persian resistance to Israelite longings to leave Babylon and return to the Holy Land. In the New Testament, Michael appears in books that took over the apocalyptic traditions of Daniel. The tiny Book of Jude refers to a fight between Michael the archangel and the devil over the body of Moses; and this fighting role is made universal in the last book of the Bible, where during war in heaven Michael and his angels fight against the dragon and his angels. Early Christian writers developed the hints implicit in these passages, so that St Michael was said to be the unnamed angel who had blocked the route of the prophet Balaam and who had routed the army of Sennacherib, the Assyrian king.

With his scriptural pedigree St Michael naturally became a popular saint in the West, as warlike barbarians were converted to Christianity. When pagan shrines on mountain tops and hill tops, home to devils, were pulled down, they were replaced by shrines dedicated to St Michael – as at Monte Gargano in Apulia, and the Tor at Glastonbury and Mont-St-Michel on the borders of Normandy. It was of St Michael *au péril de la mer* that the dying Roland, count of the Breton marches, thinks in the *Chanson* that bears his name, and in Portugal to commemorate a victory over the Moors, the monastery of Alcobaça was made home of the order of St Michael's Wings. During the Hundred Years War, Mont-St-Michel acquired a special renown in France as a symbol of national resistance, for, though surrounded by the English, the rock had never surrendered; it was fitting that Louis XI, son of Joan's king, should make the island monastery the centre of his new order of chivalry, the order of St Michael. Joan was devoted to an angel who had been a crusader and had also fought for France.

If Sts Margaret and Catherine exemplified heroic virginity, from St Michael she could learn the virtues of a warrior for God. What was startling is what they said: she must go to 'France' to raise the siege of Orléans, to help the Dauphin Charles recover his kingdom, to drive the English from France. To this end she must go to the Dauphin far away in Chinon; and she must dress as a man.

One saint Joan did not mention. As a child her life had revolved round St Rémi, to whom Domremy's parish church was dedicated. In his Latin name of Remigius he was the Bishop of Reims who persuaded Clovis, pagan King of the Franks, to be baptised a Christian, consecrated and crowned as a Christian king. By Joan's day the Franks had gone, as centuries before Francia became France, but the rite of St Remigius was still performed. Joan never spoke of St Rémi, but her voices told her to take Charles to St Rémi's cathedral; her most triumphant moment occurred not on any battle-field or at any siege, but at Reims beside the high altar, beneath the glorious Gothic arches that reach up to the heavens. But first she must be God's special, female knight.

Other country children have shown confidence in voices or visions, but Joan was unlike Bernadette Soubirous or the three children of Fatima, who proclaimed religious doctrines (in the first case) or foretold apocalyptic events (in the second). Her mission, she held, meant changing the map of political France, giving the people back to their king, making the land once more his kingdom. Her thoughts and actions were dominated by a unique brand of religious politics. She lived for this mission and she would die for it.

PART ONE

*The Maid
in Life and Death*

ONE

A Prophetess to the Rescue

England and France had been rivals for many years when, in Holy Week 1429, Joan of Arc wrote to Henry VI, child king of England and France, informing him that she was sent by God to tell him to leave France and return home. The letter was also sent to William de la Pole, Count of Suffolk, Sir John Talbot and Thomas, Lord Scales, lieutenants of the Duke of Bedford, 'who calls himself Regent of the King of France for the King of England' (Bedford, Regent of English France, was Henry's older uncle). Joan also addressed the soldiers besieging Orléans, among whom she singles out the feared English archers.

As an illiterate girl, Joan dictated her letters. How many letters in all were sent cannot be known, but about twenty are referred to in various documents, of which this letter to the English is the first complete letter to survive. It survived because it must have so incensed the recipients that it was kept and cited as evidence against Joan at her trial in Rouen. Her tone is peremptory and arrogant. The King of England must render account to the King of Heaven and return the keys of the cities he has seized. If he does not, as 'commander of the military', she will force his men to flee; and if they do not obey, 'the Maid' (Joan) will have them all killed. She is sent by the King of Heaven 'to take you out of France'. 'The King of Heaven has sent her so much power that you will not be able to harm her or her brave army.'[1]

Those before Orléans must go: 'you have no rights in France from God, the King of Heaven, and the Son of the Virgin Mary', for God has given France to Charles, the rightful heir; and he will soon enter Paris 'in a grand company'. Lieutenants of the Duke of Bedford, who 'calls himself Regent of the King of France for the King of England, make a response, if you wish to make peace over the city of Orléans!' As for the Duke, 'the Maid asks you not to make her destroy you'.

'If you come to terms, you . . . can join her company, in which the French will perform the greatest feat ever done in the name of Christianity.'[2]

Holy women on a mission are apt to be curt. Fifty years earlier, St Catherine of Siena had bullied Pope Gregory XI into going back to Rome; and when the move led to a schism in the Church, with one pope in Avignon and another in Rome, Catherine did not hesitate to maintain that the true pope was Gregory's successor in Rome, Urban VI. There were two important differences between Catherine and Joan, however. First, Catherine spoke persuasively in a melodious Tuscan Italian, whereas Joan probably never went beyond the stage of managing to write her own name, Jehanne. Second, Catherine fought for true authority in the Catholic Church, whereas Joan claimed to know the true authority in one Christian state. In 1415, shortly after Joan was born, the schism in the Church was ended at the Council of Constance, but there were doubts about the relative authority of popes and Church councils; and Joan was not sure who was the true pope. What mattered to Joan was her insistence that Henry VI was a usurper, with no rights over the lands God designed for his uncle Charles, whom his enemies had demoted to the King of Bourges; and that she, to whom she referred dispassionately as 'the Maid' (in French *la pucelle*), was to restore to Charles his undivided kingdom.

The writing of the letter was the culminating episode in a story that had begun some ten months earlier. In May 1428 Joan had gone to see Robert de Baudricourt, *châtelain*, or castellan, of the local castle of Vaucouleurs, to order him to take her to Charles. Twice he demurred, until at last, after her repeated calls that he must do what her voices demanded, he obeyed. But, even though she was admitted to the court at Chinon and she identified Charles when he pretended to hide, Charles asked the theologians of the loyal University of Poitiers to question her, before he trusted her. As the University of Paris, most prestigious of all French universities, was under Anglo-Burgundian control, this was the most prudent act he could perform. After this, her first 'trial', Joan sent her letter to the King of England.

No details of the Poitiers conversations are known; and more attention has been given by historians, playwrights and film-makers to her first meeting with Charles in Chinon. How was she able to identify him? What did she say to him in private? This encounter may have given Charles confidence in her, but it seems it was the interrogations at Poitiers that gave her confidence in herself. The university theologians found no wrong in her, but only 'humility, virginity, devotion, honesty, simplicity'. Everyone she met took an interest in her virginity. It is also obvious that she was direct, but the hectoring manner that suffuses her letter to Henry VI was not evident to the first group of clerics who pressed her closely on her mission. What worried Seguin Seguin, a Dominican friar who was dean of the Faculty of Poitiers, was that there was as yet no sign of her divine calling. 'God,' he claimed, 'did not want her to be believed unless something appeared on account of which it seemed to them that she was to be believed.'[3] It was not enough that she asserted that God had sent her nor that soldiers – he could have meant Robert de Baudricourt – believed her assertions.

A contemporary German inquisitor wrote that 'there was lately in France, within the last ten years, a maid of whom I have already spoken, named Joan, for her prophetic spirit and for the power of her miracles.'[4] When she prophesied, Joan emphasised her role as *la pucelle*, the Maid, as much as on the rights of Charles the Dauphin to be King of France. The word '*la pucelle*' is hard to translate, for although it means a girl on the threshold of adulthood, it does not have precisely the sense of our word 'nubile'. Over and over again Joan emphasised that she was a virgin, and every time her virginity was examined she was intact. To some commentators, from Voltaire to the present day, her obsession seems morbid. It places her, however, in a tradition that goes back to the beginnings of Christianity, for what distinguished the Christians from other Jewish sects, including even the Essenes of Qumran, was the value they placed on celibacy. Jesus himself was not married, his mother was said to be a virgin and of the Apostles only St Peter was known to be a married man. Even though most Christians married, even though the unmarried St Paul saw married love as an appropriate image of the love between Christ and his Church, celibacy had from the early days of Christianity a certain prestige among Christians. By Joan's time, celibacy, long cherished as a monastic ideal, had become a clerical one. While in the Eastern Church only bishops had to be monks, in the West the law prescribed that all priests should be celibate.

From the early thirteenth century, as urban society became more developed, there was a move to carry the faith to lay people in the towns, and this was carried out by the new 'orders' of friars, who took vows of chastity as well as of poverty and obedience. In Joan's day, in addition to the parish clergy there were still monks, but the storm troopers of the Church were the friars. Among their numbers were the best-trained, the most eloquent, the most admired and the most traduced of clerics. Free from working in the government of the Church, they could devote themselves to individualistic projects, such as teaching and writing – they dominated the universities – or to preaching to lay people and giving direction to their spiritual lives.

At this time, male monks or friars far outnumbered women religious, who followed slightly modified versions of male rules, but from 1300 women became more prominent and played an increasingly individualistic role in the spiritual affairs of the Church. At the age of seven St Catherine of Siena consecrated her virginity to Christ; aged sixteen she joined the Dominican third order – friars made up the first order and nuns the second – and thus was attached to a religious order while still a lay person. In her twenties, after receiving a series of visions, she began her spectacular public career. In the Netherlands, lay women lived together in *béguinages* free of vows, free to keep their property, free to leave and marry, but at least temporarily virginal, while they taught or did light manual labour or devoted themselves to prayer. Slightly further north, in Norwich, a woman who may have been a Benedictine nun, Dame Julian, lived as a recluse in an anchorage, a small house set in a churchyard, devoting herself to prayer and later, after experiencing a number of visions, to dictating her story. She claimed to be illiterate, which probably means that her Latin was not up to much, but she was well read in texts she needed to know, such as some of St Catherine's letters and some modern English clerical writings.

None of these women was a model for Joan of Arc, but it is beside this group that she belongs, both as a visionary and as a woman of action; and yet her social background was different to theirs, for whereas the others came from cities where international trade flourished, she never forgot that she was a country girl. Like her, some *béguines* were suspected of heresy; like her, St Catherine of Siena found that her life was threatened by political enemies; all were like her in their devotion to temporary or permanent virginity. Of those who 'visited' Joan, Sts Catherine (of Alexandria) and Margaret (of Antioch) reinforced her resolve to remain a virgin, though curiously St Margaret is patron saint of childbirth and as such it is probably her statue that is on the bedstead of Jan van Eyck's Arnolfini wedding portrait, which dates from 1434. There could have been many other such heavenly visitants, such as St Barbara, along with the tower in which her father had immured her to force her to marry, or the huge company, some 10,000 virgins who traipsed round Europe with St Ursula before suffering martyrdom for the sake of virginity. And besides these there were numerous virgin martyrs, set in serried ranks like those standing with loosened hair and palms in their hands among the heavenly hosts who adore the Lamb in the Ghent altarpiece that Jan van Eyck was in process of finishing while Joan became famous. One female saint, St Uncumber, had a beard to put men off; and it was for similar reasons, not as a transvestite, that Joan wore men's clothes. To accomplish what she fervently believed she was called to do, she had to neutralise men's sexual urges. She was strong and fit and became a good horsewoman, but she never struck anyone as unfeminine. To be whole-hearted, however, she had to be a virgin.

Most virgins called themselves virgins for the kingdom of heaven. What marks out Joan is that she was also a virgin for the kingdom of France or, rather, for Charles the Dauphin, whom she was sure was God's choice as King of France.

Playgoers will be familiar with Shakespeare's habit of indifferently using the words 'England' and 'France' (or 'Worcester' or 'York') for a country, a county, a city and for the person who has authority over the place. The man is identified with his title and the title with his land. In a feudal society, where a lord could expect loyalty from those who held their land from him, tight bonds kept upper-class society together; even when, by Joan's time, those bonds had been so loosened that lords thought more in terms of retainers and servants than of vassals, there was still a tendency to think of a king as sovereign, suzerain or overlord; he was the linchpin of lay society.

The King of France was also something more. As God's anointed, he was given divine authority over his people; he had a miraculous power to heal when he touched for the king's evil or scrofula, a power that his brother of England also exercised. From the 1160s, following the canonisation of Edward the Confessor, the King of England was able to claim a royal saint; a century later Henry III built a great shrine for St Edward in the abbey the Confessor had founded in Westminster and also named his son and heir Edward.

It took the French royal family 150 years to catch up, but when Louis IX was declared to be St Louis, at least every King of France since the saint's death in 1270 could claim a saint as ancestor (Edward the Confessor had died childless). The aura of holiness clung to the kings of both countries.

The lawyers of the French king drew attention to his rights as king. He could tax his subjects, lay down laws, call them to account in his courts. Indeed, in the fifteenth century the distinguished English lawyer Sir John Fortescue noted that the rights of the King of France were far greater than those of his English counterpart. Whereas the English kingdom was a *dominium regale et politicum*, the kingdom of France was a *dominium regale tantum*. Fortescue was probably writing while in exile in France in the 1460s, during the period of the dynastic civil wars known as the Wars of the Roses, when a struggle for the throne was symbolised as a contest between the white rose of the Dukes of York and the red rose of the Dukes of Lancaster. In this period English institutions were crumbling, but the point Fortescue made was still a valid one. Kings had the right and the duty to govern in a *dominium regale*, but while the English king had to consult with his peers and his commoners in parliament, the French king did not have to listen to or even summon the Estates General. In more modern terms, the King of England was a constitutional king, the King of France was an absolute monarch. Fortescue may have been too sanguine about English practice and understandably he overestimated the French king's actual freedom of action, as he was writing when Joan's Charles VII had just driven the English from all French soil except that round Calais. Throughout his reign Charles had been only too well aware that his power was restricted by the privileges of many of his subjects, above all those of his dukes, his counts and sometimes even of burgesses or bourgeois in cities. Peasants had almost no rights, but the whole pyramid of society rested on them; and there was nothing more feared than a peasant revolt.

For generations French royal power had been centred on the Île de France, the countryside round Paris, but gradually it had been extended to include neighbouring lands to the north-east, such as Artois, and in the Loire and Seine valleys, where Touraine, Anjou, Maine and Normandy were wrested from John of England. Further gains, in Poitou (also from the English), in Languedoc, in the north-east and the centre of France put most of the land now called France under the control of its king. By 1300 the King of France was the most powerful lay ruler in Latin Christendom, far stronger than the Holy Roman Emperor – whom even a man as intelligent as Dante liked to believe to be still the leading monarch in the West. Even the Church, when Philip IV cajoled the pope to move to Avignon in 1309, appeared to be a spiritual adjunct to the French Crown. A French king and pope should have been an unstoppable combination; and yet the army of Philip IV had been routed by the cities of Flanders at the battle of Courtrai in 1302.

Extensive though the royal demesne had become, four fiefs lay beyond its bounds; and, besides, the Count of Anjou, who was descended from Louis IX's youngest brother, was semi-independent both as count of Provence, a county outside France, and as sometime King of Naples. Of the four fiefs, Flanders and Brittany scarcely identified with France, as many of their inhabitants did not speak French; Burgundy, closer to the kingdom's heart, had reverted to the French Crown and would pass to the son of a king; and the English lands in the south-west, making up the duchy of Guyenne, were remote and hard to handle, as its duke was also King of England. From 1258 the English king held these lands from the French king. Philip IV made inroads into Guyenne but failed to conquer it; Philip had, however, prepared the way for France's acquisition of the duchy by making Edward I agree to the marriage of his son Edward to Philip's daughter Isabella – on condition that he, Philip, return Gascony, the southern coastal area of the duchy he had seized, to his 'dearest cousin'. With this marriage in mind, Philip could anticipate the day when his grandchild, as King of England and France, would bring to an end France's problems with English Guyenne.

It turned out that it was the Crown of France that had the problems. When Philip IV died in 1314, the French dynasty, hitherto so stable, was threatened by an unfamiliar sequence of occurrences. From 987, when Hugh Capet had become king, survival had never been an issue, because in each generation of the royal line of Capet a son had succeeded a father. Now the normal chain of events was broken. Philip's oldest son Louis X died in 1316, as did Louis's son, John I, who reigned for only ten days. The infant's uncles, Philip V and Charles IV, dying in 1322 and 1328 respectively, had no male heirs, leaving as nearest male relative the son of their sister Isabella and her husband Edward II of England. In 1327 this teenager, another Edward, became Duke of Guyenne and King Edward III of England. In Paris, his mother's representatives argued that there was no good reason why a woman should not inherit a title, but the French assembly ruled out any claim that would involve her. The French had an immediate practical problem: they needed a regent, as the late king's wife was pregnant. They chose the late king's adult male cousin, Philip Count of Valois, to take that role; and, when a baby girl was born to the widowed queen, the count quickly became King Philip VI.[5] This decision accorded later with a fundamental principle of the French constitution according to Salic Law, not only must the throne of France be inherited by a man, but also through the male line. At the time the choice of Philip VI was wise. Edward III was young, far away and apparently dominated by a mother nobody in Paris liked.

Exactly a century later, Joan too was concerned with rights of inheritance, for she held that Charles the Dauphin was the man God meant to be the king, not Henry VI of England and II of France, who was connected to the French throne by his mother Catherine, Charles's sister. Joan believed that nothing could set aside God's intended order of succession. She also valued another Frankish legacy: the work of St Remigius, apostle of the Franks, patron of her parish church in Domremy. St Remigius, in French Rémi, was the man who baptised Clovis, the first King of the Franks to extend his hold over large parts of northern Gaul.

Clovis made his ruthless way as a barbarian and a pagan until in 496, yielding to the arguments of his Christian wife and Remigius, he became a Catholic. Being Catholics did not prevent Clovis or his successors from indulging in the internecine struggles that fill the depressing pages of Bishop Gregory of Tours's *History of Gaul*. The Franks, however, were a conduit by which the Catholic faith and so the influence of the Roman Church, flowed over Western Europe. When the line of Clovis died out, it was replaced by the line of Charles Martel, who had stopped the Moors from overrunning Gaul; and his grandson Charlemagne extended Frankish rule beyond Gaul into parts of Germany, Italy and even Spain. The fame of Clovis and Charlemagne was cherished by the western or Salian Franks, whose kingdom became the nucleus of France, so that the two names most common among the kings of France were the

Frankish names of Clovis, Clodovicus or Lodovicus in Latin, Louis in French, and of Karl, Karolus or, in French, Charles. Joan's king was a Charles and his son and heir was a Louis. Both had to play a role uniquely French, for thanks to Clovis France was called the oldest daughter of the Church. But no French king, Joan believed, was truly king until he had been anointed with the oil of St Remigius in Reims Cathedral and crowned.

The legal case for English kings to be also kings of France rested on the assumption that as the late king's closest relative, Edward III should have inherited the throne of France. The assumption mattered only because some members of the English royal family were formidable generals. It was not until 1340, backdating his claim to 1337, that Edward declared he was the rightful King of France. It was a derisory assertion until first he beat Philip at Crécy and took Calais, and then his heir, Edward the Black Prince, defeated King John II, Philip's son and successor, at Poitiers. In 1361, by the Treaty of Brétigny, Edward was conceded sovereignty over the whole of Guyenne, one-third of France, in return for renouncing his claim to France. But that claim was revived when most of the duchy was won back by Charles V (1364–80). In 1369, as Charles prepared to invade Gascony, Edward reasserted his claim to France. On his royal banner, alongside the two lions of Normandy and the single lion of Aquitaine, he placed the lilies of France – which remained there until 1802 – long before the three lions had been nationalised as the emblems of England.

By the time the next English king, Richard of Bordeaux, inherited the English throne in 1377, he did not hold much land near his birthplace in Bordeaux. As an adult Richard II sought a rapprochement with France and to this effect he married Isabella, eldest daughter of Charles VI (1380–1422). He was less skilful in handling his English royal relatives; and when his cousin Henry, Duke of Lancaster, reacted to Richard's high-handedness by seizing power as Henry IV, Richard's peace policy towards France became a subject for debate. As a usurper, Henry IV hesitated to intervene, but his successor Henry V (1413–22) was confident he would show that by God's grace he was the true King of France as well as of England. He prepared to fight.

The second part of the Hundred Years War lasted less than a decade. Henry's victory at Agincourt in 1415 was effective because he followed it up by overrunning Normandy and negotiating in 1420 a treaty with the spasmodically insane Charles VI. At Agincourt large numbers of the French aristocracy, including brothers of the Duke of Burgundy, were killed and the king's nephew, Charles, Duke of Orléans, was captured. By this stage only one of Charles VI's sons had survived, another Charles, as heir or Dauphin. In 1420 at Troyes, however, the father agreed to disinherit his own child and make Henry V his heir. Within a fortnight Henry took the hand of Catherine, Charles VI's last unmarried daughter. Under the treaty, he also promised to continue with his conquests. To be acknowledged by the French as the next king of France, however, he had to outlive his father-in-law, but Henry died in 1422, some six weeks before Charles VI. His brother John, Duke of Bedford, was named regent for his son in France and his brother Humphrey, Duke of Gloucester, regent for his son in England.

Henry V's victories in France had been aided by infighting within the French royal family. The insanity of their king had encouraged his nearest relations to struggle for power. In 1407 the king's brother Louis, Duke of Orléans, had been assassinated as a result of a plot by their cousin John, Duke of Burgundy. The Orleanists were known as Armagnacs because of the second marriage of Charles, the new Duke of Orléans, to the Count of Armagnac's daughter Anne.

Throughout this period there were also rival popes. Louis of Orléans had supported the pope in Avignon, John of Burgundy the pope in Rome. Duke John took the same line as the University of Paris; and after the murder of his cousin there was a pay-off when Jean Petit, a university theologian, defended the killing of Duke Louis as the killing of a tyrant. Louis had behaved in a grand way: he had arranged the marriage of the king's elder daughter Isabella, widow of Richard II of England, to his own son Charles (his first marriage) and given her an enormous dowry out of royal funds; he had showered himself with royal gifts; he had taken land in north-east France for himself and his supporters; he had also raised unpopular taxes for war against the English. He made it easy for John to be loved in the capital. With Louis out of the way, John made Paris his power base, forced Louis's sons to be publicly reconciled with himself and purged the government of anyone he did not trust. In the end he overreached himself, however, and at a wrong moment for him, Charles VI recovered his sanity just long enough to favour the Armagnacs, so that even the people of Paris grew restive and John had to retreat to his own lands. His Flemish subjects, many of them involved in the cloth trade, were keen to have good commercial relations with the English, who supplied the cloth, so John was careful to maintain a truce with Henry V; and neither he nor his son Philip rallied to the side of their king at the battle of Agincourt in 1415.

During the chaotic aftermath of that battle, he put loyalty aside and devised a scheme to regain the dominant position in France. In 1417 he persuaded Queen Isabella of Bavaria to join him in setting up a joint government, and in March 1418 he seized Paris. While Henry V took over more and more of northern France and the Dauphin Charles set up his Parlement, or supreme court, in Poitiers and a financial court in Bourges, Duke John had a dilemma: with whom should he ally? At first he favoured the English, but Henry's capture of Pontoise near Paris made him and the queen withdraw to Champagne. He could not control Henry, but he might control the sixteen-year-old Dauphin. He met Charles for talks on the bridge of Montereau, where the Seine meets the Yonne: there was a scuffle and the duke was stabbed to death. Philip, his son, weighed advice coolly and chose to ally with Henry.

Agincourt and Montereau determined French political events wholly for one decade and largely for two. In 1415 and after 1435 most of the French, except for long-time subjects of the English like the Gascons, fought the English. Between 1415 and 1435, however, they fought each other. When Joan erupted into public life, she assumed that Burgundians were the natural enemies of France. That was what her voices told her, though most Burgundians were French and their duke was the premier peer of France.

Joan's political and military career had been determined by events in the 1420s. From 1420 France was effectively divided into three: in the north was English France, centred on Normandy; in the east, Burgundian France (Picardy and Champagne); and to the south of the Loire lay Dauphinist France, refuge of those Frenchmen who had transferred their allegiance from Charles VI to his son. By 1422, Henry V controlled most of the two northern sections and after his premature death it was from this area that his senior surviving brother, Bedford, worked to construct an Anglo-French kingdom for the infant-king Henry. Brother-in-law to Duke

1. France in 1429. Control over France was divided between the English, the Burgundians and the Dauphin.

Philip, Bedford was just and efficient; and a steady run of victories confirmed his hold on northern France. Charles's army was cut to pieces beside Cravant in 1423, his trusty Scots constable, James Earl of Buchan, was killed at Verneuil in 1424, and the logic of events persuaded Charles to avoid further military confrontation. While Bedford was in England in 1425–7 stemming a quarrel between his brother of Gloucester and his uncle Cardinal Beaufort, there was a reprieve. At Montargis the bastard of Orléans (half-brother to the captive duke) opened sluice gates to divide the forces of English besiegers and drown half of them, and soon much of Maine was in revolt. But the rising was crushed and in 1428 the English were poised to advance to the heart of Armagnac France and invest the city of Orléans itself. If Orléans fell, France would be bisected; and the richest, most populous parts of the country would be Anglo-Burgundian.

The best English commander, the Earl of Salisbury, was to direct the siege. On 12 October he was outside the walls. A few days later, however, while inspecting the walls from the twin towers of Les Tourelles, a stray piece of gunshot shattered a window nearby, an iron bar hit his visor and his head was sliced in two. After his death a lesser man, the Earl of Suffolk, took over, and a long, tough siege seemed to lie ahead. Though defended bravely by two generals, La Hire and the Bastard of Orléans in the name of his half-brother the Duke, the city was as hard to save as to take. On 12 February 1429, 500 men, mostly Scots, were beaten by Anglo-Parisian troops. The English already held the lower Seine. Strategically Orléans was the key to the Loire valley but symbolically it was even more important. Whether told by a heavenly or an earthly messenger, Joan was right to say Orléans must not fall. They were also right who held that at Orléans her mission would be tried by battle.

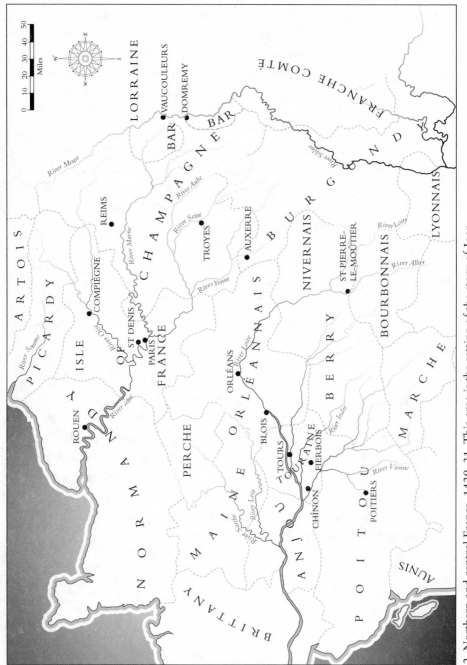

2. Northern and central France, 1429–31. This area is the setting of the story of Joan.

TWO

What Need of the Maid?

In 1429 Charles's supporters thought he needed a miracle if his cause was to recover. Those who had struggled for control of France during the past century were all related to one another; and in 1429 Charles looked like the poor relation. To Joan who had not yet met him, he was God's chosen king, Her passionate convictions about God's intentions for the kingdom impelled her on to the stage of history when, in May 1428, she arrived at the château of Vaucouleurs and demanded an audience of Robert de Baudricourt, the castellan. A century earlier, the first Valois, Philip VI, had been acknowledged as king. Joan was determined to help Philip's great-great-grandson to gain recognition too.

She had had to leave Domremy in 1428 when Burgundians raided the village and the church was burnt. Along with her family she took refuge in the nearby village of Neufchâteau. While there she was cited before a Church court in Toul in a case of breach of promise of marriage, a promise she maintained she had never made. Winning the case confirmed her belief in her call to be virginal; and the Burgundian attack gave a new sense of urgency to her mission. To go to a château alone was unthinkable for a young woman, so she made an excuse to visit a pregnant cousin who lived in a little village three miles from Vaucouleurs and then sought the help of her cousin's husband, Durand Laxart. Laxart was the first person to believe in her. Many years later, he recalled how 'Joan told me she wished to go into France, to the Dauphin, to have him crowned.'[1] In January 1429 the unlikely pair, a labourer and his cousin by marriage, turned up at Vaucouleurs to see the castellan. Without hesitation, Joan told de Baudricourt that she came in the name of her Lord; Charles must be forced to fight, he would be helped before the end of Lent, the kingdom belonged to her Lord but had been entrusted to the Dauphin, whom she would make king. Who was her Lord, the astonished castellan enquired? When Joan

replied 'the King of Heaven', de Baudricourt turned to Laxart, told him
to take her to her father and to tell him to give her a good whipping.

Historians disagree over whether she went home and came back or
whether she stayed on in the town. What is clear is that she grew
impatient and decided to set out at once, wearing her 'uncle' Laxart's
cast-offs. At the entry into a forest she stopped at the little chapel of
St-Nicolas de Septfonds, where, praying before the wooden crucified
Christ, she realised she had disobeyed her voices, who had told her to
seek the support of de Baudricourt. She went back to Vaucouleurs.
As in a good fairy story, she had failed the first time, failed a second
time and would succeed the third time; and this is what happened.
She now had useful supporters, among them two squires, Jean de
Metz and Bertrand de Poulengy; she was summoned by the ailing
Duke of Lorraine, who probably hoped she would perform a miracle.
She told him frankly that she could not oblige, but that, if he gave
her an escort, she would pray for him. Back in Vaucouleurs, she
learnt from her voices that the French had been routed near Orléans.
She told de Baudricourt what had happened and impressed on him
the urgency of her journey to the royal court at Chinon. News came
from Chinon that if nobody could find evil in her, she should be sent
for. On 23 February she appeared in the courtyard of the château of
Vaucouleurs, her escort swore their loyalty to the castellan, and,
armed with letters for the king, she set off.

Any journey in 1429 could be dangerous. It took Joan eleven days
to pass through enemy territory, where fortunately she was able to
stop at places held by Valois sympathisers or French soldiers. At no
time did she show any fear, but instead reassured her companions
that God was protecting them. What worried her was that she could
seldom go to Mass – until the party reached the monastery of Ste-
Catherine-de-Fierbois, where she felt able to relax in congenial
surroundings and where she dictated a letter to Charles to announce
that she would be with him soon.

Her arrival in Chinon is one of the best-known incidents in her short
life. High above a little medieval town on the River Vienne stands the
château of Chinon, built by Henry, Count of Anjou and soon Henry II
King of England, and from 1204 a castle of the kings of France. It was
this building with its spectacular views over a lush landscape that
Charles had made his principal stronghold. Subsequently, when Louis
XIII granted the castle to Cardinal Richelieu, the building fell into

disrepair, and today only the outlines of a few walls remain, but to one of them is attached part of the chimney of the noble fireplace that warmed the great hall; and in that hall Joan met her king.

Charles, cunning, timid and superstitious, was intrigued by Joan but was dominated by his fat chamberlain, La Trémoïlle, who paid his debts, and by his formidable mother-in-law, Yolande of Aragon, who was also the mother-in-law of Isabella, daughter of the Duke of Lorraine. La Trémoïlle would do what was needed to hold on to power: the queen mother did not mind showing that she was a keen supporter of Joan. At court there may already have been enthusiasts for Joan. Of these the most important would be John II, Duke of Alençon, a cousin of the king, a warrior and like his cousin a dabbler in astrology. Charles must have heard of a prophecy that a virgin would save the kingdom; his cousin may have encouraged him to trust in Joan; he was willing to test her out. The story goes that on her arrival he hid in the crowd of courtiers, and that once she found him, she gave him some sort of sign during a private interview. What the sign was is unclear, but Charles was no fool. He knew that the people who must investigate her claims were the clergy. Before he would do anything for her, he insisted that she should be questioned by theologians resident at the University of Poitiers at a meeting whose details are lost. Since the most famous university in the land, the University of Paris, was under Anglo-Burgundian control, this was a prudent initiative.

The examination took eleven days. The clergy questioned her at length about her voices. They also asked her that if it were God's will that the English should be driven back to England, why did she need soldiers? She snapped back that the soldiers were to fight in God's name and that God would give the victory. Their findings were cautious. The king should neither reject Joan nor be in a hurry to believe her. He should seek a sign by which he could know if she were sent by God; and she herself said that she would give the sign before Orléans. As the king could find no evil in her, he agreed to supply troops to accompany her to Orléans. There was at this stage no mention of her plans for the coronation. A follow-up to the interrogations led to a test, at Tours, to find out whether she was a virgin; the test showed that she was.

It was now time for a grander test, a test on the field of battle. Having passed her first trial before clerics, Joan moved into action. She dictated a letter to the King of England. She was sure that once she intervened, she would help to change the course of the war.

THREE

Victory at Orléans and Reims

The relief of Orléans changed Joan from God's herald into God's warrior. Joan's strident claims, her eccentric election to dress as a man, her irruption into court life could have been mere topics for gossip if she had not led men to fight and win. Against the cautious policy of diplomacy advocated by La Trémoïlle she urged decisive action – and she had succeeded in getting men to follow her. She later said she had an army of 10,000–12,000, which the chronicler Enguerrand de Monstrelet estimates at 4,000–5,000, which was still a large force for the time; and she also had an abundance of provisions (supplies often determined the result of a siege). Charles paid for them, his mother-in-law produced them and Alençon organised them.

Before being greeted at Blois by the royal commander, the Bastard of Orléans, Joan turned her army into an unusual spectacle. At its head marched a brigade of priests, who were to sing hymns to Our Lady twice a day and to hear the soldiers' confessions. As they began the march to Orléans, they held aloft their new banner, on which was painted an image of Christ crucified, while they intoned the '*Veni Creator spiritus*' ('Come Holy Spirit, Creator, come'). Joan could be practical, and so after two nights most of the priests returned to Blois. She had brought with her some of the most influential military men in France, the Marshal of Boussac, the Admiral of France, the Duke of Alençon and Gilles de Rais, the notorious bluebeard of popular legend, and the gruff La Hire. And yet, after the priests had gone, she still meant to impress on her army that her task was God-given and royally sanctioned; as proof, she had a standard, said to have been made of white canvas fringed with silk on a field of fleur-de-lis, on which was painted a Christ in Majesty flanked by two angels and inscribed at the side with the words 'Jhesus Maria'. She was clad in armour the Dauphin had ordered for her. She carried a sword that she had sent for from the monastery of Ste-Catherine-de-Fierbois. Much to the monks' surprise this had been retrieved from under an altar – a weapon located by a miracle indicated a holy cause. On the First Crusade, for example, when the crusaders wilted in Antioch, the lance that had pierced the side of Christ had been divined in a vision; and after its discovery the crusaders' fortunes had changed dramatically. Joan's sword, decorated with five crosses, may have belonged to a crusader; the weapon gave her campaigning the quality of a holy war; she carried the weapon until she was beaten for the first time at St-Denis, outside Paris. What the banner, the armour and the sword indicated for all to see was that she was no common soldier, but a knight.

Chivalry was the code of behaviour that had come to be seen as appropriate to the upper classes. Its prestige was bolstered by a military assumption, that the *chevalier*, the mounted knight, was the most effective arm in any army. Around 1100, when crusaders had just scaled the walls of Jerusalem, it was a reasonable assumption, for nothing had equalled the effectiveness of the charge of Christians clad in their chain mail. By about 1400, ways of winning wars had been transformed. At Nicopolis in 1396 mobile Turkish mounted archers routed the Latin cavalry under John of Burgundy. At Agincourt in 1415 longbow men sheltering behind stakes and English men-at-arms on foot slaughtered the French cavalry trapped in the mud. By then armour was so weighty that any knight needed a squire to help him mount, and if he fell over, he needed a squire to help him get up. Simultaneously a new weapon had been devised, the cannon that could blast a knight off his horse. And yet, socially, there was never a time when there was more cachet in being a knight. If a man joined a military order, he sported its stars and ribbons; in quarterings on his coat of arms and shield he displayed his ancient lineage; if he were captured, etiquette demanded that he should be ransomed at any cost; while in flamboyant pinnacled castles ladies and gentlemen, arrayed in the fantastic, graceful costumes, listened to improbable tales of chivalry about Arthur, Charlemagne and Alexander – and so a future King of England was named Arthur, Kings of France Charles, Kings of Scotland Alexander. Joan took for granted this aristocratic view of contemporary warfare. And for some months reality corresponded to dreams, as a maid in armour led men to victory.

Joan did not forget the practicalities of a siege. Even with the help of some 1,500 Burgundians, the English had lacked the men and the artillery to force Orléans to surrender, so they now hoped to persuade the citizens to give up the struggle by undermining their morale. They had surrounded as much of the city as they could, putting up earthworks or *boulevards* manned by small numbers of troops, four to the west, one to the north, one on an island in the river to the west and one (the boulevard de St-Loup), that was meant to block the road into the Orléans from the east. Most of the east and north of the city was not blockaded, so the English relied on the effect of capturing Les Tourelles, a stone castle that lay at the southern end of the southern bridge spanning the Loire. As the French blew up two of the arches of the bridge, Les Tourelles became just a good vantage point from which to conduct the siege, but when to the south of it the English constructed the new boulevard des Augustins, in which the new commander, the Earl of Suffolk, placed a strong defensive force, it became obvious that he and his captains were thinking that the best form of offence was defence. Unless they were dislodged, the city would fall.

Before his death, Salisbury had turned his guns on and destroyed twelve water mills that were vital to provide the besieged with bread, but the citizens quickly built eleven new horse-driven mills. Suffolk was more cautious: he intended to wait. There was no sign that the acting head of the Orleanists, the Bastard of Orléans, was enthusiastic to continue the fight. His attacks on English positions in December and January had been in vain. When he tried to surprise the army under Sir John Falstolf that was bringing the besiegers supplies, including a quantity of fish for Lenten meals, he had been mauled; and the so-called battle of the Herrings, on 12 February, could have been his last attempt to save his brother's city. That day Joan had her final interview with Robert de Baudricourt before setting out for Chinon. For the next two months the Bastard held on, and in late April he went to Blois to meet her. What may have impressed him most was that she was bringing provisions as well as men.

The problem was how to gain access to the city. Initially the French avoided confrontation by marching far to the south of the river, but eventually they knew that they would have to try to cross it. To the west of the city, on the Blois side, the English had erected the majority of their boulevards and held the towns of Beaugency and Meung. To the east, however, they held just one town, Jargeau, and had put up just one boulevard, that of St-Loup. Luckily too, for the French, they had not blocked a ford east of Orléans, near Chécy, and accordingly Joan decided to cross there. But if she could quickly get men on to the north bank, she could bring neither provisions into the city – unless the boats carrying them were helped by a favourable wind – nor her men, unless they could get past the boulevard de St-Loup. That she achieved both easily was said to be the result of two miracles: once she had made up her mind, the wind changed direction; and the English made no attempt to stop her. How provisions sent from Blois, to the west, had to cross at Chécy, to the east, is not clear, but perhaps boats were needed just to move them from one bank to the other. One chronicle, the *Journal du siège d'Orléans*, an account of the siege written probably thirty to forty years later, gives a reason for English inaction: the citizens themselves made a sortie to distract the defenders of the boulevard.[1] And yet, even if the citizens' cooperation had helped Joan to enter the city, there was still rejoicing, says the *Journal*, at the 'divine virtue that was said to be in this simple maid'. The Bastard, however, remembered she had rebuked him for making a cautious entry rather than precipitately rushing at the English.

> I am bringing you better help than ever came from any soldier or any city, as it is the help of the King of Heaven. It comes not from me but from God Himself, who, on the petition of St Louis and St Charlemagne, has had pity on the town of Orléans, and has refused to suffer the enemy to have both the body of the lord of Orléans (still in prison in England) and his city.[2]

The Bastard was unmoved, so Joan next tried to convince the English that they must leave. She went to the boulevard de Belle Croix on the bridge and talked to soldiers in Les Tourelles, but Glasdale, their leader, replied only with insults. She next demanded the return of her herald, perhaps the man who had delivered her letter to the English, and threatened she would kill all the English prisoners in Orléans. This time they did what she requested, but added that if they captured her they would torture and burn her. If she had a plan, it was to be provocative to those who opposed her.

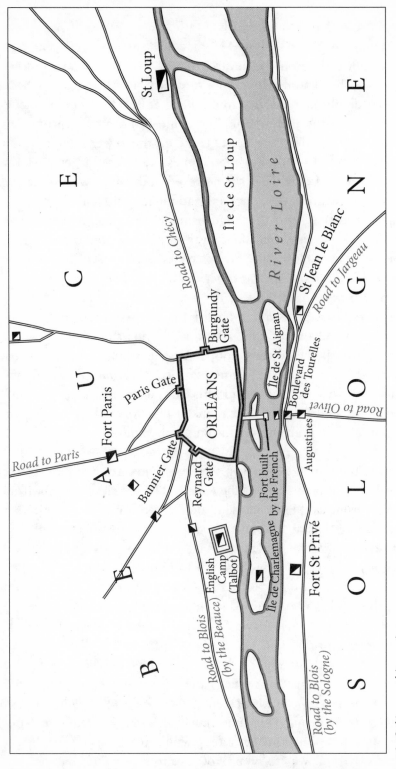

BEAUCE

SOLOGNE

St Loup

Île de St Loup

River Loire

Road to Chécy

Burgundy Gate

Road to Paris

Fort Paris

Paris Gate

Bannier Gate

Reynard Gate

ORLÉANS

Île de St Aignan

St Jean le Blanc

Road to Jargeau

Boulevard des Tourelles

Road to Olivet

Augustines

Fort built by the French

English Camp (Talbot)

Road to Blois (by the Beauce)

Île de Charlemagne

Fort St Privé

Road to Blois (by the Sologne)

3. Orléans and its environs.

At the same time, as she showed while the Bastard was away seeking more men, she was adept at winning friends and influencing the people she needed, in this case the townsfolk. On 4 May she got her way when the French attacked and took the isolated boulevard de St-Loup. She may have wept over the English who died without having been to confession, but she also was thrilled that she was proved right. Attacking worked. On the following day she wrote another, but more terse letter to the English, and took another, deserted boulevard; and yet she was clear in her mind that picking off such weak points one after another might make decisive victory harder to achieve. Her preference was for taking risks, a preference that was realised when the boulevard des Augustins, which lay at the south end of the bridge, was taken. Those in Les Tourelles were now caught between the citizenry of Orléans on the north bank and the relieving troops on the south bank. Though wounded, Joan was not to be deflected from her course, and, after the bloodiest fighting since Agincourt, the castle fell, Glasdale fell into the river and was drowned and Joan was left to weep for the foes who had died for not listening to her words. Although the English were undefeated to the north of Orléans, without Les Tourelles they had little chance of investing Orléans. They realised that to continue the siege was pointless, and on 8 May they withdrew.

According to the *Journal du siège d'Orléans*, 'everyone was filled with great joy and praised the Lord for the great victory He had given them'.[3] The clergy and people alike sang the *Te Deum* and Joan had time to have her wounds treated. She then joined the soldiers who were preparing to fight any English who continued to resist, and watched her foes slink away. The mud boulevards had not been a strong defence; the English would put their trust henceforward in the stone fortresses that they still held on either side of Orléans. To her Orleanist followers, however, it was clear that God was with the Maid. After her death she would be called 'the Maid of Orléans', and until her collateral heirs died out her family would be Orléannais and 8 May, the day on which the English marched away, became a day of celebration in the city, with a re-enactment of events in her honour. In London, Charles, Duke of Orléans, rejoiced that his city had not fallen. He must have been grateful to his half-brother but showed his gratitude to Joan by sending her a beautiful robe.

There was a pause for a month, perhaps so that new recruits could be found to replace those killed during the siege. Two strategies were debated at Charles's court. One idea, supported by the lords of the blood royal and the captains (said the Bastard) was to move on Normandy, and then on Paris. The other idea, Joan's idea, was to clear the route to Reims so that Charles could be crowned. Joan won the debate by pleading to her lord on her knees. Charles put his cousin Alençon in charge of the army as lieutenant-general and told him to 'do entirely according to her counsel'. That meant there would be direct assaults on other Loire strongholds.

The first objective was Jargeau to the east, a town strongly defended with five towers, three fortified gates and a fortified bridge over the river, full of gunpowder weapons and protected by some 700 troops under the command of the Earl of Suffolk. The French leaders hesitated until Joan shamed them, saying that if she was not sure God was on their side she would rather have stayed at home to herd her sheep. This led to an attack that was countered by an unexpected sortie. When the French faltered, Joan picked up her standard and encouraged them to fight back. Her resolution paid off and the counter-attack was beaten off. Joan sent a peremptory letter telling the enemy to give up: 'Surrender this place to Heaven's King and to gentle King Charles, and you can go. If not you will be massacred.'[4] Suffolk tried to negotiate with La Hire rather than with Alençon or Joan. In any case, his offer was rejected and yet he did not leave. While Alençon wished to continue bombarding, Joan urged an immediate assault on the walls. On Sunday 12 June the French put ladders in the ditch and Joan went forward with her standard. After some three or four hours, just as the French were at the point of clambering into the town, Joan was struck on the head with a stone that broke on her helmet. Quickly on her feet again, she cried out: 'Our Lord has condemned the English. At this hour they are ours. Have courage.'[5] Her words seem to have prevented any last-minute attempt at a negotiated surrender. One of Suffolk's brothers was killed, another was captured and for social reasons – a nobleman could not surrender to a commoner – the noble lord felt compelled to knight a squire from Auvergne before allowing himself to be taken alive. Other Englishmen were less distinguished and less fortunate. Many were killed and many prisoners executed on their way to Orléans.

Back in Orléans, Joan went to Mass and told Alençon that she wished to leave for Meung next day. As had happened so often before, she had to accept an unwelcome delay, in this case for three days, while Jargeau was garrisoned, the army prepared and the gunpowder weapons shipped downstream. This time she would go west.

On 15 June the French marched on Meung, halted to take the bridge and then set out to besiege Beaugency. By then the repute of Joan had attracted many volunteers, including the Lord of Laval, the Lord of Lohéac and his brother, the Lord of Chauvigny de Berry, the Lord of La Tour d'Auvergne and the *vidame* of Chartres, and, most important of all, Arthur de Richemont, brother of the Duke of Brittany and Constable of France, who had recently been banished from court. Being threatened by an English force under the redoubtable Sir John Falstolf, Joan needed Richemont's men. Seeing the large numbers ranged against him, however, Falstolf left Beaugency and did not offer battle. He withdrew on 17 June, by which time the French had been steadily bombarding the town for two days, and the commanders of the garrison decided to leave if they could get favourable terms. They were offered free passage if they did not fight for ten days; they accepted, and in the meantime Falstolf, without the use of artillery, made a botched attack on the bridge at Meung. The failure of this effort and English awareness that their enemy was superior in forces and morale persuaded the leaders in Meung that this stronghold too was indefensible. The English army under Falstolf and Talbot withdrew northwards in good order, yet dispirited and feeling weak.

Falstolf prepared for one last stand before he abandoned the Loire valley. Adopting the defensive tactics that had worked so well in the past, he concealed his vanguard, provisions and artillery in a wood on the way to Patay, a village on the road from Orléans to Chartres. Talbot meanwhile hid 500 mounted archers between two strong hedges, where he believed the French must pass. Unluckily for him a stag rushed through this position, so disclosing the intended ambush to the pursuing French cavalry. The archers fled into the woods, where they collided with the other troops whom Falstolf had not had time to deploy. On the heralds' count 2,200 English, now in disarray, were slaughtered. Talbot could not escape and Falstolf fled with as many men as he could save. Joan's role in the victory is unknown, for no chronicler mentions her, but at the rehabilitation trial, her page, Louis de Coutes, tells how she held a dying Englishman's head in her hands while hearing his confession. Thanks to this action, the Loire was once again a French river. Joan prepared to go to Reims.

Joan, who had seen off the English, now had to contend with the Burgundians too, for Reims, her destination, was under Burgundian control. The route there was not as difficult to follow as might appear, for neither the English nor their French allies had the men to garrison all the intervening villages and towns. Many in territory held by the Burgundians were sympathetic to the Anglo-French monarchy of Henry VI only because they preferred being on the winning side; and as this was no longer the case, feelings of loyalty to Henry evaporated. After Patay, the people of Janville closed their gates to the fleeing English and opened them to the pursuing French; and this pattern of behaviour became common as Joan and the Dauphin's large army made their way first east and then north into the heart of Champagne. Besides, Joan had promised to save Orléans and had done so. As she had said that Charles would be crowned in Reims, people assumed that that too would happen.

In mid-June Charles moved to Gien, east of Orléans, from where it was relatively easy to set off for Champagne. At court, however, La Trémoïlle was all for temporising. The way ahead was not safe; it would be wiser to wait till relations with Philip of Burgundy had improved; the king should go to Bourges. On 25 June Joan sent a letter to the citizens of Tournai in which, after outlining the recent triumphs of French arms, she invited the citizens to the anointing of the king at Reims, 'where we shall soon be'. This must have been one of several such letters. Clearly she had every intention of setting out in the near future. But as so often, she was frustrated that others, in this case Charles, did not share her sense of urgency. For two days she camped with the soldiers outside the city, which showed Charles how devoted his troops were to her. He could not afford to pay them; they knew they could get him safely to Reims; he gave way.

On 30 June Charles's troops came to Auxerre, which for ten years had been pro-Burgundian and had even been ruled by Burgundians. The sight of a huge French army, numbering perhaps 10,000, encouraged the town council to make terms. After three days of negotiation, Charles magnanimously pardoned anyone who had sided with his enemies. No one was killed, the gates were opened and the army was reprovisioned. The army next passed through a succession of villages until it came to Troyes. A town long famous as a market town on important trade routes, to Charles Troyes was infamous as the place where nine years earlier his father had denied his right to the French throne, with the added humiliating condition that his sister Catherine, who was to marry Henry V of England, would be wife and mother to future kings of France – in fact she never became queen but was mother to Henry VI and II. With this past in mind, the people of Troyes had reason to reflect. To direct their thoughts to the future, on 4 July Joan wrote yet another letter instructing the citizens to recognise the true King of France, her master, 'who will soon be at the city of Reims and at Paris . . . And with the aid of the King Jesus he will be in all good cities in his holy kingdom.'[6] To this Charles added a practical incentive to make them submit: if they did so, he would grant them an amnesty.

At first the drawbridges were raised, the gates shut and soldiers from the garrison made a show of a sortie, with one beneficial effect: it made the defenders realise they were far outnumbered by the force beyond the walls. Once again days passed while heralds and envoys went from town to camp and from camp to town. The citizens sent their own holy person, Friar Richard, a Franciscan with a line in prophesying the end of the world, to see Joan. When he had made the sign of the cross and sprinkled her with holy water, she told him to approach: 'I will not fly away.' On 8 July Charles called a council of war, from which Joan was excluded, to debate whether to bypass the town, as Archbishop Regnault of Chartres urged, or to attack it. Joan was called in to give her views, and she proposed an attack. The very sight of her preparations was enough for the people of Troyes. Once she began the attack, the rules of war meant that the besieged would have no legitimate defence against whatever fate Charles might allow. The prospect of the terrible consequences that could follow from their defiance made Troyes submit. A triumphal entry and the free gift of supplies was enough to buy Charles off. In return he freely pardoned the people of Troyes their offences. The march to Reims was turning into a procession.

The people of Reims were now the only possible obstacle left to the coronation. Charles was anxious because he was aware that if they resisted he had inadequate artillery and siege machines. Joan reassured him that they would come to meet him; and once more she proved to be right. She was almost in her home country. A neighbour, a farmer called Gérardin d'Épinal, came with four friends to see her. He would recall that previously she had told him that she had a secret she would not disclose because he was a 'Burgundian' and that now she was afraid of nothing except treason. On Saturday 16 July the royal party reached Reims. On the following day Charles was crowned.

The lengthy coronation service in Reims Cathedral was the happiest time in Joan's short life. The ceremony enacted publicly Charles's calling to be the sacred monarch of a holy kingdom; it was for his role in life that she had fought; it was his vocation that gave her life its meaning.

Reims was the royal, national cathedral of France. On its façade is a sculptural group consisting of Clovis, King of the Franks, his Christian wife Clotilda and St Rémi. The pagan chief is being baptised while the saint receives the ampulla from a dove; in the ampulla is the holy oil that will be used to anoint all Frankish and French kings; and the dove stands for the Holy Spirit. There are variations on the royalist theme. The priest-king Melchisedek gives communion in bread and wine to the patriarch Abraham, clad in the armour of a thirteenth-century knight. King Solomon, standing for Christ the King, stands beside the Queen of Sheba, representing the Church. Inside the nave are representations of twenty kings, beside the bishops who consecrated them. Only Karolus (Charlemagne) is named, as he is the most important of all since Clovis. In other French Gothic churches are other examples of devout kingship: at Chartres the story of Charlemagne; at St-Denis the story of Godfrey de Bouillon, the Frankish leader chosen after the First Crusade to rule in Jerusalem; in the Ste-Chapelle in Paris the story of St Louis. Nowhere else, however, is there so much emphasis on the Most Christian King as there is at Reims. On the western front by the great rose window King David is anointed by the prophet Samuel, King Solomon by the prophet Nathan. David shows kingly courage by slaying Goliath, Solomon kingly justice by returning the disputed child to its true mother and kingly piety by building the Temple. Above all these scenes God gives his fatherly blessing to the kings.

Nobody knows if Joan studied these figures, but they were biblical stories familiar to the illiterate poor, from which class she sprang. Nobody knows what exactly she witnessed; for 1429 there is no equivalent to the *Coronation Book of Charles V* that contains the liturgy by which Charles's grandfather had been consecrated King of France. We do know, however, that from nine o'clock in the morning until two o'clock in the afternoon the drama moved steadily towards its climax, when Charles was anointed on the head, hands and chest with the holy oil from the ampulla of St Rémi by the saint's living embodiment, the Archbishop of Reims; and then he was crowned. In October 1422 Charles had been acknowledged as king at Mehun-sur-Yèvre by a forlorn group of followers. From the moment his father died, according to his lawyers, he had the legal authority of a king, yet he was still known as the Dauphin. What made him the Most Christian King were the sacred mysteries of 17 June, *le beau mystère* as it was described. His anointing made him, unlike all his lay subjects, a priest-king after the order of Melchisedek, who had the right to take communion in both kinds; and it prepared him to become, by a separate rite, a thaumaturge who could 'touch' for the tubercular condition called scrofula, the so-called king's evil. His anointing also gave him, unlike many other kings, some authority within the Church.

Certain traditional parts of the ceremony could not be followed at Charles's coronation. At one stage, the twelve peers of France, six ecclesiastical and six lay, should have been summoned to stand before the high altar. Three of the clerics were present – the Archbishop of Reims, the bishops of Laon and of Châlons – but three were absent, among whom Pierre Cauchon, Bishop of Beauvais, was deeply involved in Burgundian politics. Among the laity, the Duke of Burgundy, conspicuous by his absence, alone was a peer in his own right; the other five peerages had reverted to the Crown. Of the twelve peers, then, nine had to be substituted. Another official who should have been present was the leading military officer in France, the Constable, but Richemont, who had fought alongside Joan in the Loire valley, had since been disgraced, so his ceremonial sword was carried by the brother-in-law of Joan's critic, Georges de La Trémoïlle. Other than the king, however, the person most prominent in the cathedral was Joan. She stood beside him, holding her banner, next to him the focus of attention. At the end of the ceremony she knelt down, and clasping him by the knees wept tears of joy. 'Gentle King,' she exclaimed, 'now is God's pleasure fulfilled. He desired that the siege of Orléans be lifted, and that you should be brought into this city of Reims to receive your holy consecration, so showing that you are the true king, the man to whom the kingdom of France should belong.'

It is not clear if Joan was present at the banquet mounted to celebrate the coronation. If she was not, the reason must have been because she had not yet been ennobled. Among the people of Reims, however, she was revered; and as Charles rode round the city, his crown on his head, she rode at his side. The crowds pressed towards her to touch her. She was thrilled that the great aim of her mission had been accomplished. She remained sure that she was called to do more; but what precisely and how precisely she would do it, she was uncertain.

Joan's days in Reims were the high point of her public career, for the coronation ceremony gave meaning to everything she had done for her king. A modern visitor to the cathedral may be awe-struck by its beauty and in looking to explain such feelings will probably point to the daring of the masons' work. Gothic engineering was a new skill, which facilitated the building of churches much taller than Roman and Romanesque arches could sustain. The pointed arches at the royal abbey of St-Denis led to a proliferation of glass where before there had been massive walls; the use of flying buttresses at Chartres produced higher, lighter walls and yet more glass; at Reims and then more ambitiously at Amiens, the pitch of the nave was still steeper. Finally, the Ste-Chapelle in Paris was made into an exquisite glass house and at Beauvais the pillars strained so high till the nave came crashing down.

We cannot tell whether Joan had an aesthete's eye. What we can believe is that for her Reims was the home on earth of St Rémi, a saint she had known as a child in Domremy. Reims Cathedral was the holy place where kings of France were consecrated by God for the sacred task of ruling France. What mattered to Joan was her assurance of God's presence and action there. During the final year of her life she would find that such convictions were to be harshly tested by events.

FOUR

Defeats and Capture

In her letter to the English, Joan had asserted that 'Charles, the rightful heir, to whom God has given France . . . will shortly enter Paris in a grand company.'[1]

Charles was in an anomalous position: he was now a consecrated king who had no control of his capital. Paris had been the capital of the duchy of the west Franks before it became the capital of France. The treasury of the kings of France was kept on the Île de la Cité. The Parlement of Paris was the supreme court of appeal for most of northern France, and the University of Paris had long been regarded as the first seat of learning in Latin Christendom. Paris may also have been the most populous city north of the Alps. The defences of the city had been so strengthened by Charles V that it had the most formidable walls to the west of Constantinople. All the same, in 1429 the English and their Burgundian allies had reasons to be anxious, and the defenders of the city were far from complacent. Other than the duchy of Guyenne, nearly all France south of the Loire was in the hand of Charles and now much of Champagne had fallen to him too. Anglo-Burgundian lands in Picardy and Normandy were vulnerable and would be more so were Paris to fall.

Work began to make the city virtually impregnable. Boulevards were placed before the gates, houses by the walls were pulled down, gunpowder and stones were stored ready for use, ditches and moats were cleared of debris. A diplomatic campaign was also set in motion to win friends for the Anglo-Burgundian cause. The English concluded an alliance, for what that was worth, with the changeable Jean V, Duke of Brittany, and offered his younger brother Richemont, the Constable of France currently out of favour with Charles VII, a similar rank in the English army; though Richemont was not drawn, he remained detached from the French cause. At the same time, Bedford still defied Charles, saying to him '[you] now without reason call yourself king' in the name of his nephew, 'Henry, by the grace of God, true, natural and lawful King of France and England'. He blamed Charles for trusting in the ignorant people who were seduced by 'a disordered and defamed woman, dressed in man's clothing and base in conduct'. He blamed the French for disturbing the peace and to secure it he took command.

Philip of Burgundy, as so often, was devious. On 17 July, the day of the coronation at which he should have been present, Joan wrote to him in her inimitable style: 'the Maid calls upon you by the King of Heaven, my rightful and sovereign Lord, to make a firm and lasting peace with the King of France'. She goes on to say that he and Charles should pardon one another – she must have thought of the bridge of Montereau – and, if Philip must fight, then he should fight the 'Saracens', that is the Turks. She assured him that Charles wished to make peace with him and warned him that he would win no more battles against royalists. Cunning as ever, Philip did offer Charles a truce of fifteen days, at the end of which he would surrender Paris and then prepare for further negotiations. Joan, rightly, was not convinced that Philip was trustworthy and told the people of Reims that she retained her instinct for fighting. After the two weeks were up, Paris had not yielded; instead it had been made harder to capture. Joan began to move against Paris early in August. Hitherto she had acted in accordance with the advice of her voices, but on this occasion there are grounds for arguing that she was acting as a leader of a faction rather than as the inspiration of the royalist cause. Her letter to the English had mentioned Paris; at the nullification trial Seguin Seguin, who had interrogated her at Poitiers, and Alençon, her chief royalist supporter, both asserted that the capture of Paris was a part of her mission; during the heresy trial at Rouen, after she had failed to take the city, she maintained that she had acted to please certain noblemen, in other words the war party. Even before the coronation she had ignored the king's wishes in accepting Richemont's help. In the last months of her military career less and less did she seem to act as the king wanted and less and less confident was she that she was following the advice of her voices. The tone of her own voice became shriller, her actions became more independent and she lost her reputation for invincibility.

In 1453 Sultan Mehmet II was to demonstrate how to conduct a successful siege against an enormous city – with overwhelming superiority in numbers, with inventiveness and with well-directed cannon. A generation earlier, Joan had lacked such advantages. Unlike Constantinople, which was almost deserted by 1453, Paris in 1429 had a population large enough to frustrate a besieger; only a vast army could invest it on all sides and make its inhabitants hunger; only an army with the appropriate siege machines could damage its defences. Joan's preferred idea of attack was direct assault. Charles did not yet have the resources that at the close of the war would enable him to eject the English from city after city. Yet he would never have what he needed to take Paris by force, and he was only to win the city as a reward for a policy of dogged diplomacy of the kind favoured by Joan's opponent at court, the rich, obese and wily Georges de La Trémoïlle. Against Paris Joan's stubborn impetuosity never had a chance.

On 21 July the army left Reims and on the 23rd reached Soissons, which surrendered to the king. It moved on to Château-Thierry four days later, where it stayed until 1 August. While there, Joan was enough in royal favour to ask the king to exempt Domremy and the neighbouring village of Greux from taxation, a privilege they retained until 1789. At Provins on 2 August the army was joined by René of Anjou, duc de Bar, son-in-law of the Duke of Lorraine and thus again connected with Joan's part of the country; but even more important was the fact that yet another royal relation pledged himself to support the head of the family. The army marched to the northern side of Paris, and on 15 August was camping outside the cathedral city of Senlis when at last the English under Bedford offered battle. Though it was the feast of the Assumption, Joan was keen to fight, preferably to attack first, but the army commanders, only too aware of how unwise French armies had been in the past, had no intention of being caught yet once more in an English defensive trap. As a result, in the field near the village of Montépilloy, between 6,000 and 7,000 Frenchmen spent the day staring at 8,000–9,000 English soldiers, among whom were between 6,000 and 8,000 Burgundians. Joan, accompanied by Alençon, tried to taunt the English into coming out from behind their stakes, ditches and wagons, but they equally would not be moved. As night fell, the French returned to their lines. At break of day the English left for Senlis and Paris.

Like the English, Charles also left, in his case for the royal residence of Compiègne, which he found so agreeable that he stayed there for days. Joan remained with him, fretting at her inactivity. Philip of Burgundy had not given up Paris; surely now was the time to take it from him? La Trémoïlle spoke against the idea, Charles was unwilling to press forward and Joan had to be content that he allowed her the Dukes of Alençon and Bourbon and lesser nobles such as Gilles de Rais and professionals such as La Hire to march towards Paris; she would have been disillusioned had she known that while she went south, Regnault of Chartres, the Archbishop of Reims, was in touch with Philip the Good. Remorseful perhaps for the death of Philip's father and anxious to detach Philip from the English alliance, Charles asked Philip what his terms would be. He promised to vacate Compiègne, Senlis, Creil and Pont-St-Maxence, all towns that had submitted to him, in return for a four-month truce (he did not know that simultaneously Philip was offering more troops to the English, in return for titles to Brie and Champagne). It was then, and with half-hearted support, that Charles sanctioned the attack on Paris.

The army made for St-Denis, home of the royal abbey where traditionally kings of France were buried. From there skirmishers were sent out to discover the weakest point in the walls, but no attack could start without Charles's permission. Eventually, on 7 September, the king arrived and ordered the attack. The assault, made the following day, failed, and Joan was wounded. On 9 September Charles suspended the siege.

The failure before Paris proved that Joan did not always win. Her enemies were quick to learn from her recent successes and failure. While Paris was Anglo-Burgundian in sympathy, its university regarded her as a foe to the faith and its Parlement still upheld the Treaty of Troyes that had disinherited Charles. Inevitably, Paris became the setting for a ceremony to rival the one Joan had inspired for Charles at Reims. In November 1431, when Joan was dead, King Henri II (Henry VI of England) came to St-Denis, as Joan had done, and on 2 December, unlike her, from the abbey made a *joyeuse entrée* into Paris. In the cathedral of Notre-Dame his uncle Cardinal Beaufort anointed him as true King of France, although without the oil of St Rémi. The occasion was mismanaged, however: English lay peers had to take the place of the lay peers of 'France' (as none of the appropriate French ones was available); the rights of the Bishop of Paris were ignored; the feast was chaotic and the food stale. Nevertheless, the people of Paris were loyal to their Anglo-

French king. His rival, Charles VII, was not yet *de facto* master of the country; and until arms had settled the question *de jure*, the canny Parisians waited to decide whom to back.

Philip of Burgundy learnt a second lesson about Paris. In 1429 he was still hedging his bets, still trying to keep the kind of watch over French affairs that his father had done. But in 1430 he married into the pro-English Portuguese royal family and he began to think that his future lay in acquiring yet more of the Netherlands, so that spending money on fighting in France began to look like a bad investment. Others around him had their own reason for wanting an accommodation with Charles. Georges de La Trémoïlle had a brother at the Burgundian court. If Joan were out of the way, such men were thinking, the tortuous route to a Franco-Burgundian rapprochement could be opened. Voices at the court of France began to speak in the same sense. In late September the king dissolved Joan's army and sent Alençon home. In late October Joan was sent off to the upper Loire.

Joan had her uses. Much of the upper Loire was dominated by a freebooting captain, Perrinet Gressaert, nominally an ally of the English and Burgundians, but in fact a self-seeking mercenary, one of the last survivors of a military type that the Hundred Years War had fostered. Gressaert was not much more than an irritant, a fly soon forgotten when he was swotted. In October Joan set out from Bourges on her least memorable and least-known campaign. She moved on St-Pierre-le-Moûtier, a stronghold on the River Allier – and therefore difficult to help – and in early November she took the town, retaining enough authority to be able to prevent a massacre. For the last time her characteristic plan of impetuous frontal attack was successful. But on turning east to the River Loire she was faced with the formidable defences of La Charité-sur-Loire. In vain she pleaded for reinforcements from local people, as in Riom. The weather was harsh, the bombardment had little effect and in a grim mood the siege had to be lifted. Back at Jargeau, which she had attacked so enthusiastically and taken just six months earlier, Joan learnt that she and her family had been ennobled. It was perhaps a pay-off, but she did not take the hint.

In 1430 she acted on her own initiative. One of the terms of the truce between Charles VII and Philip the Good had been that Charles would give up certain towns he had recently captured, including

Compiègne, while his cousin of Burgundy had earlier promised to vacate Paris. Alhough the duke had not yet surrendered the capital, the king wanted to keep his part of the bargain by returning Compiègne. At the end of March Joan heard that the townsmen were preparing to disobey Charles's wishes. She hurried off to help them and on the way defeated an Anglo-Burgundian force at Lagny. On 14 May she reached her target, and entered the town; her objective, to relieve it, proved beyond her. Eight days after her arrival an Anglo-Burgundian force surrounded Compiègne and during a sortie on the following day she was cut off and pulled from her horse by an archer called Lyonnel. She was handed over to Jean de Luxembourg, who, according to a later testimony, was willing to have her ransomed if she would cease to fight the Burgundians. According to the witness Haimond de Maincy, she refused. She would have been cheered to find out that Compiègne was to humiliate the troops investing it by not falling to them. To her captors she was worth more than any royal city, since her capture discredited her cause.

FIVE

Coming to Trial

In late April 1429 Joan joined the royal army at Blois. In late May 1430 she was captured outside Compiègne. At the end of May 1431 she was burnt to death in Rouen. Her public career is thus neatly divisible into two nearly equal parts, the first involving her military career, the second her trial and execution; but this division does not correspond to a neat division in her way of thinking or of behaving. Her voices impelled her to take up arms and her voices were tested by her judges. Her masculine dress and political pronouncements scandalised her foes long before she was questioned, judged and condemned. The mission she had fulfilled so spectacularly in 1429 was vilified for its seeming ultimate failure in 1431.

There was never any doubt that she would be put on trial and found guilty; the only point at issue was how. She was a prisoner of war and therefore she might be worthy of ransom, although not as much as a king, like John II of France who had died in England before the ransom money could be paid, or as a royal duke, like Charles of Orléans, who was still in gaol fifteen years after Agincourt. That she was valuable was indicated by English anxiety to pay a significant amount to have her, but the purpose of the money exchange was to gain control of her fate: she was bought so she could be given a show trial. She could have been accused of treachery to her lawful king, Henry, and yet Bedford, acting in Henry's name, was keen to arraign her before an ecclesiastical court. The only court considered suitable was an inquisitorial court.

Historical myth has given the inquisitions a bad name, but in 1430 an inquisitorial trial properly conducted was probably the fairest trial anywhere in Europe. In England at this time, for example, whereas the local courts did not allow the accused to have counsel or to produce witnesses on their behalf and did not grant them time to prepare a defence, an inquisitorial court conceded a right to be informed of any charges, to know the names of the prosecution witnesses (except in cases where the witnesses' lives would have been put at risk), to receive copies of their depositions, to have the help of counsel, to dispute and challenge charges. Inquisitions also conceded to the accused a right of silence.

Clearly, Bishop Cauchon, the man who masterminded Joan's trial and sentenced her, despite his expertise as a licentiate in canon law, with his unrivalled experience of pleading a hard case at a General Council of the Church, was disqualified from presiding by one simple fact: he, like all the assessors, was her avowed enemy. But he claimed he had the right to try her because she had been captured in his diocese of Beauvais, and yet, even though one of the spiritual peers of France, he had stayed away from Charles VII's coronation. He had also been ejected from his diocese by Joan's supporters, so that he had a possible motive of revenge that was in itself enough to disqualify him from acting in the case. Worse still, his whole career had been based round the cause of the Anglo-Burgundian alliance and its current concomitant, the 'dual monarchy' (Henry V's rule as King of England, and, in his eyes, King of France also). In 1397–1403 he had been Rector of Paris University, an institution committed to political policies he shared. In 1415, at the Council of Constance, he had defended the view of the Paris theologian Jean Petit that John, Duke of Burgundy, had been right to murder Louis, Duke of Orléans, and on that occasion he had shown a precise knowledge of correct procedure. When trying Joan, however, he interrogated her under oath before she was charged; he also demanded answers to questions she was not obliged to reply to and never allowed her advice, never sought out evidence that might conflict with his case. It may well be that he genuinely believed her guilty of sorcery and heresy, and that his opinions were sound; but the trial he conducted violated the best practices of inquisitions.

How such a trial should be conducted Cauchon had seen at the Council of Constance, when the Czech priest John Huss and a lay disciple of his were examined on charges of heresy and condemned. There was a difference between Huss and Joan, however: Huss was an educated man who believed that he could demonstrate the soundness of his personal interpretation of Christianity, whereas Joan had no special doctrine to teach and was marked out from other lay Christians only by spiritual experiences she thought authentic. As such experiences are rare, Joan needed to be examined not by dialecticians but by experts at discerning spirits, who might discover if she were deluded. The trial she was in fact granted was technically unfair, on a par with the average secular trial in England or France at the time, where those in power did not lose.

The English did not have much experience of inquisitions till their recent experience of heresy. Inquisitions had been set up in southern France, where they had been used to root out the Cathars, a sect who held a dualistic view of God and the world. Although by about 1300 the Cathars were vanquished, inquisitions remained a procedure useful to the Church, and so they survived. They were employed partly to keep religious dissenters of any kind under control, the most dangerous of whom were university lecturers, with the training to question Church teaching. Such a person was John Wyclif, an Englishman prominent at Oxford, the country's one influential university, before becoming notorious nationwide for his attack on authority. While the bishops took steps against him, they remained worried at the attraction his anticlerical theology held for leading laymen. They wanted the cooperation of the ruling classes in parliament, lay as well as clerical; and this they obtained when the statute *De haeretico comburendo* laid down rulings similar to Continental practice: heretics whose guilt had been proven in Church courts – and by definition a heretic was guilty of bad faith – could be liable to the penalty of burning under the secular law if they 'relapsed', that is, if they obdurately stuck to their heresy or, worse still, reverted to it. The statute became law in the reign of Henry IV, whose uncertain title to the throne made him all the more keen to please the Church. No king, however, was so enthusiastic to crush heresy as his son, Henry V.

Although when he was Prince of Wales, Henry was squeamish about the horrid fate awaiting heretics, he changed his mind at the beginning of his reign when he had to cope with heretics who turned rebels. In 1413, proceedings were begun against the well-connected knight Sir John Oldcastle for possessing heretical tracts. Sir John was put in the Tower to reflect on his errors, but when friends contrived his escape he moved from religious to civil disobedience and plotted to kill the king and his brothers. When the plot was discovered, the government reacted swiftly and decisively against the knights who led the 'Lollards', as Wycliffites were called, and those, drawn mainly from the artisan class, society's natural nonconformists, who made up the mass of the dissenters. As a political threat, Lollardy was finished, and until the coming of the Reformation survived only as an underground movement. The shock of these events, however, left Henry V and probably also his brother John of Lancaster, later Duke of Bedford, with a pathological hatred of heresy. It was at the same time as the Lollard revolt that Huss became an internationally renowned heretic; he could be regarded as a scion of England's religious deviance, for the spread of Wycliffite ideas to the Czech people had coincided with Richard II's first marriage to Anne of Bohemia. The Lancastrian dynasty dedicated itself to the uprooting of dangerous beliefs; in 1428 Cardinal Beaufort, half-brother to Henry IV, was charged by the pope with leading a crusade against the Hussites; and Bedford, the conscience of the Lancastrians in France after the death of his elder brother Henry V, called Joan 'a disciple and limb of the fiend', who 'used false enchantments and sorcery'.[1]

Bedford held the conviction, prevalent among the English, that Joan was a witch. In claiming to identify a witch he showed himself to be a thoroughly modern man. Witchcraft was a recent craze. For centuries intellectuals trained in Arab science had valued the occult knowledge transmitted through alchemy – by which a 'projector' could change 'base' or common metals into gold – and astrology, by which future events could be predicted from the movements of the heavens. These studies, which would lead to the evolution of modern chemistry and astronomy, were forms of magic attractive to the learned. There were other, less salubrious forms. Necromancers conjured up spirits within their magic circles, healers effected cures with magic potions and spells, sorcerers used holy objects for malicious purposes. All these had one thing in common: they dabbled with supernatural powers. No one, however, was as evil as those practising black magic or witchcraft, for the essence of witchcraft, the theologians said, was a pact with the devil. One revivalist preacher, Bernardino of Siena, told his listeners that anyone who failed to denounce a culprit to an inquisitor must answer for the omission on the Day of Judgement.

In the English royal family, Bedford shared his elder brother's horror of anything connected with witchcraft. The pressure of investigations, whether carried out by inquisitorial methods or not, required a clutch of erudite theologians and canon or Church lawyers. Since the early years of the thirteenth century the life of the Church had been transformed by the founding and dissemination of the orders of friars.

It was above all the manpower of the first two orders, those founded by St Francis and St Dominic, and of these above all the Dominicans or Friars Preacher, who provided the Church with the men it needed. The long hours of study to which Dominicans were committed, made easier by opportunities afforded by the universities, prepared them for the arduous work of assessing who was or was not a heretic or a witch. They compiled books on procedure, kept records of their cases and outlined the symptoms they were looking for. Often, as in Joan's case, they were dealing with illiterate suspects. Usually, as in her case too, they had a clear idea of what they were trying to find out; they wasted no time on confusion or contradiction. Once brought before an inquisitorial court, Joan might not have a technically correct trial – in her case prima facie she did not – but she would have her presuppositions clearly defined, she would have her words redrafted in technical, precise theological terms, she would have subtle arguments debated before her. What is astonishing about the surviving records is that in whatever circumstances they were compiled, they capture the tone of her spoken French, urgent, colloquial, direct. No one else talked so freely to Church lawyers and theologians, men of acumen and authority. Joan did not go quietly into the night.

The Burgundians removed Joan from the war; the English kept her out of the war for good.

One of her first enemies to interview her, according to an early chronicler, was Philip of Burgundy. He perceived her capture as a sign of God's favour, in particular His wish that the affairs of the true King of England and France should prosper. Like many involved in French politics in the early fifteenth century, including Henry V and probably Joan herself, Philip viewed victory as a sign of God's favour and defeat of His disapproval. Although from 1215 the Church no longer sanctioned priestly blessing of trials by battle, the attitude that God was on the side of the winners persisted and was to persist at least till the time of Oliver Cromwell. Joan was now a loser, and any lingering aura of invincibility was gone. She was a liability to those who had believed in her, for she was incapable of leading any more men to victory; and her prediction that the English would be driven first from Paris, then from France appeared incredible. She was a fantasist; there had been fantasists before.

And yet her enemies began to take her more seriously, treating her less as a fantasist than as someone who was wickedly deluded.

Philip was keen to send letters to cities in his lands, among them
Leiden, Delft, Dordrecht, Zevenbergen and Amsterdam, telling them
that she had been captured. His fame needed boosting. His men had
taken Joan outside Compiègne: they could not take Compiègne
itself. In August French troops began an attack on the southern
Burgundian county of Charolais, which eventually fell in the spring
of 1431. They also attacked the northern frontiers of the duchy near
Auxerre, which had fallen to Joan, and defeated a Burgundian army
at the battle of Chappes, near Bar-le-Seine. And although during the
year the French assault came to a halt, Charles VII was able to keep
up the pressure by enlisting the help of the Duke of Austria. Charles,
it seems, was coming to share the opinion of the war party, who had
agreed with Joan that Philip's endless truces were not worth much.
But for some time Charles still kept Georges de La Trémoïlle as his
main adviser and was still persuaded that Trémoïlle's belief in
accommodation with Philip of Burgundy was a sound instinct.
While the king's son and heir, Louis XI, set out to destroy
Burgundian power, Charles needed to neutralise that power to
defeat England. In 1430–1 he could not do so, because Philip was
content to remain an ally of the English.

In November 1430 Joan was sold by Jean de Luxembourg, Comte
de Ligny, vassal of the Duke of Burgundy, to the highest bidder, who
just happened to be the English. It may seem strange that it took the
best part of six months to decide who would be her gaoler. On
26 May 1430, a letter from the Vicar General of the Inquisitor was
sent to Philip, asking that Joan be sent to the city of Paris for trial, on
the grounds that she was suspected of having committed crimes
'smacking of heresy', and promising to act in accordance with the
advice and favour of the good men of the university. This letter was
followed up by two more letters from the university itself, one for
Philip and another for Jean de Luxembourg; that to Jean expressed
concern that there had been talk of Joan being ransomed, as indeed
there had been. The two men were invited to hand her over for trial
to the Bishop of Beauvais, 'within whose diocese she has been
apprehended'. Both the university and the bishop were to get what
they wanted, but not in the manner that they wanted. The letters,
dated 14 July, were brought to the Burgundian camp by Pierre
Cauchon, who demanded that he handle Joan himself. Cauchon was
determined to cope with a heretic who had defied his English masters

and who was indirectly responsible for his being driven fom his see. He had an inducement for those whom he met: he could offer good English money, either a pension of 2,000–3,000 *livres* for Guillaume de Wandonne, the man-at-arms who had taken Joan prisoner, and 6,000 *livres* for his lord or, in Henry's name, 10,000 francs 'according to the right, usage and custom of France'. The terms made clear one fact that was bound to have a bearing on the trial: Joan was to be not a prisoner of the Church, but a prisoner of the English.

Jean de Luxembourg hesitated. He was in no hurry to give Joan up. He wanted cash and Bedford was short of cash. Bedford persuade the Estates of Normandy to grant an aide of 120,000 *livres tournois*, of which 10,000 was to 'purchase . . . Joan the Maid, who is said to be a sorcerer, a warlike person, leading the armies of the Dauphin'; the cash, most of it in gold, had to be advanced by the English exchequer. Cauchon reported back to the Earl of Warwick that his negotiations were going well. Joan stayed with Jean, first at Clairoix near Compiègne, then at Beaulieu-les-Fontaines, near Noyon. At first her steward, Jean d'Aulon, attended her, but when she tried to escape from Beaulieu Castle, she was put alone into a tiny, dark cell. Eventually she was transferred to Jean de Luxembourg's principal château at Beaurevoir, and it was there that she gained powerful friends in Jean's wife, his wealthy aunt Jeanne and possibly his stepdaughter too. They tried to persuade her to wear women's clothes; and the discussions that Joan had with the ladies has given the impression that this was a pleasant period for her. But while for Jean and the Earl of Warwick she was a counter worth bargaining for, to some of the French her value had vanished. Archbishop Regnault of Reims told his people peevishly that she 'had not wanted to take advice, but to do everything according to her wishes', and as for Charles, it may have been as a gesture of his admiration of her when in 1437 he entered Paris that he asked the devoted d'Aulon to walk beside him holding the bridle of his horse. In 1430 he may have thought of trying to help her, but he did nothing. There was in fact little he could do.

Joan jumped from the Beaurevoir tower, either as a bid for freedom or as a gesture of despair. Jean took no chances: he wanted his money. She was therefore sent under close guard to be imprisoned in the duke's city residence, the Cour Le Comte at Arras. On 21 November the University of Paris wrote to congratulate

King Henry that she was in his power and to ask that she be transferred into the custody of Cauchon and the Inquisitor. The request was premature – she was then only at Le Crotoy – and naive – the English had no intention of handing her over to anyone. Five weeks later she was already in Rouen. On 28 December Cauchon arranged to be conceded a territorial jurisdiction so that she could be tried as though in Beauvais; and on 3 January she was technically handed over to him by the English, technically because she remained an English prisoner. As a lawyer who had tried heretics once before (in 1426), Cauchon wanted to make the trial appear to be fair. Equally, the English lay authorities wanted only one result: her death.

SIX

The Preparatory Trial

The first stage of any inquisitorial process could involve a
lengthy inquiry, during which the judges attempted to find out
the precise grounds on which the accused could be indicted for
heresy. In Joan's case this led to cross-questioning, as the judges
often seemed to go round in circles, like some bird of prey seeking
the best way to attack its victim. By comparison, the subsequent
'ordinary' or actual trial was short and to the point.

The record of the trial is couched in the sonorous phrases beloved
of grand ecclesiastics. 'Pierre, by divine mercy Bishop of Beauvais,
and brother Jean Lemaître, of the order of Preaching friars . . . and
venerable master Jean Graverent of the same order . . . eminent
doctor of theology, by apostolic authority Inquisitor of the Faith and
of Heretical perversity in the whole kingdom of France' sent greeting
in the author and accomplisher of faith, Our Lord Jesus Christ.
They knew of the reputation of a woman 'of the name of Joan,
commonly called the Maid', who 'had immodestly put on immodest
garments suited to the male sex' and who besides had the
presumption to 'perform, to speak, and to pass on many things
opposed to the Catholic faith and detrimental to the articles of
orthodox belief'.[1] Cauchon explained how he and the Christian
prince, 'our lord the King of France and England', had summoned
the most illustrious lord the Duke of Burgundy and the lord Jean de
Luxembourg to surrender this woman 'to us, that we might, hold a
complete inquiry into her acts and sayings before proceeding further,
according to the Church's laws'. The inquest was to be carried out in
Rouen, beginning on 9 January 1431. Some distinguished men were
asked to act as advisers: abbots Gilles of Ste-Trinité de Fécamp,
doctor of sacred theology, and Nicolas de Jumièges, doctor of canon
law; Pierre, prior of Longueville, doctor of theology; Raoul Roussel,
treasurer of Rouen Cathedral, doctor of both canon and civil law;

Nicolas de Venderès, Archdeacon of Eu, licentiate in canon law; Robert Le Barbier, licentiate in both canon and civil law; Nicolas Couppequesne, bachelor of theology, and Nicolas Loiselleur, master of arts. Jean d'Estivet, canon of the cathedral churches of Beauvais and Bayeux, was to exercise in the trial the office of prosecutor or procurator general, Master Jean de La Fontaine, master of arts and licentiate of canon law, was made councillor, commissary and examiner, and as notaries or secretaries were chosen the 'prudent and honest' Master Guillaume Colles, also called Boisguillaume, and Guillaume Manchon, priests, notaries by apostolic and imperial authority at the archiepiscopal court of Rouen; and Master Jean Massieu, priest, ecclesiastical dean of Rouen, was appointed executor of what was decided. The trial was recommended by the University of Paris.

It is worth commenting briefly on some of these men. Many were officials from Normandy, which was then still firmly under English control, and most were from Rouen. Some were notable, not always for good reasons. Estivet specialised in coarse language, Lemaître in evasion; he avoided taking part in the proceedings for as long as he could and did not appear till 13 March. Others obviously depended on the English: the Abbot of Fécamp received 1,000 *livres* a year from them, Roussel, also in their pay, was rewarded for his long service with the archbishopric of Rouen in 1444, five years before the city fell to Charles VII. As for the University of Paris, which provided expert comment, for some years now only those in favour of the Burgundian alignment with the Anglo-French monarchy had been employed.

The evidence against Joan was read out on 13 January, and further experts appointed. Ten days later articles were drawn up and discussed. On 13 February the officers appointed took the oath; on 19 February the court decided to summon the Inquisitor, but, as Lemaître refused to act, it wrote directly to the Inquisitor in person. Clearly the chief inquisitorial officials were not as committed to the cause as Cauchon and friends. The court reminded them that 'heresy is a disease which creeps like a cancer, secretly killing the simple, unless the knife of the Inquisitor cuts it away'. Cauchon added that the king (that is, the child-king Henry) had graciously invited him to act in the case. In all the proceedings that followed it was Cauchon who took the lead.

At last, at eight o'clock in the morning of 21 February, a Wednesday, the first public session was held in the chapel royal of Rouen Castle, an English property. The court announced that Joan could not go to Mass, since she wore men's clothes. She was required to take an oath: 'we lawfully required the said Joan to take proper oath, with her hands on the holy gospels, to speak the truth in answer to such questions put to her, as before said'. For the first time she had the chance to show how sharp she was. She replied correctly: 'I do not know what you wish to examine me on. Perhaps you might ask such things that I would not tell.' She was then asked if she would answer questions on the faith, to which she replied that

> concerning her father and her mother and what she had done since she had taken the road to France, she would gladly swear; but concerning the revelations from God, these she had never told or revealed to any one, save only to Charles whom she called king; nor would she reveal them to save her head; for she had them in visions or in her secret counsel; and within a week she would know certainly whether she might reveal them.

She did take an oath to answer on questions of faith. In this, as in subsequent exchanges, she was to show she was a better lawyer than her accusers, for good inquisitorial practice did not allow them to ask her to give evidence that could be used against her, let alone to answer every question they asked her. So was established a pattern of dialogue between legalistic, moralistic, literal-minded clerics concerned with self-justification and a free spirit without any theological training.

The first questions were routine and seemingly trivial, concerning her life at home. The overall aim of the questioning first became obvious when she was asked to say her Paternoster and she told Cauchon that if he would hear her in confession then she would gladly say it. Cauchon knew that a witch would not dare say the Paternoster: she guessed, with disconcerting shrewdness, that he would not dare hear her confession.

Cauchon changed the subject. He forbade her to try to leave her prison: she would not promise, in case she tried to escape and succeeded. The court then ordered her to be put in chains, thus once again failing to observe good legal practice. She was defiant: 'It is true that I wished and still wish to escape, as is lawful for any captive or prisoner.' English soldiers, again in defiance of correct legal practice, were appointed to guard her.

On Thursday 22 February, in the second session, after an altercation about oath-taking, she was questioned by Jean Beaupère. The court had made inquiries in her neighbourhood and learnt that she had been a pious girl, which she confirmed; the one sign that marked her out as unusual, she declared with startling assurance, was that she had heard voices. She claimed the voice she first heard 'taught her to be good and to go to church often; and it told her that she must come to France'. She added that Beaupère would not learn from her

> in what form that voice appeared to her. She further said this voice told her once or twice a week that she should leave and come to France, and that her father knew nothing about her intentions. She said the voice told her to come, and she could no longer stay where she was; and the voice told her again that she should raise the siege of the city of Orléans. She said too that the voice told her that she, Joan, should go to Robert de Baudricourt in the town of Vaucouleurs of which he was the captain, and he would provide an escort for her.

She volunteered to say how she came to Vaucouleurs, how she easily recognised Robert de Baudricourt, though she had never seen him before, how her voice identified him, how it told her he would refuse her twice, how the third time he would provide her with an escort. She offered to fill in many details about her journey to Chinon, but on the question of men's dress 'she several times refused to answer' and also said 'that it was altogether necessary to change her women's clothes for men's'. She believed her idea was sound. At Chinon, her gift for recognising a stranger was evident once more, and this time it was the man whom she called the king; and once more she did so by the 'advice of her voice'.

She told him she wanted to make war on the English; then she started to hedge. Asked whether there was any light when the voice revealed her king, she answered: 'Pass on to the next question.' Asked if she saw no angel above the king, she answered: 'Spare me that. Continue.' She added that before the king put her to work he had several apparitions and beautiful revelations. Asked what revelations and apparitions the king had had, she answered: 'I will not tell you.

It is not now the time to tell you; but send to the king and he will tell you.' She knew and they knew that they would never do that.

About her voices she became more explicit. 'There is not a day,' she told them, 'when I do not hear this voice; and I have much need of it. I never asked of it any final reward but the salvation of my soul.' It 'told me to remain at St-Denis in France', and she 'wished to remain; but against my will the lords took me away . . . If I had not been wounded, I would not have left; I was wounded in the trenches before Paris, after I left St-Denis; but recovered in five days.' She admitted that she caused an assault to be made before Paris on a feast day. Asked if she thought it was a good thing to do, she answered: 'Pass on.'

By the date of the third session, on 24 February, it became obvious what the court was trying to do. Every time Joan was asked to tell the truth, the whole truth and nothing but the truth, she invoked a medieval equivalent of the Fifth Amendment: she refused to say she would tell the whole truth, for it might be wrong of her to do so. In the end she settled for promising to say what was relevant to the case. On this occasion she said that 'of her coming to France she would willingly speak the truth, but not the whole truth; and a week would not be enough for that'. Yet once again she was the better lawyer, but the court advised her that she would make herself seem in the wrong if she would not swear. She was unmoved, saying that she came from God, and that there was nothing for her to do here, and she asked to be sent back to God, from whom she came. When they told her she would be charged with what she was accused of, she simply replied: 'Continue.'

The court got down to the day's theme. Beaupère was soon questioning her about 'the voice'. How did she react to it, what did it tell her, what had it said when she woke up? A look of defiance flashed across her face as she told Cauchon to be careful what he did, as she was sent by God and he put himself in great danger. Had the voice forbidden her to reply to all that she was asked? 'I will not answer that, I shall not tell you everything I have been told about the king.' She was sure, as she was sure of the Christian faith, that the voice came from God. Would it obey her? Only if God willed it. Had she seen a light when the voice came? Yes, the light comes with the voice, but she would not say if she saw anything else with the voice; and she had not promised to answer everything she was asked. She quoted the proverb, 'Men are sometimes hanged for telling the truth.'

What must have annoyed the men facing her became clear when she was asked if she was in God's grace. This was a trick question to see if she was presumptuous, but Joan answered with great astuteness: if she were not in God's grace she would pray that God would put her there; if she was, may she be kept there; and if she were not, the voice would not come to her. She also irritated them because her voice sided with the king of France against the Burgundians. A line of questioning they could have developed, but did not, was that if the Church is universal, why should God prefer one group of people to another? The reason perhaps that this argument was not deployed is that her judges too had taken a political stance, so that a criticism of her support of 'France for the French' could be turned equally against their belief in France for the Anglo-Burgundians.

The court made its first clumsy attempts to prove she was a witch. She was vague about life in the fields and could not remember when she had helped with the animals. She had little to say on the so-called fairies' tree or the fountain nearby. Sometimes she had made garlands for Our Lady of Domremy there, but she had never seen fairies there or anywhere else, nor did she trust the story that from the local wood would come a maid who would work miracles. She was not even superstitious. What made her singular was her insistence on wearing male attire.

During the fourth session, on Tuesday 27 February, the court tried to go more deeply into the question of the voices. She came round to the subject of St Catherine and St Margaret, of the crowns on their heads, of how she had been asked all this before at Poitiers – not a happy reference, as the theologians there had supported her king – and how they were easy to distinguish from one another. She had known them for seven years, but she would not tell them more, she had said it all before at Poitiers, and some revelations were for the King of France alone, not for them. She could not say if the saints were the same age, if they spoke at the same time, which appeared first, but she had been comforted by St Michael – yes, he had come first. Was it a long time since she had first heard him? She was speaking not of his voice but of the comfort he brought her, since she was about thirteen; and he had first come with many angels. She came to France only at God's command. She had seen St Michael with her own eyes, but what he looked like she was not allowed to say, nor was she going to tell them what he had first said, though she had once told the king everything. She wished her questioner had a copy of the record made at Poitiers, she was not sure what she could reveal to him now, but she would not have come to France without permission. And she wore male costume only because commanded to do so.

At the moment when the topic changed, the records stop citing her own words. Her voices, the lawyers noted, had told her about the sword unearthed at Ste-Catherine-de-Fierbois. She carried it continually from the time she had got it till she left St-Denis, after the assault on Paris. But she had not regarded it as a talisman, it had not been specially blessed, nor did it bring her better fortune and she did not know where it was. Besides she preferred her standard to her sword; and the painting on it was put there by God's command.

The dialogue turned naturally to her military exploits. How many troops had she been given? Ten to twelve thousand, she thought. She was certain she would relieve Orléans, it had been revealed to her and she had told the king that she would. She had been wounded but she was comforted by St Margaret and the wound healed within a fortnight; she knew she would be wounded. She was questioned over her behaviour at Jargeau – at this point the questioning was broken off until later in the week.

On 1 March, at the start of the fifth session, Joan put her hands on the holy gospels and said: 'Of what I know concerning the trial I will willingly tell the truth, and will tell altogether as much as if I were before the pope of Rome.' Which pope, they asked? 'Are there two?' she countered. The Count of Armagnac had asked her which of the three sovereign pontiffs to obey, and she had said she would give him an answer when she was in Paris, or anywhere where she was at rest. She thought she should obey the pope in Rome.

Did she put the names of Jesus and Mary with a cross in her letters? Sometimes yes, sometimes no. The court quoted from her correspondence with the count and also with Bedford and the King (Henry). She said, where one letter said 'Surrender to the Maid' it should say, 'Surrender to the King'. She, not any lord, had dictated the letters, she said, and within seven years the English would lose a greater stake than they had done at Orléans, for they would lose everything in France. (As so often before, she was over-optimistic: the English did indeed lose Paris, but little else for fifteen years.) She wished it would all happen by St John's day, in other words by midsummer. Perhaps, by Martinmas (in November), 'it might be that the English would be overthrown'.

Over and over again she was questioned about her voices, how often they talked with her, what they looked like, what language they spoke (why would St Margaret speak English, if she is not on the English side?). The questions moved to her rings; were they in some way magical? Next, she would not tell them what promises the voices had made, except that the king would regain his kingdom and they would take her to Paradise. She would not say if they would release her from prison, nor what was for the ears of the King of France only. She had nothing to say about a mandrake – they were back to the subject of superstition – and robustly rebuked them for thinking St Michael was naked. Not much on sexual fantasies, then, not even much to savour when they moved the discussion from saintly crowns to the king's crown at the coronation. Throughout this session a record of her words was preserved.

In the sixth session, on Saturday 3 March, she was pressed to speak about the bodies of her saints. She would not be drawn, she would not incriminate herself; she knew she would be delivered, but not how or when. Why had people at Poitiers not pressed her on the matter of her dress? They had only asked when she changed, to which the answer was at Vaucouleurs. Had her voices ordered it, had the queen asked her about it, had the Demoiselle of Luxembourg and the Lady of Beaurevoir offered her a woman's dress, or the cloth to make one, and told her to wear it – she had replied God had given her permission, it was not yet time. She said she should obey God in this matter. She would not say who had told her to wear men's clothes.

She was questioned about the pennons on her standard. Had holy water been thrown on them? Had any of her companions-at-arms written on their pennons the names Jhesus Maria? Had she worn something round at the back of her helmet before Jargeau? Had she known brother Richard? How had he greeted her? Had she seen pictures of herself in circulation? Yes, at Arras. The court was pressing her to admit to some superstitious practice or to show pleasure in being considered a saint. Did her own party think she was sent from God? Had they kissed her hands and feet? Had she been a godmother? Had women touched her hand and her rings? Who had caught butterflies in her standard? Had she received the sacraments in men's clothes? Why had she taken the Bishop of Senlis's horse? How old was the child she restored to life in Lagny? Had she seen Catherine de La Rochelle, a woman who had turned out to be a fraud? – they were trying to show that she was a fraud too.

At Beaurevoir, during her four-month stay, she had jumped, though her voices had forbidden her to do so. She would rather commend her soul to God than fall into the hands of the English. Had she not blasphemed the name of God? Never: it was not her custom to swear. At Soissons she had never said she would have the commander drawn and quartered.

The first part of the public sessions finished in the first ten days of March. They had been too animated, with too many people talking at once, so the judges and assessors decided to continue the preliminaries without any interruption and make it easier for the theologians to study Joan's answers. To modern observers, a trial in secret session smacks of a denial of human rights, but in the fifteenth century there was nothing strange in the procedure, partly because an inquisitorial trial was then the most open available; and, besides, nobody talked about human rights.

Jean de La Fontaine was charged to make legal inquiries; and when the hearings resumed in prison on 10 March, he was Joan's interrogator. After asking her about her capture and the voice's reaction to it, he moved on to ask about her banner, her shield and her coat of arms, her horses, her wealth. What she had was her king's own money, given so that she could fight. What was the sign she gave the king? It is with the king's treasure, and she would not say what it was. An angel had borne it to her king and after she left more than 300 had seen it.

On Monday 12 March the Dominican Brother Jean Lemaître, the Inquisitor's vicar, was summoned, together with another Dominican, Brother Ysambard de La Pierre; the Inquisitor himself, Jean Graverent, had excused himself. In prison on the same day, Joan was brought before Jean de La Fontaine, who went straight back to the angel that brought the sign to her king. 'He told the king to set me to work straightaway to free the country.' By this time it must have been dawning on her that there was an intellectual barrier between her and her judges: she was sure she had experienced a series of private revelations, while they were sure she had not. This explains the literalistic line of the questions: had she received letters from St Michael? 'Give me a week and I shall give you an answer,' she replied. She did not help her cause by her lapses into hyperbole, claiming this time that in three years with the help of her saints she would bring the Duke of Orléans back to France.

By Tuesday 13 March Jean d'Estivet had been made Prosecutor and Jean Massieu ordered to carry out Cauchon's citations and summonses. Lemaître and Cauchon continued with their examination. Joan refused to be drawn to speak about the sign of the crown, as this would mean perjuring herself, but she did say that Charles would have the whole kingdom. Had she spoken to St Catherine? Yes, and she was told to answer boldly. The crown she had seen at Chinon and at Reims meant that Charles would rule all France. It had been borne by an angel, which she thought the Archbishop of Reims, the lords d'Alençon, de La Trémoïlle and Charles de Bourbon had seen, while many churchmen and others had seen the crown but not the angel. The judges pressed her further on the crown and the angel; the clergy, she said, knew about it by their learning. Was this a crack at the clergy ranged before her? She was fearless, but also incapable of irony.

On Wednesday 14 March, the Inquisitor's vicar appointed a notary, Nicolas Taquel, a priest of the diocese of Rouen. Joan's recent behaviour was scrutinised. Why had she jumped from the tower at Beaurevoir? She had heard that the people of Compiègne, all of them, were to be put to fire and to the sword, and she would rather die than live after such a destruction of good people. That was one reason why she jumped: the other was that she knew she had been sold to the English, and she would have died rather than fall into the hands of her enemies the English. Had the leap been made at the counsel of her voices? St Catherine told her almost every day not to jump, and God would help her, and the people of Compiègne too. As she leaped she commended herself to God. She hoped that by the leap she would escape from being given to the English. She added touchingly that because of the noise of the prison and the tumult made by her guards she did not always understand her voice, yet every day it came to her. She asked for freedom for France and herself.

She also asked for the salvation of her soul. She was still bright enough to ask for a copy of the questions and of her replies, so that she might give it to the people at Paris if she went there. Her judges must watch out; she would be helped. This led them to touch on her apparent presumption: was she sure she would be saved?

That same Wednesday afternoon in the prison the inquisitors came back to the same subject. She was sure she would be saved if she kept her word to God and guarded her virginity. She was not aware of any mortal sin, but was keen to go to confession as much as possible. They pressed her further: had she committed a mortal sin by taking a man at ransom and then putting him to death, by attacking Paris on a feast day, by wearing men's clothes, by taking a horse belonging to the Bishop of Senlis? On the last point she was scornful: the horse was no good for fighting.

On the following day, still in prison, Joan was 'charitably exhorted, admonished, and required' to defer to any decision by 'Our Holy Mother the Church', if she had done anything contrary to our faith. The court explained the distinction between the Church Triumphant, the Church in heaven, and the Church Militant, the Church on earth, and she was told to submit to the Church's decision whatever it was. She temporised: 'I will not give you any further answer for the present.' This was to be the crux of her debate with her judges. They expected her to accept whatever they decided. She could not see how what God told her in one way, by her voices, could conflict with what she learnt in another way, by the Church's teaching.

They asked her about her attempt to escape from the castle of Beaulieu; she would try to escape from anywhere. She admitted that so far her voices had not given her permission to escape from prison, but, if the door was open, that would mean God allowed her to do so. '*Aide toy, Dieu te aidera.*'

Since she wanted to hear Mass, why not in women's clothes? 'Would you promise I could go, if I was so dressed? And what do you answer, if I have sworn and promised to our king not to put off this dress? Yet I will tell you: have made for me a long dress reaching down to the ground, without a train, and give it to me to go to Mass; and then, on my return, I will put on once again the dress I have.' For the honour of God and of Our Lady could she please go to Mass 'in this good town'?

They asked her again about submitting to the Church. 'Everything that I have said or done is in the hand of God, and I commit myself to Him. I would do or say nothing against the Christian faith.

Would she submit in matters of faith to the Church's command? Her line was the same as it had been. She could not see how God's command, transmitted through her voices, could conflict with what she learnt in another way, through the Church's teaching. 'I will not add anything to my answers now, but next Saturday send me the priest, if you do not wish to come, and I will answer him with God's help, and it shall be set down in writing.'

She must have been puzzled: how had she done or said anything against the faith? She taught no special doctrine, like Wyclif or Huss. She claimed only that she had had certain religious experiences. They therefore asked her more about her voices, whether she bowed to them, whether she lit candles for them and had Mass said to them, if she always did what they told her to do, how she could tell if they were good spirits. On the first occasion it was St Michael who had appeared to her, 'the first time she was a young girl and was afraid; since then St Michael taught her and showed her so many things that she firmly believed it was he'. Asked what doctrine he taught her, her response was that 'in all things he told her to be a good child and God would help her'; among other things, he told her she should go and help the king of France. A great part of what the angel taught her is 'in this book', and the angel told her of the 'pity' that was in the kingdom of France. What her judges wished to imply was that her private revelations were unorthodox.

On Saturday 17 March they asked further questions about the appearance of St Michael and she told them something about him, but nothing about any other angels she had seen. She believed, she said, what St Michael did or said, as firmly as she believed that Our Lord Jesus Christ suffered and died for us. Did she wish to submit all her acts or sayings, either good or evil, to the decision of Our Mother the Church? She said she loved the Church and would support it with all her might for the Christian faith; and she was not a person to be forbidden to go to church or hear Mass. As for the good works she performed, and her coming, she must commit herself to the King of Heaven who sent her to Charles, son of Charles King of France, who would be king of all France, even though she could not predict when this would happen. As for the Church's decision, 'I commit myself to Our Lord, Who sent me, to Our Lady, and to all the Blessed Saints of Paradise.' She emphasised her point by asking, 'Why do you make difficulties when it is all one?' They told her that the Church Militant cannot err. Would she then submit to it? Cauchon noted that she would not give any further answers.

The inquisitors went back to the question of her dress – she said she wanted a long dress when she died – and of her grandmother, who saw the fairies, but was not a witch or a sorceress. As to her dress, she understood that it implied her military calling. And her saints' attitude to the English? 'They love those whom God loves, and hate whom He hates.' But her male costume still riled the court: did Our Lord approve? What armour had she offered in the church of St-Denis and why did she want her armour to be revered? Why were there five crosses on the sword she found at Ste-Catherine-de-Fierbois? Why were angels painted on her standard?

That afternoon it was natural for them to ask if the angels on her standard were St Michael and St Gabriel. The standard, she said, was just meant to honour Our Lord, who was painted on it holding the world. They asked if this standard gave her the power to win all the battles in which she fought; and what was the purpose of the sign she put on her letters, and the names Jhesus Maria? Devotion to the names of Jesus and Mary was a new devotion; Joan said that the clergy who wrote her letters put those words on the letters.

The court went on to graver matters, asking what would happen if she were to lose her virginity, would her voices stop coming to her? Had her king been right to have the Duke of Burgundy killed? Would she tell the pope more than she had told the court? Was she not bound to tell him everything? She then demanded to be brought to him. This time the court changed the subject. Her questioners wondered if she was superstitious about the power of her rings and presumptuous about claiming to be intimate with St Catherine: did she know anything about fairies? Apparently not.

Why was it her standard, they asked, rather than the standards of other captains that was carried into the Reims Cathedral at the consecration? 'It had been present in the perils; that was reason enough for it to be honoured,' she replied.

On Passion Sunday, 18 March, Joan's statements were presented to the assessors and on the following Thursday they were condensed into a small number of articles. On Saturday 24 March the interrogations were read in Joan's presence. She told them that her surname was d'Arc or Romée and that in her part of the country girls bore their mother's surname. She also asked that the questions and answers should be read consecutively to her, and she admitted as true whatever she did not then contradict. But she added these words to the article touching her taking woman's dress: 'Give me a woman's dress to go to my mother's house, and I will take it.' She would do this, she claimed, to escape from prison, and once outside she would find out what she should do. Finally, after the contents of the register had been read to her, 'the said Joan' confessed that she believed she had spoken well according to what had been written in the register and read to her, and she did not contradict any other saying from the register.

On Palm Sunday, 25 March, Joan asked permission to go to Mass in the male costume she was wearing and to receive the sacrament of the Eucharist on Easter Day. Would she give up male dress if she were granted permission? She answered that had not had any advice on the subject and could not yet wear women's clothes. The inquisitors pressed her to ask her saints if she could wear female dress, to which she replied she might be allowed to hear Mass as she was, but she could not change her costume. Neither side was capable of dialogue. The court would not give way, nor would she; indeed, she said that wearing men's clothes 'was not against the Church'. The court made a note of the conversation.

The interrogations had revealed the challenge that Joan's assertions made to the conventional wisdom of her interrogators. Did she believe that she had magical powers? Did she claim to be impeccable, that is sinless? Could she justify her unnatural style of dressing? Could she justify her claim to hear the voices of angels and saints? Would she accept the Church's authority? If the respective answers to these questions were yes, yes, no, no and no, then she was a witch and a heretic. The interrogators had a further concern: her confidence that Charles VII was God's elected, the man chosen to be the king of France. Her mission was a political one antithetical to their own politics. In the eyes of her English gaolers she was a prisoner of war already guilty of treason. In the eyes of her French judges, she was liable to the punishment of a heretic and a witch. What her trial had to prove was that her treason derived from her heresy and witchcraft.

This preliminary trial was only a preamble, a foretaste of what was to come. It was the decision of the subsequent 'ordinary' trial that would determine Joan's fate.

SEVEN

The Ordinary Trial

On Monday 26 March, the day after Palm Sunday, Joan's 'ordinary' trial opened. The court decided to draw up articles. If Joan refused to answer them, she would be said to have admitted them. Accordingly, on the following day the articles drawn up by the Prosecutor (or Promoter) were read out and Joan was questioned in French. Her battle for the right to silence had won a slight victory, for the Abbot of Fécamp asserted she should swear to tell the truth 'in all things concerning the trial' and would have problems only if she thought some matters the court considered were matters on which she would not give a full reply. Further, the Prior of Longueville thought she should not be compelled to answer yes or no.

Joan was willing to take an oath to tell the truth about anything relevant to the trial but refused an offer of advice, since she had no intention of not taking God's advice. Then, that day and the next, the charges were read out to her in French. She was suspected of being

a witch, enchantress, false prophet, a caller-up of evil spirits, superstitious . . . given to magic arts, thinking evil in our Catholic faith, schismatic . . . sacrilegious, idolatrous, apostate of the faith, accursed and working evil, blasphemous . . . scandalous, seditious, perturbing and obstructing the peace, inciting to war, cruelly thirsting for human blood, encouraging it to be shed, having utterly and shamelessly abandoned the modesty befitting her sex, and indecently put on the ill-fitting dress and state of men-at-arms; and for that and other things abominable to God and man, contrary to laws both divine and natural, and to ecclesiastical discipline, misleading princes and people; having . . . permitted and allowed herself to be adored and venerated, giving her hands to be kissed; heretical or at the least vehemently suspected of heresy.[1]

There followed a list of seventy articles of accusation, against which Joan's replies in the preparatory trial were carefully noted. The process of reading and recording took the court till the end of Holy Week. On Easter Eve she gave answers to some questions she had asked for time to think about. By Easter Monday the charges had been reduced to twelve key points, which the judges read over and reflected on during the next two days. By Easter Thursday, 5 April 1431, the final version was ready for detailed analysis by all the local experts.

Joan was to be investigated under twelve headings: her claim to 'see' Sts Michael, Catherine and Margaret; the sign 'the prince' had received; her conviction that she was visited by St Michael and the saints; her claim to knowledge through them of future events, such as an impending French success; her use of male clothes; her letters in the name of Jhesus Maria; her approach to 'a certain squire', in other words Robert de Baudricourt; her leap from the tower against the instruction of her saints; their promise to lead her to Paradise; her conviction that the saints speak to her in French, not in English, as they are not on the English side; her conviction that the voices come from God; and, finally, her conviction that what she had done had been done in God's name.

Sixteen doctors and six licentiates or bachelors in theology stated that they believed her revelations did not come from God, as there were lies, improbabilities and misleading fictions in what she maintained. To this they each added their individual comments. A few, such as Guesdon, made excuses and left, but most, with no more than a nod to papal or conciliar authority, agreed to condemn Joan unconditionally. On 18 April Joan was exhorted 'charitably'; on 2 May publicly admonished. 'We first tried to lead her back [to the truth] by means of many notable doctors of theology whom we sent to her on many different days . . . but the cunning of the devil prevailed and they have not yet been of any effect.' To this Joan replied: 'I trust in my judge. He is the King of Heaven and of earth.'

The judges explained to her that they represented the Church Militant here on earth, 'incapable of error or false judgement', yet she persisted in her own obstinate trust in her private line to God. What struck them as abominable was her assurance that she had private relations with angels and saints, that she did not have to wear conventional feminine clothes, that she had been given a special role in French politics by God – in short, it was her belief in a unique destiny that appalled them. 'I have a good master, Our Lord, to whom I refer everything, and to none other.' She was ambiguous about submitting to the judgment of a council, but when asked if she would submit to them, she said, 'Take me to him, and I will reply to him.' In conclusion, she was keenly urged anew to submit to the Church under pain of being abandoned by it; she replied with seeming arrogance: 'You will not do as you say against me without evil overtaking you, in body and soul.'

On Wednesday 9 May she was brought into the great tower of the castle of Rouen before her judges. Threatened with torture, she said, 'if you were to tear me limb from limb and separate my soul from my body, I would not tell you anything more: and if I did say anything, I should afterwards declare that you had compelled me to say it by force.' Then she said that on last Holy Cross Day she had been comforted by St Gabriel. She said she asked her voices whether she should submit to the Church, since the clergy were pressing her hard to submit, her voices told her that if she desired Our Lord to aid her she must wait on Him in all her doings . . . She asked her voices if she would be burnt and was told to wait on God, who would help her. Seeing the hardness of her heart and her manner of answering, the judges, 'fearing that the torments of torture would not do her much good', decided to postpone their application till they received more complete advice on the question. Loiseleur said he thought it good for the health of her soul to put her to the torture, but he deferred to other people's opinions.

On Saturday 19 May the University of Paris addressed its official response to the 'King of France and England', who 'with God's grace began on a fine course of action for our holy faith, that is the legal proceedings against this woman known as the Maid, against her scandals, errors and crimes, which are evident throughout the kingdom.' Beaupère, de Touraine and Midi had enlightened the university on the affair and in its turn the university asked their gracious Lord to end the affair as soon as possible. Master Jean Lefèvre and Brothers Martin Ladvenu and Ysambard de La Pierre hoped Joan would be charitably admonished and on 23 May her faults were publicly expounded to her in French by Pierre Maurice. The trial was over.

Joan had been unwilling to listen. All she said in her defence was 'As for my words and deeds, which I declared in the trial, I refer to them and will maintain them.' If she were condemned, she added, and 'she saw the fire and the faggots lit and the executioner ready to kindle the fire, and she herself were in it, she would say nothing else and would maintain till death what she said in the trial.' But on 24 May, after the public sermon, the proceedings took an unexpected turn. Quite suddenly, in her own style she recanted: 'Let all I have said and done be sent to Rome to our Holy Father the Pope to whom after God I refer myself. As for my words and deeds, they were done at God's command.' If there were any fault it was hers and no other person's. She referred herself 'to God and our Holy Father the Pope'. This, she was told, was to no avail, as they could not seek the pope 'at such a distance', and anyway a bishop in his own diocese was a competent judge. Then she recanted in French and the document was then translated into Latin; it was said that she had renounced her apparitions, had broken God's law by dressing like a man and having her hair cropped like a man's, by bearing arms, by wishing to shed blood, by calling up evil spirits.

And I vow, swear and promise to you, to my lord St Peter, Prince of the Apostles, to Our Holy Father the Pope of Rome, His vicar and his successors, to you, my lords, to the lord Bishop of Beauvais and the religious Brother Jean Lemaître, vicar of the lord Inquisitor of the faith, my judges, that I will never let myself be persuaded or for any other reason return to the said errors, from which it has pleased God to free me; but I will always live in the unity of Our Holy Mother Church and the obedience of our Holy Father the Pope of Rome. This I say, affirm and swear by God almighty and the Holy Gospels. In sign of which I have signed this schedule with my mark.

Signed 'Jehanne +'

For this statement she was sentenced to 'perpetual imprisonment, with the bread of sorrow and water of affliction', so as to weep for her failings and 'never from this time on commit anything to make others weep'.

On the afternoon of 24 May Joan put on woman's dress and she was visited in prison by Jean Le Maistre, Nicolas Midi, Nicolas Loiselleur, Thomas de Courcelles, and Brother Ysambard de La Pierre, who said how mercifully she had been treated. She said she would willingly wear women's clothes and would let her hair be shaved off. Her resolutions did not last, for on 28 May she went back to male costume – 'a short mantle, a hood, a doublet and other garments used by men' – which she claimed she preferred to women's clothes. 'She was told she had promised and sworn not to wear man's dress again, and replied that she never meant to take such an oath.' The reason, she added, was that promises to her had not been kept; she was not allowed to go to Mass and she was still in chains and she was not put in a prison with a woman companion. 'We her judges had heard from certain people that she had not yet cut herself off from her illusions and pretended revelations.' Her voices had told her to answer boldly. The preacher, she said, had falsely accused her of many things she had not done. She said too that what she had declared and recanted on Thursday was done because she was afraid of the fire. She believed her voices to be those of St Catherine and St Margaret and that they came from God. If her judges wished it, she would wear women's clothes. To nothing else would she agree.

Accordingly, on 29 May in the archiepiscopal chapel of Rouen, Cauchon sentenced her as a lapsed heretic. 'We exhorted her to believe the advice of the clergy and the distinguished people who instructed and taught her things relevant to her salvation, and especially that of the two venerable Preaching brothers who were then standing near her' – he was referring to Martin Ladvenu and Ysambard de La Pierre – and 'we denounce you as a rotten member, which, so that you shall not infect the other members of Christ, must be cast out of the unity of the Church, cut off from her body, and given over to the secular power: we cast you off, separate and abandon you.' He prayed that the secular power would be merciful to her if there were any signs of repentance in her. Her death sentence, however, he knew was now inevitable. The sentence was witnessed by the three notaries, Boisguillaume, Manchon and Taquel.

EIGHT

The Maid's Death

On 30 May 1431, in the market square of Rouen, Joan was burnt to death. She died quickly. There are many affecting descriptions of her last moments, but all date from the 1450s; not a single one was written down in 1431. Her judges had not worried about the manner of her death. What concerned them was an urge to justify themselves to the world beyond Rouen. On Thursday 7 June 1431, they announced that they had received sworn information on certain words, before many trustworthy persons, spoken by the late Joan while still in prison and before she was brought to judgement.

First, the 'venerable and circumspect' Master Nicolas de Venderès, licentiate in canon law, Archdeacon of Eu and canon of the church of Rouen, aged fifty-two or thereabouts:

> declared on oath that on Wednesday the last day of May, on the Eve of Corpus Christi last, the said Joan, being still in the prison where she was detained in the castle of Rouen, said that since the voices who came to her had promised her she should be freed from prison, and she saw the contrary, she realised and knew that she had been and was deceived by them.

Brother Martin Ladvenu, Dominican priest, aged about thirty-three,

> said and declared on oath that this Joan on the morning of the day on which sentence was passed against her . . . admitted before she was brought to judgement, in front of Masters Pierre Maurice, Nicolas Loiselleur, and the Dominican brother Toutmouillé, that she knew and recognised she had been deceived by the voices and apparitions which came to her; for these voices promised her, Joan, that she should be saved and set free from prison, and she clearly realised the opposite had happened.

Asked who induced her to say this, he said that he himself, Master Pierre Maurice and Master Nicolas Loiselleur urged her for the salvation of her soul, and they asked her if it were true that she had received these voices and apparitions. She answered that it was but she did not precisely describe . . . in what form they came to her, except as far as he could recall, that they came in large numbers and in the smallest size. Besides, he heard Joan 'say and confess that because the clergy held and believed that any spirits which might come to her came and proceeded from evil spirits, she also held and believed in this matter as the clergy did, and would no longer put trust these spirits'. And in his opinion when she said this Joan was in her right mind.

Brother Martin said that on the same day he heard Joan say and admit that though in her confessions and answers she had boasted that an angel from God had brought the crown to the man she called her king, and that she had gone with the angel when he brought the crown, and many other things that were reported at greater length in the trial, all the same, with no use of force and of her own free will she saw and admitted that in spite of all she had said and boasted on this subject, there was no angel who brought the crown; that she, Joan, was the angel who had told and promised her king that she would have him crowned at Reims if she were set to work; that there has been no other crown sent from God, whatever she had said and affirmed in the course of her trial on the subject of the crown and of the sign given to the man she called her king.

The 'venerable and discreet' Master Pierre Maurice, professor of sacred theology, canon of Rouen, aged about thirty-eight years, had asked her if they really had appeared to her: she replied, in French: '*Soint bons, soint mauvais esperits, ilz me sont apparus*' ('whether good or evil spirits, they appeared to me') and she usually heard them at the hour of Compline, in the morning when the bells were rung. Brother Jean Toutmouillé, a Dominican priest, about thirty-four years old, told how on the Eve of Corpus Christi he and Brother Martin Ladvenu had visited Joan to exhort her to save her soul, and heard her tell Pierre Maurice that what she had said about the crown was pure fiction, and that she herself was the angel. This 'the said Master Pierre' took down in Latin.

Her voices had deceived her, she told the good bishop, for they had told her she would be freed. She would trust herself to the judgement of the Church or 'to you who are of the Church'. Jacques

Le Camus, a canon of Reims, about fifty-three years old, swore to much the same story, stating: 'I believe in God alone, and will no longer put faith in these voices, because they have deceived me.' Master Thomas de Courcelles, master of arts and bachelor of theology, aged about thirty years, also heard her say she had been deceived by her voices. So too did Master Nicolas Loiselleur, master of arts, canon of the churches of Rouen and Chartres, about forty years old. Asked if she had really sent a crown to the man she called her king, she replied that there was nothing beyond the promise of coronation which she herself made to him, promising him that he would be crowned. Loiselleur thought that Joan was of sound mind, for she showed great signs of contrition and penitence for the crimes she had committed. He heard her, in prison before many witnesses and in public afterwards, ask with great contrition of heart pardon of the English and Burgundians for 'having caused them to be slain, put to flight and sorely afflicted'.[1]

The English and Burgundians had reason to be content. No divine agent had rescued Joan. Her painful death confirmed her military failure to transform the unrelenting, harsh, meaningless nature of the war. She would soon be a distant memory.

In the harsh winter of 1434/5, while the Thames was frozen over and wine ships from Bordeaux had to dock at Sandwich, authorities in Arras kept records of the special snowmen set up in the town streets and squares. They included the figure of Danger, the Grand Veneur or huntsman with his dogs, the Seven Sleepers, the Danse Macabre and Joan of Arc and her men. Once spring came, the figure of Joan melted away. In Arras, however, only a few months later, her cause, the cause of Charles VII, started on a long, arduous route towards vindication and final triumph.

PART TWO

The Maid Vindicated

NINE

The King on Trial

Everyone knew that in condemning Joan, the court was judging her king. If Charles had been deceived by a witch and heretic, then her role in the relief of Orléans, her part in the victories in the Loire, even his own anointing and crowning might be the work of the devil. Charles had been the unmentionable presence at her trial, just as he had been that mission's chief concern, the beneficiary of her success and the man whom his enemies wished to associate with her final failure.

> Upon the King! Let us our lives, our souls,
> Our debts, our careful wives,
> Our children, and our sins, lay on the King!
> > . . . I know
> 'Tis not the balm, the sceptre and the ball,
> The sword, the mace, the crown imperial,
> The intertissued robe of gold and pearl,
> The farced title running 'fore the king,
> The throne he sits on, nor the tide of pomp
> That beats upon the high shore of this world,
> No, not all these, thrice-gorgeous ceremony,
> Not all these, laid in bed majestical,
> Can sleep so soundly as the wretched slave,
> Who with a body filled and vacant mind
> Get him to bed, crammed with distressful bread.[1]

Shakespeare portrayed Henry V as his ideal king of England. It is an ideal of kingship that Joan would have recognised, even though she would have added that the actual Henry V had been wrong to claim the throne of France. From Charles VII's point of view and hers, the Treaty of Troyes had justified the unjustifiable – an act of usurpation.

In Henry V's soliloquy before Agincourt Shakespeare takes for granted the sacred nature of Christian monarchy. This assumption, as fundamental to Joan as to the real or imagined Henry V, was dramatised symbolically in the ceremony of anointing and coronation. As the soliloquy also reveals, there was another side to kingship: the lonely role of one born to rule, a burden taken up at the moment of succession that must be endured to the moment of death. As far as the lawyers were concerned, this truth was expressed by the declaration, 'The King is dead, long live the King!' From the moment the old king died, the new king took over his authority. For this reason, all laws made in a new reign were dated from this moment. Charles VII may have been known as the Dauphin to his friends and as the King of Bourges to his foes, but in the eyes of his legal officials all laws he approved were royal.

When he first met Joan in March 1429, Charles the Dauphin was isolated partly by feelings of inadequacy; and it is possible that her private interview with him and the spectacular change in French morale that ensued in the following few weeks began a transformation in his character that helped make him a formidable politician. But he remained isolated by his office as well as his character. To such a man Joan had her uses, but he also understood, which she did not, that he could not fight continuously and might have to treat with his cousin of Burgundy and even his nephew of England.

The king, the only person who was always at the centre of affairs, might discard Georges de la Trémoïlle or Alençon or Joan, but never his own kingship, for it was as king that he, not his generals or his counsellors, would earn the title of *le très victorieux* (the very victorious) by winning the Hundred Years War; and, when the final triumph was imminent, it became timely to remember the strange, difficult girl who had held such a high view of his own authority and yet had not always obeyed him, who was uncommonly Catholic and yet would not yield to bishops and priests who did not accept her private revelations. On the nullification of her sentence depended the silencing of any doubts that he was indeed God's anointed.

TEN

National Salvation

Joan had first been examined by theologians at Poitiers. The opening words of the so-called Poitiers résumé make clear why Charles VII had asked their advice about Joan.

> The king, in view of his necessity and that of his kingdom, and considering the continuous prayers of his poor people to God and to all other lovers of peace and justice, should not turn away nor reject the Maid who says she is sent by God to give him help, even conceding that her promises consist only of human works.[1]

The theological wording means that the 'necessity' in which the king finds himself is the need for salvation. This may involve material salvation, but the emphasis is on the peace and justice that the Maid may bring to those who pray. The way she will achieve her aims, however, is purely human and material. Those who examined Joan knew that she was committed to war, unless the English and their allies withdraw from the lands that were not theirs by right; but it was a special kind of war. It was a moral commonplace that a war of self-defence is just; and this right of self-defence could cover attempts to recover what had been unjustly taken away, in this case parts of the land of France. But Joan did not see her war as merely a just war. It was also in some sense a holy war, as the king held France from God as a sacred trust. This was not quite like struggling to regain Christ's lands, which was the business of a Crusade, but it was analogous to crusading. It is not surprising that once her work in France was accomplished, Joan thought of crusading against the Hussites in Bohemia.[2]

The résumé concludes with a recommendation on the immediate action to be taken:

The king, in view of the testing carried out on the said Maid, so far as he can, and that no evil is found in her, and considering her answer, which is to give a divine sign at Orléans; seeing her constancy and perseverance in her purpose, and her instantaneous requests to go to Orléans to show there the sign of divine help, must not prevent her from going to Orléans with her men-at-arms, but must have her led there in good faith, trusting in God. For doubting her or dismissing her without appearance of evil, would be to repudiate the Holy Spirit, and render one unworthy of God's help, as Gamaliel stated in a council of Jews regarding the apostles.[3]

The reference to Gamaliel, the Pharisee who advised caution to the Jews who condemned the early preaching of St Peter and St John, makes clear that at least some Poitiers theologians, being of the party of Gerson, were familiar with his persistent researches into the art of the discernment of spirits. In her trial at Rouen, Joan was wronged partly because correct inquisitorial procedure was not followed and partly because her judges chose to see certain aspects of her behaviour, notably her decision to wear men's clothes, as inherently heretical. The fundamental point at issue, however, was her willingness to trust her voices rather than what her judges told her she should believe. Her voices did not teach her any doctrine opposed to the Catholic faith, and, if they did, then it was the opinion of the leading theologian of the Middle Ages, Thomas Aquinas, that such questions should be referred to the pope. But her judges refused to allow her appeal to the pope. In so doing they were arrogating to themselves the right to decide the doctrine of the Church.

In the nullification process, the new judges concerned themselves largely with matters of procedure. It was more prudent to declare that the verdict of the Rouen court was unsafe than to defend the right of certain women to wear men's clothes, which many clerics would have found shocking in fact, even if defensible in principle. But it was hard to deny that if Joan should not have been condemned, the overriding reason for that view was that a devout Christian has a duty to obey the Holy Spirit. As one of the theological consultants wrote, 'they who are led by the private law are moved by the spirit of God and are not under the public law, because where the spirit is, there is liberty'.[4]

Between Joan's first examination by clerics at Poitiers in March 1429 and the nullification in 1456 of her condemnation by clerics at Rouen in May 1431 there had been a theological sea change. In 1456 it was clear that in certain rare cases the clergy had to learn to be sensitive to the workings of the Spirit in private individuals, and that included the laity and, worse still, lay women. Further, the surest sign that the Spirit was working in an unusual person was that person's holiness of life; and many of the witnesses to Joan's life attested to her holiness.

There was another consequence of the nullification. Joan always claimed that her mission was to restore the kingdom of France to France's rightful king. She did not live to see this happen, but by 1456 it was hard to deny that Charles VII, anointed and crowned for a sacred charge, was God's chosen to be King of France. After the raising of the siege of Orléans and subsequent victories in the Loire valley, Joan had seemed to be the person who had saved France for its sacred king. Another 450 years elapsed before she was considered to be the girl who had saved France and a saint of the Catholic Church.

ELEVEN

The Alliance of 1435

Arras was one of those Franco-Flemish towns that had grown rich on the textile trade, and was especially well known for its tapestries. In the 1430s it was one of several such towns in the lands of Philip, Duke of Burgundy, and a fit meeting place for kings and grandees. Accordingly, from 4 August 1435 the town's abbey of St-Vaast, or Vedast, was the setting for a conference meant to bring about a general peace between England, France and Burgundy. Two cardinals presided at the sessions. The pope, anxious to encourage Latin Christians to combine against the Turks, had sent one, the Council of Basel another.

The Duke of Burgundy, ever a man for gesture politics, was good at entertaining heralds in gorgeous costumes and hundreds of retainers, but less effective in achieving his grandiose ambitions. The English and the French representatives at the conference refused to be in the same room, even in the same chapel, and early in September the English walked out. One week later the English Regent, John Duke of Bedford died and was buried in the heart of English France, in Rouen Cathedral. A week later still, the French and Burgundians made terms. The French delegates, led by Philip's brothers-in-law, the Duke of Bourbon and Arthur, Count of Richemont (who had once come to Joan's aid) had much to offer Philip, who was preoccupied with the conquest of Holland and the pacification of Flanders. Towns he held without royal sanction, such as Auxerre, would be his; for a mortgage he could hold towns like Abbeville, Amiens and St-Quentin in the Somme valley; and in return, as a sign of his good intentions, Charles VII promised to make a formal apology for the murder of Philip's father at Montereau. Some in Philip's council argued vehemently that any quarrel with the English would be harmful for Flemish trade, but many councillors had been bribed, among them the chancellor, Nicolas Rolin.

While Philip indicated his willingness to resume the role of a Valois, Rolin commissioned a painting, *The Madonna of Chancellor Rolin*, from Jan van Eyck. Van Eyck lived in Bruges, in Flanders, while Rolin came from Autun, in Burgundy; and it was the union of the international commercial towns of the coastal county with the inland vineyards of the royal duchy that had made Philip incomparably rich.[1] For the merchants of Bruges and Ghent, the Liverpool and Manchester of the day, it was vital to keep the sea lanes to England open. In the long run, the 1435 treaty probably did not promote the cause of either Flanders or of the dukes of Burgundy; it certainly weakened England, but for Charles VII and, briefly, for a subtle Burgundian like Rolin, it was a diplomatic triumph. Rolin behaved in a suitably pious way. In the foreground of van Eyck's picture he kneels in prayer before a Madonna being crowned by angels, a scene that refers to his gift of a statue to his native cathedral, while in the middle distance on a bridge tiny figures re-enact the murder of Montereau. At the same time Rolin gives thanks and celebrates forgiveness. With a mixture of hypocrisy, calculation and fine feeling, the Burgundians – Joan's captors – at last made possible the attainment of her ultimate goal: the expulsion of the English from France.

There were other ironies in the new situation. The policy of the Franco-Burgundian rapprochement had been the policy of Joan's arch enemy at the French court, Georges de La Trémoïlle, but he had fallen from power in 1433, largely through the restoration to favour of Richemont, the man whom Joan had been criticised for dealing with. It can be argued that the Treaty of Arras did little more in the short-term for Philip the Good than to make him feel good. He was assured by the papal envoy Cardinal Albergati that he had done no dishonour to his English allies, whom he might attack only if they first attacked the French. Van Eyck had meticulously studied the cardinal's patient features, as he had the harsh traits of Rolin; and like Rolin, his motives deserve close scrutiny. Both would benefit from the reconciliation, but, whereas Rolin was after riches, the cardinal was more idealistic: he hoped to save Constantinople. Those who thought like him were to suffer the worst form of disillusionment. The Treaty of Arras did not bring the Hundred Years War to a rapid end; instead it dragged itself on wearily till 1453, the year when Constantinople became Istanbul.

It was their use of cannon that enabled Sultan Mehmet II to defeat the Greeks and Charles VII to drive out the English. Joan herself had been modern enough to see the advantages of guns. When talking about this method of warfare, Alençon had had to use the new French word, *artillerie*, for there was no equivalent term in Latin, the ancient tongue of learned men.[2]

TWELVE

The End of English France

Shortly after Joan of Arc's death the English had a symbolic success. Days before Christmas 1431, on a dais whose steps were painted blue and which was studded with golden fleur-de-lis, young Henry was anointed King of France according to the English Sarum rite in the cathedral of Notre-Dame, Paris, by his uncle Cardinal Beaufort. The manner of the ceremony confirmed Joan's view that in France the English were foreigners. Worse still, while the king was present, the cardinal insisted that Bedford resign as regent. This was not only an imperious but also a foolish act, for the Regent had many French admirers. The following year the tenuousness of the English hold on French land was revealed by the temporary capture of the Grosse Tour at Rouen and the conclusive capture of Chartres. At Lagny, too, the Bastard of Orléans beat off Bedford's attack. Bedford's position was further weakened by the death of his wife Anne of Burgundy, sister of Duke Philip, and he then annoyed Philip by marrying the wealthy Jacquetta de Luxembourg without first gaining the duke's approval.

Bedford lacked the financial resources and manpower to prosecute war as vigorously as he wanted to. Although Talbot took numerous fortified towns in Normandy during 1434 – but not Mont-St-Michel – a peasants' revolt briefly threatened Caen and Bayeux and the Estates of Normandy could not raise enough money for war. As Duke Philip was putting out feelers for a grand meeting of the main belligerents, Bedford lay dying in Rouen. Unwilling to compromise, Cardinal Beaufort had marched away from Arras in a huff, so ensuring that England was excluded from the peace.

The French army operated with new vigour. After Dieppe, Fécamp and Harfleur had fallen, and in February 1436 Joan's former friend the Bastard of Orléans and Richemont invested Paris with 5,000 men. Whereas Joan's frontal assault in 1429 had been beaten off, her former supporters now effectively starved the citizens until some let down ladders to invite the royalists in. When the youngest of Henry V's brothers, Humphrey, Duke of Gloucester, repelled a Burgundian attack on Calais, the contrast between the royalists' success and the Burgundians' failure revealed how the power balance within France had shifted towards King Charles. In 1437, just under six years after Henry VI's coronation there, Charles VII made a solemn entry into the cathedral of Notre-Dame.

Those who had united against Joan in 1429 during the siege of Paris and in 1431 during her trial in Rouen, were only too anxious to show that they welcomed her king into his capital. At St-Denis, her base in 1429, the provost of the merchants, the aldermen and some burgesses met the royal cortège. Charles was offered the keys of Paris; and provost and aldermen then 'raised up a blue canopy covered with fleur-de-lis over the king, and thenceforth carried it above his head'. Further on, people dressed up as the Seven Deadly Sins and the Seven Virtues rode before representatives of the Parlement, which had once ratified the Treaty of Troyes that deprived Charles of his throne. By four o'clock the king had reached the cathedral, to be greeted there by the clergy and representatives of the university, which had staked its reputation on Joan's conviction for heresy. The prince, who by implication had accepted the advice of a witch and a sorceress, prayed as the undisputed king before the statue of Our Lady, venerated relics and heard the choristers singing the *Te Deum* in his honour. At that moment Joan's assessment was proved sound.

Joan's own case, however, was not clear. The English had still not left France. In 1440, the ransom of the Duke of Orléans was paid at long last and the noble poet, who from the Tower of London had asked for a beautiful robe to be sent to Joan as a token of gratitude, was freed. In 1441 Pontoise fell and the English were driven from the Île de France. During the mid-1440s there was a short truce, but war soon resumed: in 1448 the English had to evacuate Maine; in 1449 Charles VII invaded Normandy and took Rouen, its capital, and so enjoyed yet another *joyeuse entrée*; by the end of 1450 the French controlled the whole province. Guyenne collapsed in 1451 and two years afterwards its capital, Bordeaux, became French territory once more.

The dual monarchy controlled Paris for less than twenty years, from 1422 to 1437. The English had regained Normandy, a duchy that had been previously linked to their country for 150 years, and held it for just 30 years. A much more severe blow was struck by the loss of Guyenne, which had belonged to English kings since Richard I had inherited it from his mother. The Gascons much preferred the light rule of a far-off Englishman to the exacting commands of a French monarch, often nearby in the Loire valley; and the English wished to keep open the sea route to the south-west, for they had long acquired a love of claret that no other wine could satisfy.

From the duchy of Normandy, only the Channel Islands, which the French consider Anglo-Norman, then remained and still remain English. Of all the lands and cities conquered or re-conquered during the Hundred Years War, the only place left to England was Calais; and over Calais an English king or queen reigned for just over 200 years. At enormous cost to lives, money and land, almost the whole of France had been secured for the King of France. From 1453 until his death, Charles VII was king of a nation as well as of a country. Posthumously, in a way and at a time that in her impatience she could never have endured, Joan's prophecies had come true. Her fame, which at her death seemed destined to be transitory, would have an astonishing and enduring afterlife.

THIRTEEN

Voices in Defence

By 1450 it was safe to remember Joan of Arc. Even when she was a figure who divided Frenchmen against one another, there were impressive defenders of her Valois cause.

Of these the most renowned was Jean Gerson, former Chancellor of the University of Paris, who spent his last years in Lyons, deep inside the lands favourable to Charles VII. Gerson was Paris's leading theologian in a period when the city was still reputed to have the most famous university in Christendom. With his mentor and predecessor Pierre d'Ailly, he worked energetically to end the Great Schism; and the two put forward the theory of conciliarism as a response to a choice Catholics must make: which pope to obey. From 1378 to 1415, when there was one pope in Avignon and another in Rome, the French usually sided with the Avignonese and the English with the Roman pope. In the end there were three rival popes. In these circumstances it was hard to sustain the papal lawyers' view, which was given its most magniloquent form in the final ringing sentence of Boniface VIII's Bull *Unam Sanctam*: 'it is altogether necessary for salvation that a human being should be subject to the Roman pontiff'. It is hard to see how this declaration could apply to a Chinese mandarin or a Persian sufi, of whose existence some Catholics had heard, let alone to an African south of the Sahara or to an American or an Australian *in terra incognita*. Philip IV of France was equally unimpressed, and his agents captured Boniface, while the next popes relied on France's favour. A century later the papacy seemed such a derisory institution that it could be rescued only by the intervention of a general council of the Church. If the popes had lost their authority, what authority did a council have? The answer must be that, as the epitome of the Church, the council had authority over a pope, still more over two or three popes, and indeed, as a last resort, a council could depose a pope. Gerson expounded such ideas at the Council of Constance in 1415.

Gerson's theories are apposite to Joan's trial, for as late as 1431 she learnt that churchmen were not sure who should be pope; but it was not Church politics that made Gerson sympathetic to her mission. At Constance he had a moral cause to defend. He had been outraged not only by the murder of Louis, Duke of Orléans, at the instigation of John, Duke of Burgundy, but even more by Jean Petit's defence of the act as justifiable tyrannicide. To Gerson this seemed a travesty of Christian ethics, and despite able pleading by a university lawyer, one Pierre Cauchon, who showed an assured grasp of inquisitorial technicalities, Gerson, in the name of Charles VI of France, secured the condemnation of Petit's views if not of the duke who inspired them. While arguing his case he was ranged against a group of men who were to be Joan's prosecutors: Jean Beaupère, Erard Emengard, Jean de Châtillon, Pierre Miget, Guillaume le Boucher and the future grand Inquisitor of France, Jean Graverent. Back in Paris, Gerson had to cope with the duke's bullyboys, who plundered his house and tried to kill him. He learnt that the duke had vowed to destroy him; and the 'nation' of Picardy in the university, who came from the duke's lands, urged that he be punished *atrociter*.

When the Council ended Gerson slipped away, and at the invitation of the archbishop, eventually settled in Lyon. One of his brothers was the prior of a religious house in the city; and it was here, in July 1429, that he died. His enemies dismissed him as an Armagnac spokesman who stuck by the discredited French king and the king's closest relatives of the house of Orléans, but in fact Gerson was the only Parisian theologian who counted as an international figure. Not one work by any of those who at Joan's trial laboured to impress her with their erudition has ever been published; at their best they were acute debaters, at their worst time-servers. Only Gerson has been studied; only he can be studied.

As a clerical man of affairs, he followed the contemporary events in northern France. Just before he died, two tracts began to circulate, one cautiously, the other clearly in Joan's favour, and both from his entourage. The first was *De quadam puella*, or 'About a certain girl', the second *De mirabili victoria cujusdam puellae*, 'On a certain girl's wonderful victory'. As *De quadam puella* shows no knowledge of Joan's military achievements it must have been written before the relief of Orléans. *De mirabili victoria* does not make sense unless written after the relief of Orléans. The first treatise is probably more authentically Gersonian, as it focused on an issue that preoccupied Gerson: the discernment of spirits.

De quadam puella has a detached, academic tone, constructed in the form of propositions for and against Joan. The author argues first that Joan is a real person and a true maid; second, that the Church still needs prophets; third, that now and again there are some prophets who work miracles; fourth, that women and young people can bring about salvation, for example Deborah, Esther, Judith, Daniel and David; fifth, that no evil man appears in Scripture as if he were a woman; and sixth and lastly, that this girl is a real human person, sent by God to act with His powers, and that she is to be trusted. The author's long training then leads him to examine the opposing case. First, many false prophets arise, claiming to be sent from God. Second, false prophets can see into men's hearts and foretell the future. Third, it is hard to distinguish between a true and a false prophet by exterior signs. Fourth, it is implausible that a mission sent by God will have a worldly end. Fifth, despite the prohibition in Holy Scripture, this girl wears men's clothes and a mission from God ought to relate to an interior state, so 'it seems indecent that such a person may transform herself into a secular man of arms'. Sixth, it cannot be shown convincingly that this girl has been sent by God, that God works through her and that she should be trusted.

De mirabili victoria may sound convincing to anyone already convinced. In a 2,000-word treatise, the author urged his readers not to judge the Maid hastily. He carefully distinguished between two ideas of faith. Anyone trifling with one category of beliefs, the truths of faith, could be tried before an ecclesiastical tribunal, as in the case of Huss. In the case of beliefs or pious opinions, the principle to be followed is well expressed in the popular phrase, '*Qui ne le croit, n'est pas damné*' ('he who does not believe is not condemned'); on her 'pious beliefs' the reader must not rush to judge Joan; any decision in this respect ought to be left to the Church, its officials and theologians. Secondly, the author argued that restoring a king to his kingdom, instead of seeking her own ends or working by spells, is a 'just enterprise', and therefore a sign that her mission is providential. Thirdly, the author argued that the Old Testament prohibition of men's dress for women does not necessarily bind women who live under the New Testament. The author was circumspect: 'a certain maid' must defer to the Church's judgement.

While *De mirabili victoria* is exultant because the relief of Orléans seemed to prove that Joan's mission was God-given, *De quadam puella* shows the caution more typical of Gerson. He believed in the Valois cause, but he may not have been a supporter of Joan. Probably he saw in her another test case: was hers a true prophetic gift? He had been exercised by the case of St Bridget of Sweden, whose prophesyings of the disasters to befall France had not stopped her from being canonised by the Church. The Church accepted that St Bridget, for all the problems in her writings, was a true saint. Gerson may well have been uncertain if the same could be said of Joan.

Such caution is not the case of a women friend of his, the poet Christine de Pisan, who has become a feminist heroine. In 1418, after the Burgundian seizure of Paris, Gerson was driven into permanent exile and Christine retreated to the convent of Poissy. Safe there from the Burgundians, and still near the capital, she was well informed about what was going on in the world and could hope to influence opinion outside the conventual walls. From her enclosure, in the last months of her life, she took up the case of the most extraordinary woman of the age with more eloquence and partisanship than the great theologian she was proud to think of as her ally.

Less famous than many of her other poems or prose works, but more remarkable in its own time, is the *Ditié de Jehanne d'Arc*, which probably dates from 1429 and must be Christine's final work. What marks out Christine from earlier women writers is her zest for the defence of womankind. A virgin who was a soldier in man's armour – Christine could not have a better theme, for God had wished to save France by a '*jeune pucelle*':

> *Chose est bien digne de memoire*
> *Que Dieu par une vierge tendre,*
> *Ait adès voulu (chose est voire)*
> *Sur France si grant grace estendre.*[1]

('It is worth recalling/that God by a tender maid/should have wished {and this is the truth}/to grant France such a great grace'.)

Christine continued, declaring that she wept over the state of France since the Dauphin had fled from Paris and she had been forced into a convent, but her tears changed to song, when in 1429 the sun had begun to shine again on the kingdom: the rejected child of the previous king is coming as a crowned King, let us praise God as we greet him. In matters of faith the lilies have never erred; and the renown of Charles, seventh of that noble name:

> ... *Dieu grace, or voiz ton renom*
> *Hault eslevé par la Pucelle*
> *Qui a soubzmis soubz ton penon*
> *Tes ennemis (chose est nouvelle!)* ...

('has been raised up by the Maid, who by God's grace/has laid low your enemies under your standard {a new event})'.

She then turns in her mind to address the Maid directly:

> *Et toy, Pucelle beneurée*
> *Y dois-tu estre obliée*
> *Puis que Dieu t'a tant honorée*
> *Que as la corde desliée*
> *Qui tenoit France estroit liée ?*

('And will you be forgotten, happy Maid,/as God has honoured you/so much that you untied the rope/holding France so tightly bound'.)

Christine compares Joan to the Old Testament heroines Esther and Judith and Deborah, and she is well informed about Joan's examination at Poitiers and her journey with Charles through the countryside en route for Reims. Her power was first made apparent at Orléans:

> *Hee! quel honneur au femenin*
> *Sexe! Que Dieu l'ayme il appert,*
> *Quant tout ce grant peuple chenin,*
> *Par qui tout le regne est desert,*
> *Par femme est sours et recouvert* ...

('What an honour to the female/sex, it seems that God loves it/when this whole great, wretched people/by whom the whole kingdom is wrecked,/is recovered and made safe by a woman'.)

Joan will conquer the English, bring harmony to Church and Christendom, overrun the Holy Land. When Christine ends the poem, Joan was at a decisive moment in her career: would she and the king enter Paris? The poetess died before Joan's tragedy unfolded after she failed to take the capital, failed to drive out the English, failed to take Jerusalem. Joan would not end her days, as the poetess hoped, in peace, for ever faithful to her king.

What is true of almost all those who put the case for Joan, however tentatively, is that they wrote before her trial and death. Eminent among Charles's theological advisers was Jacques Gélu, first Bishop of Tours and later Archbishop of Embrun. Initially a sceptic, by mid-1429 he was able to declare 'we piously believe'. Similarly, Jean Dupuy, a Dominican Inquisitor living in Rome, had heard of Joan through the *De mirabili victoria*. What neither of them faced was how to defend her once she had been burnt as witch and heretic. That dilemma, oddly, was confronted by Martin Le Franc, a priest in the service of the Duke of Burgundy. In 1442 Le Franc completed a mediocre poem, *Le Champion des dames*, that belatedly addressed questions about the roles of the sexes debated some forty years earlier by Christine de Pisan, Gerson and some royal secretaries. As a cleric, if not as a writer, Le Franc was a figure of some importance, who worked for an anti-pope and a pope, but who for a long time was in the service of the Duke of Burgundy. He dared to wonder if the verdict against Joan was safe; but he was not entirely brave, for the verses in which he puts his dangerous case were preserved in only one manuscript, which does not seem to have been published.

After 1450, Philip the Good was no longer the force in French politics he had been; Henry VI no longer counted at all; Charles VII governed more of the country than any of his predecessors and for almost the first time in the fifteenth century it was clear who was the true pope. A brave man might ask Le Franc's dangerous question: was the verdict against Joan safe? By 1450 most of Joan's judges were dead; and it seemed a good moment to apply one of Gerson's most radical ideas – not the view that a council can depose a pope, but the view, ultimately more important, that in judging the state of a soul men need the gift of *discretio spirituum*, the discernment of spirits, the ability to assess aright the tendency of a personality in its intimate relationship with God.

Some of Joan's defenders were more intelligent than her attackers. Gerson or a Gersonian had set out the theological arguments raised by Joan's case, but the master had not lived to resolve them; and those who judged Joan were lawyers not theologians. The most important of them, Cauchon, had never finished the lengthy course that would have led to a doctorate in theology. He had been diverted into clerical politics; and it was as a clerical politician that he judged Joan. Her assertions needed to be analysed, their implications established, but what concerned Cauchon and his fellow judges was the necessity of her condemnation. They lacked detachment. They had a job to do and they did it. They were professionals in the art of evading awkward questions. By 1450 it was possible to ask those awkward questions.

FOURTEEN

The Case Reopened

By 1450 the political hesitations of 1429 were long forgotten by Charles VII. He was king over a greater area of France than any of his predecessors; he had shown his independence from the papacy by announcing in the Pragmatic Sanction of Bourges (1438) that he not the pope would nominate bishops; he had provided his country with an heir who would be an even more skilful politician than himself, the Dauphin Louis (Louis XI), and until 1450 he had enjoyed the favours of a famous mistress, Agnès Sorel, who may have posed for the Virgin Mary in Jean Fouquet's masterpiece, the Melun diptych.

In 1450, with Normandy occupied and Rouen submissive, Charles VII realised that he could investigate Joan's condemnation, for if she had been a witch and heretic then his status as Most Christian King was impugned. On 13 February he told his counsellor Guillaume Bouillé to inquire into the conduct of the trial undertaken against Joan by 'our ancient enemies the English', who, 'against reason, had cruelly put her to death'. Bouillé was Rector of the University of Paris, the post once held by Cauchon, and Dean of the Theological Faculty, Dean of Noyon, a member of the Great Council, and one time ambassador to Rome. He may have been the first to argue on parchment that the Rouen verdict was unsafe, and at any rate it was he who on 4 and 5 March held an official inquiry at Rouen into events that happened nineteen years earlier. He questioned seven witnesses: four Dominicans from St-Jacques, Rouen, Toutmouillé, de La Pierre, Ladvenu, and Duval; the notary Manchon, the usher Massieu, and Beaupère, a chief examiner. But, although several he consulted thought the original trial was illegal, the case was dropped.

In 1452 Guillaume d'Estouteville, Cardinal-bishop of Digne, Legate of Pope Nicholas V, returned to the subject, at the request of

Joan's mother, Isabelle Romée, who urged her daughter's rehabilitation on both civil and ecclesiastical grounds, claiming that the family had been damaged by the imputation of heresy to Joan.

It is said that the rehabilitation process was vitiated by its political nature. In 1431 the English and Burgundians had not worried that they might offend the French. In 1450, however, the king of France knew that he might offend the English, the inquisitors and the University of Paris, but using Joan's family made the case a private one. It was a clever ruse, which would restore Joan's honour and indirectly the honour of the Inquisition and the king.

The cardinal was careful to invite the help of Jean Bréhal, Inquisitor of France and Prior of the Convent of the Jacobins in Paris; and, together, they opened their inquiry at Rouen in April 1452. They heard the evidence of twenty-one people, including some of those who had given evidence in 1450. When the cardinal had to leave Rouen, the inquiry was left in the hands of Bréhal and Philippe la Rose, the treasurer of the cathedral. The pope was concerned. He did not wish to offend the English, then enduring the death throes of the Hundred Years War, and once more an inquest lapsed. It was not till 1455, after Pope Nicholas had died, that Pope Calixtus III, of the Spanish Borja family (Borgia in Italian), agreed to the petition of the d'Arc family, granting a rescript authorising the process of revision, and naming Jean Jouvenal des Ursins, Archbishop of Reims, Guillaume Chartier, Bishop of Paris, and Richard de Longueil, Bishop of Coutances, as delegates for the trial. These three then invited the Inquisitor, Jean Bréhal, to help them.

The case was solemnly opened on 7 November 1455 at Notre-Dame, in Paris. Joan's mother and brothers came before the court to present their humble petition for a revision of her sentence, demanding only 'the triumph of truth and justice'. The court heard the request with some emotion. Isabelle Romée threw herself at the commissioners' feet, showed the papal rescript and wept aloud, while her advocate, Pierre Maugier, and his assistants urged justice for her and for the memory of her martyred daughter. Many of those present joined aloud in the petition, so at last it seemed as if one great cry for justice broke from the whole crowd. The commissioners formally received the petition, and chose 17 November, ten days later, for its consideration, warning the petitioners that the 1431 trial could be confirmed, not reversed, as they had hoped, but promising them careful consideration of the case were they to persist in their appeal.

On 17 November the court met in Notre-Dame for a second time, the papal rescript was solemnly read and the advocate for the petitioners made a formal accusation against the judges and Promoter of the earlier trial, none of whom, as has been said, was still alive. They took care to exclude the assessors involved in the case, whom, the advocated declared, had been led to wrong conclusions by false deductions. When the advocate finished, the Archbishop of Reims and the Bishop of Paris said that, with the Inquisitor, they were ready to act as judges in the appeal case. They appointed 12 December for the inaugural sitting and cited all concerned in the case to appear before them on that day.

At the opening of the trial on 12 December, the d'Arc family was represented by the procurator, Guillaume Prévosteau, formerly prosecutor in the case started by Cardinal d'Estouteville, but only the plaintiffs were represented, as no one was there to answer for either of the accused judges or for the Prosecutor Estivet. The case was adjourned until 15 December so that advocates for the defendants could be summoned to appear. Yet, when the court met, no one was there to represent the accused, and therefore five days' further delay was allowed. Court officials were appointed; and the registrars of the former trial, who were present, were asked if they wished to defend the process in which they had been involved. When they said no, they were told to produce any documents of the 1431 trial still in their possession. In this way the commissioners had before them the actual minutes of the previous trial, written in Manchon's own hand and presented by him, and also his formal attestation of the authenticity of the official *procès-verbal*, on which further inquiries would be based.

The proceedings of the preliminary inquiry of 1452, which had been initiated by Cardinal d'Estouteville and his delegates, were added, at the request of the prosecutor, to the official documents of the trial of rehabilitation, but as the inquiry of 1450 had been made under secular authority, it was treated as valueless and therefore not included in the authorised case. On 18 December the prosecutor lodged his request for the d'Arc family and begged that the previous sentence should be declared null, on the grounds that as in both form and substance it was null and void, it should be publicly and legally declared so. On 20 December, the final day appointed for any representative of the accused to appear, the one family to produce an advocate was the Cauchon family. In their name, the advocate stated that the late bishop's heirs had no wish to defend the soundness of a trial they had not been concerned with and that took place either before they were born or when they were very young children; that Joan, despite her pure and innocent life, had been a victim of English hatred, and that for this reason the responsibility for her death fell chiefly on the English; and, finally, they requested that the rehabilitation of Joan might not prejudice their own interests, as they had a large house in Rouen, and they invoked the benefits of the royal amnesty granted after the conquest of Normandy. With these words perhaps the name Cauchon could have moved for ever out of the glare of historical notoriety into decent obscurity; but it did not.

Other defendants were declared contumacious for not appearing and cited once more to appear on 16 February. On 20 December the prosecutor formulated his accusation and drew the court's attention to some features of the previous trial that tended to vitiate the whole: first, the intervention of the hidden registrars and the alterations, additions and omissions found in the twelve articles; second, the suppression of the preliminary inquiry, and the obvious prejudices of the judges; third, the incompetence of the court and the unfairness of the treatment received throughout by the accused, leading as it did to an illegal sentence and an irregular execution.

The Promoter then asked for inquiries into Joan's life and conduct and into how she had taken on the reconquest of France herself. Orders were then given for Reginald de Chichery, Dean of Vaucouleurs, and for Wautrin Thierry, Canon of Toul, to go to Domremy and Vaucouleurs to collect information. Meanwhile, a document containing articles was drawn up, on the first thirty-three of which are based the later inquiries made at Paris, Orléans and Rouen. These set out the plaintiffs' case for the benefit of the still absent defendants, and stated at great length why, on grounds both of fact and of reason, the sentence should be revised.

On the very last day for the citation of the defendants, 16 February 1456, the court met again. This time the accused were represented by legal successors: the Promoter of the diocese of Beauvais, Bredouillé, as that of Bishop Guillaume de Hellande; and Chaussetier, Prior of the Evreux Convent, as that of the Beauvais

Dominicans, to whose order Joan's other judge, Jean Lemaître, belonged. The representatives denied responsibility for the previous trial, but submitted themselves to the court's judgment; and, as no objection was offered to the 101 articles, the judges accepted these and the case could proceed.

The 1456 inquiry lasted several months. Thirty-four witnesses were heard, in January and February, at Domremy and Vaucouleurs; forty-one, in February and March, at Orléans; twenty at Paris, in April and May; nineteen at Rouen, in December and May; and on 28 May, at Lyon, the vice-inquisitor of the province received the solitary deposition of Jean d'Aulon, whose evidence has a special importance, as he had been the steward of her household and her most devoted follower.

The d'Arc family's advocate asked the judges to read the comments of various learned men on the case, which documents he begged should be made part of the trial's formal proceedings. Eight such comments were filed away as documents of the *procès-verbal*; the views were summarised in a 'Recollectio' drafted by the Inquisitor, Jean Bréhal; and this document in its turn was later the basis of the eventual sentence of nullification.

FIFTEEN

Witnesses to the Life

One witness stands out from all the rest, as only he gave evidence in Lyons and only his evidence is preserved in the original French. Curiously, this makes the voice of Jean d'Aulon, once Joan's steward, now Seneschal of Beaucaire, sound as formal as any of the other witnesses whose words are recorded in Latin, as the notary has kept carefully to the form of a legal document. Like their words, d'Aulon's are always recorded in the third person, from the time in Poitiers when he first heard of Joan until the last time he was with her as a fellow prisoner at Beaulieu. During the year he knew her he had privileged access to certain moments in her public life: he was there when she learnt the verdict from Poitiers, when she was declared a virgin by the Queen of Sicily, when she was given armour to fight at Orléans. With her he entered Orléans, and he remembered how she leaped from her bed to encourage the attack on the boulevard of St-Loup, how before the assault on the bridge she was wounded by an arrow and he had her wound dressed, how she fought bravely in the upper Loire valley. He remembered her being examined by 'certain masters in theology' who had found her 'a good Christian and true Catholic', and by ladies, who found her a true virgin.[1] Having told the story of her exploits, he then added, 'he had never seen or known in her anything that should not be found in a good Christian'. She tried to go to Mass every day, she confessed and went to communion, she never swore or blasphemed. She loved a good honest man ('*bon prudhomme*') whom she knew to have led a chaste life. When the Maid had to do anything concerning war, she told d'Aulon that her 'Counsel' had advised her what she ought to do and she told him she was visited by three 'counsellors', but when asked for details of her 'Counsel', she told him sharply that he was not worthy to be told. He was sure 'she was full of all the virtue which could be or should be in a good

Christian', and he said this 'without love, favour, hate, or any suborning, but only for the truth, and as he has seen it and known it in the Maid'. He was one of those who, as a young man living beside her, said that although he had seen her naked body, he had never felt any sexual desire for her. He was also unique in that he added a piece of information about her sexuality; he had been told by her women that she had never known the 'malady of women'. D'Aulon's remark has inspired much speculation in the last hundred years. Perhaps Joan never menstruated, or perhaps nobody knew if she did or not. No other witness suggests that Joan had not reached puberty. What we do know is that one man who knew her well thought she had not done so, but then no witness had ever seen Joan relieve herself when on the march.

Many witnesses had memories that went back longer than d'Aulon's, witnesses who had known Joan as a child; and in their cases there is nothing exciting to relate. In the region of Domremy, Greux and Epinal, labourers, wives, widows and sons remembered the girl who became a woman so fast. Jean Morel from Greux, her godfather, knew all about the fairies' tree that had so fascinated Joan's interrogators. He had heard that the fairies used to dance underneath it but came no longer, since the Gospel of St John had been read there; young girls used to dance there on Laetare Sunday in the middle of Lent and had feasts there on holy days; Joan had been there with the others, but she never went alone. He was glad to speak of her piety and the love she inspired in the village; and he was delighted to mention that when she was famous he had met her at Châlons, when the king was going to Reims to be anointed, and she had given him a red dress she had been wearing. Others had seen her pray, work in the fields, go to confession, knew she did not swear, recalled how she said 'Adieu' to her father when she set out for Vaucouleurs, and that later she had gone to 'France'. Hauviette, a wife from Syonne, near Neufchâteau, had been with Joan to the well of the thorn on Laetare Sunday, and wept when her friend went away – Hauviette's name was used by the poet Charles Péguy when he imagined Joan's time in Domremy. Joan was kind, and she looked after the sick.

The picture these reports build up is of a simple, pious, serious girl, of no special status in her village, and one whose strong convictions alone marked her out from her friends. Before her original trial, investigators had been sent to Domremy, but they were searching only for evidence with which they could convict her; and they found none. Nicolas Bailly, Notary of Andelot, had come one day to the village with several other persons and, at the request of Jean de Torcenay, bailly of Chaumont for the 'pretended King of France and England' (Henry VI), he set about inquiring into Joan's conduct and life, but could not 'induce the inhabitants of Vaucouleurs to depose'. Now he admitted he had seen her often in her father's house and said 'she was a good girl, of pure life and good manners, a good Catholic who loved the Church and went often on pilgrimage to the church of Bermont, and confessed nearly every month', as 'I learned from a number of the inhabitants of Domremy, whom I had to question on the subject at the time of the inquiry that I made with the Provost of Andelot'.

At Vaucouleurs Joan moved for the first time into a grander world; and she astonished those she met with her assurance. Jean de Metz or de Novelompert, the first knight to follow her, heard her say that before the middle of Lent she must be with the king, for 'no one in the world, neither kings, nor dukes, nor the King of Scotland's daughter [Margaret, daughter of James I, who was betrothed to Louis, afterwards Louis XI] nor any others can recover the kingdom of France'; only she could provide the help that was needed. Who had told her that, he asked? 'God,' she replied. Jean was willing to take her to the king, but would she go dressed as she was? 'I will willingly wear men's clothes,' she replied, so Jean then gave her the dress and equipment of one of his men. He was impressed by her lack of fear: 'I had absolute faith in her, her words and her ardent faith in God inflamed me, I believe she was sent from God; she never swore, she loved to attend Mass, she confessed often, and frequently gave alms.'

Catherine Leroyer (who with her husband, a wheelwright in Vaucouleurs, had become an early convert to Joan's cause), took Joan as a guest in her house at Vaucouleurs, where Durand Laxart had brought her to stay, and got to know her well. Joan, she said, was 'good, simple, gentle, respectful, well behaved, and went freely to Church and to confession'. She believed that through Joan the prophecy, of which Joan reminded her, would be fulfilled, that France, which had been lost by a woman (presumably Charles VII's mother), would be saved by a virgin from the borders of Lorraine. Bertrand de Poulengey testified that on the journey to Chinon 'at night, Joan slept beside Jean de Metz and me, fully dressed and armed. I was young then; still I never felt for her any physical desire: I would never have dared to approach her, because of her great goodness.'

In Chinon Joan first came across the great of the land. The courtiers of the 'King of Bourges' may have lacked the glamour she would have expected, as they were dispirited by repeated failure. Of the people she met there none was so important to her as Charles himself, who could not testify on her behalf; and none was so true to her as one of the royal cousins, John II, Duke of Alençon, a descendant of Philip III (1270–85), so third cousin to Charles VI, and nephew by marriage to Charles VII's sister. Although of the blood royal, he was yet more closely related to Charles by his recent marriage to Joan, daughter of Charles of Orléans, the king's cousin, which firmly attached him to the loyal side of the royal family. He was young, handsome, brave, passionate. His father was killed at Agincourt and he himself had been captured at Verneuil in 1424 and ransomed for the huge sum of 80,000 *saluts*. To help raise his ransom money his wife pawned her jewels, while he had to give up the barony of Fougères to his uncle the Duke of Brittany and a property in Touraine to the Bishop of Angers; he was released from his oath to surrender his lands only after victory at Orléans. As Henry V had bequeathed Alençon itself to Bedford, now English Regent, Alençon's true duke was a natural foe of Henry VI.

Once Alençon heard that a girl had arrived at Chinon declaring she was sent by God to defeat the English and raise the siege of Orléans, he hurried to greet her from St-Florent, where he was hunting quails. The two took to each other at once. She welcomed him as a man of the blood royal and named him '*mon beau duc*'. He was charmed to find she was a tomboy. After dinner the following day, while the king went for a walk, Alençon watched as Joan coursed, and when he saw how well she managed her lance, he gave her a horse. He was a witness to her first interrogation by senior clergy and knew she told them she heard voices and received advice as to what to do, but he was not sure if she told them what the voices told her. Once when they dined together she told him she had not told the clergy everything. He did not go to the more searching examination at Poitiers, but knew the clergy there told Charles that in his dire troubles he could make use of her. He was then sent to the king's mother-in-law, Queen Yolande of Sicily, to ask for supplies to be prepared for the army of Orléans. Alençon did not set out with her, but he joined her later. He remembered how the captains and soldiers who took part in the siege said that what happened was a miracle.

He joined her after Orléans had been saved. He came to love her habit of taking risks. Outside Jargeau she urged him to attack. 'On, gentle Duke, to the assault!' (*Avant, gentil duc, à l'assaut!*) she called out; and, when he told her it was too soon to attack so quickly, 'Have no fear,' she said to him, 'the time is right when it pleases God; we must work when He wills it. Act, and God will act!' Later she added, 'Ah! gentle Duke, are you afraid? Did you not know that I promised your wife to bring you back, as safe and sound as you were?' His wife was anxious he should not be captured and ransomed again. Joan had promised to return him in one piece or in even better shape than he was. They spent several days together with his wife and mother at St-Laurent, near Saumur.

Despite being the commander, Alençon did not object to Joan's advice. He was conscious that during the attack on Jargeau Joan had told him to move from his current position just before enemy shot killed the Sieur de Lude beside him. It was she who led the attack and Alençon who followed. Forced to the ground by a stone that hit her helmet, she immediately got up and encouraged the troops: 'Our Lord has condemned the English.' Alençon yielded to her: she begged him to cooperate with Richemont, the disgraced Constable, who was Alençon's uncle; and so together they won the battle of Patay. When the fighting was over, the defeated Talbot came into the presence of Joan, the Constable and Alençon, who said how surprised he was at what had happened. It is the fortune of war, commented Talbot tersely. And so they rejoined the king and went with him to Reims for the coronation.

Joan had said many times that she wished to accomplish four things: to beat the English, to have the king crowned and consecrated at Reims; to deliver the Duke of Orléans from the hands of the English; and to raise the siege of Orléans. She did not live to see her four wishes achieved, but Alençon did. Twenty-five years after he last saw her, he still thought of her as a chaste young woman, who hated women camp followers – at St-Denis, sword in hand, she had once chased one away – and was angry with him if he swore. He had seen her clad in armour, he had seen her naked breasts. She was an excellent Catholic, so far as he could tell, who communicated often,

To enter Chinon Castle to meet the Dauphin, Joan went under this clock tower, now a minor museum dedicated to her. *(Author)*

LE TRESVETORIEVX ROY DE FRANCE

CHARLES · SEPTIESME · DE CE NOM ·

Jean Fouquet's fifteenth-century *Charles VII* is the best-known portrait of the 'very victorious' king. *(Musée du Louvre: AKG-Images/Erich Lessing)*

In 1451 Charles VII struck the first French medal, known as a *Calaisenne*, to celebrate his victory over the English. This one, however, dates from 1454. *(Lane Fine Art)*

In this fifteenth-century French illumination taken from the *Chronique de Charles VII*, Jean Chartier's artist sees the 1429 battle of Patay as a chivalrous encounter. *(MS Fr. 2691, f. 38, Bibliothèque nationale, Paris, France: AKG-Images/Jérôme da Cunha)*

In a fifteenth-century life of Charles VII, Joan is shown chasing prostitutes from an army camp. *(MS Fr. 5054, Bibliothèque nationale, Paris, France: The Bridgeman Art Library)*

In the fifteenth century, Martin Le Franc's artist for *Le Champion des Dames* compares Joan to Judith, slayer of Holofernes. *(MS Fr. 12476, Bibliothèque nationale, Paris, France: The Bridgeman Art Library)*

In a sixteenth-century picture, Joan wears her hair long. *(Musée des Beaux-Arts, Orléans, France: The Bridgeman Art Library)*

In 1825, Delaroche illustrates the fiction that Cardinal Beaufort threatened Joan with hell. *(Wallace Collection, London: The Bridgeman Art Library)*

In 1854, Ingres makes Joan the principal figure at the coronation of her king. *(Musée du Louvre: AKG-Images)*

Emmanuel Fremiet's statue of Joan (1874), once in Place des Pyramides in Paris, became dear to the far Right (1899). In 1959 De Gaulle gave a copy to the city of New Orleans. *(AKG-Images)*

Jules-Pierre Rouleau's Joan (1893) charges furiously above the cars in Chinon, where once she trained troops. *(Author)*

On 30 May 1920, the anniversary of the Maid's death, a procession celebrates the canonisation of St Joan as it passes through place de la Concorde, Paris. *(AKG-Images)*

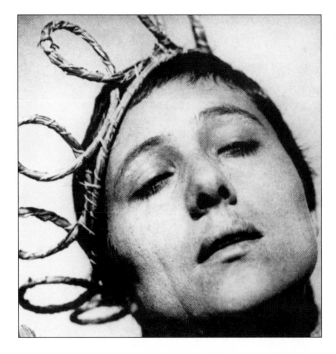

Left: Maria Falconetti expresses the silent anguish of Joan in Carl Dreyer's film *The Passion of Joan of Arc* 1928). *(Soc. Gle. Films/Gaumont/Album/AKG-Images)*

Below, left: Rue Jeanne d'Arc, leading up to Orléans Cathedral, is decked out to honour the patron saint of France on a national holiday (9 May 2004). *(Author)*

Right: Marie d'Orléans' statue of Joan, a bronze copy (1840) of the original in Versailles (1836), quietly stands before the Hôtel de Ville, Orléans. *(Author)*

and when not fighting was 'a simple, young girl', but when 'bearing the lance, bringing an army together, making war, directing artillery' she was as skilful 'as a captain who had fought for twenty or thirty years'. In the use of artillery she was marvellous.

This testimony is impressive since Alençon himself was hardly straightforward. Like his cousin Charles VII he dabbled in astrology. He was anti-English, but not always loyal to his king. During the Hundred Years War he rebelled with his godson Louis, the future Louis XI, and in the course of the nullification trial the king had him arrested. In 1458 he was condemned for treason by his peers, but on the accession of Louis in 1461 he was released. Louis, however, did nothing to prevent his being ruined from the results of his waywardness; and on his death the duchy of Alençon reverted to the crown. In fifteenth-century French history, Alençon was an erratic figure: in his unquestioning devotion to Joan, however, he was constant and consistent.

Another John played an almost more important part in Joan's story. The Bastard of Orléans, half-brother to Charles, Duke of Orléans, who was famously imprisoned in England for twenty-five years after Agincourt, had been brought up as a member of the Orléans family after the murder of his father, Duke Louis. Born in 1402, he grew up with the Dauphin Charles. This shared upbringing, together with the fact that his half-brother was out of the country for such a long period, gave him a prominence in national affairs rare even for the illegitimate son of a peer of royal blood. From his mid-teens he was a professional soldier determined to avenge the wrongs of his house, of which he was the virtual head. His marriage in 1422 to the daughter of Louvet, president of the Parlement, linked him to the legal and bureaucratic classes who ran the administration; but when Louvet fell from grace the Bastard fell too, and was sent into exile. The English attempt to overrun the duchy of Orléans brought him back into the war, and when Orléans itself was under threat, he was the obvious leader of the defence. It was this task that first brought him into close contact with Joan. She died long before he had turned into the statesman who as 'one of the finest French speakers there is of the French language' used his eloquence to draw up the Treaty of Arras in 1435 between France and Burgundy; who was made count of Dunois in 1439; who ransomed his half-brother the duke in 1440; who reconciled the king and the Dauphin Louis; whose capture of Dieppe in 1443 prepared the way for the reconquest of Normandy; who eventually became the Count of Longueville; and who marched towards Guyenne in 1451 near the end of the Hundred Years War. Apart from a short period of falling-out with Charles VII in the 1420s and a longer period of falling-out with Louis XI in the 1460s he was in royal favour for most of his fifty years in public life. To Joan, however, he was merely 'the Bastard', and it was as 'the Bastard' that he testified in 1455: 'I think that Joan was sent by God, and that her deeds in war were divine rather than human in inspiration.

'I was at Orleans, then besieged by the English, when the rumour spread that a young girl, commonly called the Maid, had just gone through Gien, on her way to the noble Dauphin' so as to raise the siege of Orléans and take Charles to Reims for his anointing. 'I was the man put in charge of the town of Orléans and was Lieutenant-General of the King in affairs of war.' To find out more about Joan he sent the king Sieur de Villars, Seneschal of Beaucaire, and Jamet de Tilly, then Captain of Blois, later Bailly of Vermandois.

They came back and told him publicly that the king had at first refused to see her, while she continued to repeat her views on her mission to save Orléans and take Charles to Reims. She also asked for men, arms and horses. For three weeks the king had theologians examine her, then he gave her what she asked for, sent her to Blois with the Archbishop of Reims and the Grand Steward; and there they joined Gilles de Rais, de Boussac, La Hire and others. As the English blocked the route, supplies had to be loaded on boats, but the winds blew in the wrong direction. The first time Joan met him, she asked him if he were the Bastard of Orléans and enquired about his plans. Dismissing his ideas of avoiding the English, she told him that God had better plans: He had taken pity on the town and would not let the English hold both town and duke. At that moment the wind changed and so supplies could be taken into Orléans by boat; and ever after the Bastard believed in her. She went with him, clutching her banner, on which Our Lord held a lily in His hand. Joan said she had seen St Louis and St Charlemagne (patrons of France) praying God for the safety of the king and the town.

Other reasons led him to believe Joan was from God: her letter to the English that told them if they did not retreat she would attack and defeat them; her capture of the boulevard des Augustins, where she was wounded by an arrow; the capture of Les Tourelles the next day and the relief of the city. Where he was cautious, she was reckless; and yet events proved she had been right. Only when the siege was over did she receive the care her wound needed and did she have a few slices of bread to eat.

Once Orléans was safe, the Bastard and Joan went to see the king at Loches and begged him to let them attack other towns in the Loire valley. The Bastard, Alençon and other captains were given troops and the towns fell quickly – thanks, the Bastard believed, to the Maid's intervention. At Loches he saw Joan on her knees begging the king to go to Reims –her 'counsel', she said, told him he must do so. When the king's confessor, Christophe d'Harcourt, Bishop of Castres, queried her about her 'counsel', she blushed and replied that when people doubted how God advised her, she sought solitude to pray, grumbled to God and a voice told her 'Daughter of God! Go on! Go on! Go on! I will be thy help: go on' (*Fille De, va, va, va, je serai, va*). She said that when she heard this voice she was filled with joy.

After the capture of so many strongholds, the nobles of the blood royal and captains urged the king to go to Normandy instead of Reims. But Joan insisted on his going to Reims, so that he could be consecrated, giving as her reason that once he were consecrated and crowned, his enemies' power would decline, and so they would be unable to harm him or his kingdom: 'All accepted her opinion.'

Before the town of Troyes, the council debated what to do. Joan's suggestion was followed, and the town was besieged. Once the city had surrendered to him, the king went to Reims, where everyone submitted and he was consecrated and crowned.

While in Reims, Joan used to go every day to church at Vespers or towards evening; she had the bells rung for half an hour, collected the friars who were with the army and had them sing an anthem in honour of Our Lady. She was also preoccupied with her future: what was she to do? When the king was at La Ferté, Joan rode between the Archbishop of Reims and the Bastard and said she would love to be buried there. 'Where do you want to die?' asked the archbishop. 'Where it pleases God,' she replied, 'for I cannot know either the time or the place, any more than you do.' If it pleased God, her Creator, she would retire then, give up arms, go back to serve her father and mother and look after their sheep with her sister and brothers, who would be happy to see her again.

The Bastard knew no one more sober, just as d'Aulon had known no one more chaste. 'Neither I nor others when with her ever thought of her as a woman to be desired: she seemed holy.' Fifteen days after the Earl of Suffolk had been made prisoner at the taking of Jargeau, someone sent him four lines, in which it was said that a Maid should come from the oak-wood and ride on the backs of the archers and against them (this was the so-called prophecy of Merlin). If some of Joan's prophecies did not come true, she was sure that she had been sent to raise the siege of Orléans and lead the king to Reims.

By the time these words of prophesy had been spoken, the Bastard had seen his cousin the king enter Paris, his half-brother the duke return to the city of Orléans, and the English driven from the mainland of France, with the exception of Calais.

An even more intimate insight into Joan's public life comes from the witness Louis de Coutes. Louis was the brother-in-law of Beauharnais, a bourgeois of Orléans, and a son of Jean de Coutes, captain of Châteaudun and chamberlain to the Duke of Orléans. Louis met Joan when he was fourteen or fifteen years old and page to Sieur de Gaucourt, captain of the castle, during her visit to Chinon with two gentlemen, who took her to the king. He saw her many times going and coming to the king. She was housed throughout her stay there in the tower of Coudray, and he passed the whole days with her, until night, when she always was with women. 'He [Louis] remembered well while she was living at Coudray many days high-ranking people came to visit her there. He did not know what they did or said, because when he saw them coming he retired, nor does he know who they were.' While she lived in that keep he often saw her on her knees praying, without knowing what she said, and sometimes she was weeping.

Joan was taken to Poitiers, then to Tours, where she lived with a woman called Lapau. There the Duke of Alençon gave her a horse, which he saw at the home of the woman Lapau, and the king gave her a whole suit of armour and a military household. Louis became her page there, along with a boy called Raymond, and from then onwards he stayed with her 'as her page, at Blois, at Orléans, and until she came to Paris'. From Tours she went with the army to Blois, where she remained for a while with them – how long he did not remember. Then she went to Orléans via the Sologne and set out fully armed, along with her men-at-arms, whom she constantly told to trust in Our Lord and confess their sins. Once she reached Orléans 'he saw her receive the sacrament of the Eucharist'.

When she reached Orléans on the side of the Sologne, Joan, many others and Louis were taken across the Loire, to the side of the city of Orléans; and from there they entered the town. During the journey from Blois to Orléans, Joan got badly bruised, as she had slept fully armed. In Orléans she lived at the house of the town treasurer, Jacques Bouchier, facing the Banner Gate, and there she received the Sacrament. The day after her arrival she went to seek the Bastard of Orléans, with whom she had an interview, and when she came back, she was annoyed because the captains had decided not to attack the English that day. All the same she went to a boulevard occupied by the French, opposite one under English control, and urged them in God's name to leave or else she would drive them away. In response the Bastard of Granville said insultingly: 'Do you want us to surrender to a woman?' Although at first she retired to her lodgings (when Louis thought she would go to bed), she soon got up again saying, '*Ha! sanglant garçon, vous ne me dyriez pas que le sanc de France feust repandu!*' ('Ha, bloody boy, you didn't tell me French blood was being spilt!') He was sent to get her horse while Joan was dressed in her armour with the help of the ladies of the house; and so the French took the fort of St-Loup. She saw to it that clerics in their robes were spared, but Louis heard that all other English were taken away and killed by the local French. Once it was all over Joan came back to eat and Louis was amazed that as so often she ate only a piece of bread, and that just twice a day. Every night when women were with her she changed out of her armour, but if she could not find any women she slept fully clothed.

Joan went on and on fighting until 'the fort of the bridge' fell, and once Orléans was relieved, she went after the English at Beaugency and Meung. She was distressed at the brutality evident at Beaugency – she was very humane – and when a Frenchman struck a prisoner and left him for dead, she got off her horse, had him make his confession and comforted him as best she could. She went with the army to Jargeau, which was taken by assault, along with many English (among them the Earl of Suffolk and John de la Pole, his brother), and then to Tours to join the king and to Châlons and

Reims. Louis stated: 'There our king was crowned and anointed in my presence for I was, as I have already said, page to Joan, and never left her. I stayed with her till she came to Paris.

'She was a good, upright woman, living a good Catholic life, and, when possible, never missing Mass,' de Coutes continued. Swearing in God's name distressed her. If Alençon swore or blasphemed before her, 'she told him off'. Soldiers dared not use bad language in front of her, for fear of being rebuked. She allowed no women in her army. 'One day, near Chateau-Thierry, seeing the mistress of one of her followers riding on horseback, she pursued her with her sword, without striking her' and gently and charitably told her she must no longer be . . . with the soldiers', or she would be in trouble. 'He know nothing else, not having seen her since Paris.'

The last of the intimates who were with Joan during her few months of glory was her chaplain and confessor, Jean Pasquerel. Like that much more famous cleric Martin Luther, Jean Pasquerel was an eremitical friar of the order of St Augustine. He was at the convent of Tours in 1429 and at the convent of Bayeux in 1456. He first heard of Joan when at Anche, a place whose exact location is unknown. One day he was invited by a group of people to join them in visiting her; they told him they would not leave him until he had seen her. So he went with them to Chinon, then to Tours, where 'he was then a reader in a convent'; and there they found Joan staying with Jean Dupuy, a burgher of the town. His companions spoke to her: 'Joan, we bring you this good father; if you knew him you would love him very much.' She said that 'she had already heard of me and would like to confess to me tomorrow'. On the following day he heard her confession and sung the Mass before her. 'From that day on, I always followed her and was constantly with her, until Compiègne, where she was captured.'

At Chinon, Father Jean heard that she had been visited on two occasions by women, the Lady de Gaucourt and the Lady de Trèves. Like many other witnesses he recalled how she went away to be examined at Poitiers, where Maître Jourdin Morin, Maître Pierre de Versailles, later Bishop of Meaux, and many others decided that 'in view of the necessity weighing on the kingdom', the king could use her help. They found nothing in her 'against the Catholic Faith'. She returned to Chinon and thought she would be allowed to speak to the king but had to wait for the council to agree:

On the day when she was to speak to the king, just as she was going into the castle, a man on horseback said, 'Is that the Maid?' and insulted her and swore. 'In God's Name,' she said to him, 'do you, who are so near your death, take God's name in vain!' And an hour later he fell in the water and was drowned. The friar said he heard this from Joan and many others who said they had witnessed it.

Father Jean then tells the familiar story, according to which she told the king he was the true heir to the kingdom and other things that only he could know. That at any rate is what Joan told him, but there was no witness to corroborate her version of events. What sounds typical of her is Father Jean's assertion that she was angry at being cross-questioned so much, since it stopped her from acting. She told him she had asked 'the Messengers of her Lord, that is of God, who appeared to her', what she should do; and they told her to take her Lord's banner. And so she had her banner made, with the image of Our Saviour in judgement on the clouds of heaven and an angel holding in his hand a fleur-de-lis which Christ blessed. Father Jean was with her at Tours when the banner was painted. His account ties in with the treasury note that twenty-five *livres tournois* were paid to one 'Hauves Poulnois, painter, living at Tours, for painting and getting materials for a great standard, and a small one for the Maid'.

When she went to help Orléans, Father Jean went with her and did not leave her till the day she was captured at Compiègne. As her chaplain, he confessed her and sang Mass for her. She was, he said, full of piety to God and Our Lady, confessed almost daily and communicated often. If near a friary, she told him to remind her of the day when the children of the poor received the Eucharist, so she might receive it with them; and this she did often. When she made her confession she was in tears.

When she left Tours to go to Orléans, she begged him to stay on as her Confessor; and this he promised to do. At Blois she asked him to have her banner made, which he did, and once in the morning and once in the evening he was to bring priests together 'to sing anthems and hymns to the Blessed Mary'. Joan was with them and allowed only the soldiers who had confessed that day join her; she told her people to confess if they wished to come to the meeting, and the priests were always at hand to hear confessions. On the march to Orléans the priests were placed at the front of the army and sang the *Veni Creator Spiritus* and other antiphons.

Father Jean's version of how the supply boats got into Orléans differs slightly from that of the Bastard of Orléans. He says just that the water rose. Then he and the other priests went back to Blois, but some days later he got into the city by way of the River Beauce. Neither the priests nor their convoy were attacked by the English. He tells a familiar story about the capture of the fort of St-Loup on the eve of Ascension Day and about Joan's distress at the sufferings of the wounded soldiers. She was worried particularly that so many English had died without having confessed. Making her own confession on the spot, she told him to invite the whole army to do so too and to thank God for the victory – and if they would not, she would give them no more help. That day she predicted that the siege would be raised within five days, and so things turned out. She would not fight on Ascension Day, but went to confession and received the host.

On that day too she dictated yet another letter to the English, telling them to leave France. She did not send it in the normal way, by means of a herald, since her herald Guyenne had not been sent back, so she attached it to an arrow and told an archer to shoot it at the English. The gesture merely provoked yet more insults, which reduced her to tears, but she soon recovered because she had received good news, she said, from God – and on the following day the Fort des Augustins fell. Although wounded by an arrow, she refused to let any of her soldiers use charms to heal the wound. She was hurt by yet more coarse language from the English commander Glasdale, but when soon after he fell into the Loire and was drowned, she wept for his soul.

Nothing about Joan's life remained so vivid in Father Jean's memory as the days that led up to the relief of Orléans. He may have put words in her mouth, for as late as May 1430 he wrote for her to warn the Hussites of Bohemia that if they persisted in their heresy, she might well come to sort them out when she had finished with the English; such sentiments confirmed her orthodoxy. He was content to make general comments, and his testimony omitted many details of her later story.

He believed firmly that she was sent by God because of her good works and her many virtues. So much did she fear God, that not for anything in the world would she displease Him. He then repeats himself. When wounded in the shoulder by an arrow, which went through from one side to the other, and some spoke of charming her, promising in this way to cure her on the spot, she answered that it would be 'a sin', and said she would rather die than offend God 'by such enchantments'.

His final remarks were bolder. He was amazed that clerics as distinguished as those who caused her death at Rouen should have dared to commit such a crime as to put to death so poor and simple a Christian, cruelly and without a cause, or at least not one grave enough for capital punishment; they might have kept her in prison or elsewhere, but she had annoyed them so much that they had become her mortal enemies; and so, it seems, they were responsible for an unjust sentence. He stated that her actions and deeds were all perfectly known to the king and the Duke of Alençon, who held certain secrets they could tell if they wanted to. As for himself he had nothing more to say, 'unless it be that many times Joan expressed to me a desire that, if she died, the king would build a chapel, where men could pray for the souls of those killed in defence of the kingdom'.

Nobody else who came across Joan from the day she arrived in Chinon to the day she was captured at Compiègne knew her as well as d'Aulon, Alençon, the Bastard, Louis de Coutes and Father Jean, but others had encounters with her they still liked to recall twenty-five years after they had occurred. Many such comments repeat tales that other witnesses had given. For example, she was a 'simple shepherd-maiden', who often went to confession and took communion, who ate and drank moderately, who tried to be rid of all women camp followers unless soldiers would marry them and that she was 'good not only to the French, but also to the enemy'. Those who had examined her at Poitiers had found 'nothing but good in her', and discovered nothing against the Catholic faith. Joan had a great horror of dice, was generous in giving money away and astonished soldiers for the way she handled a lance or a horse. Thibauld d'Armagnac said she was like 'the most skilled captain in the world who all his life had been trained in the art of war'.

Some witnesses are valuable because their evidence fills in gaps in the standard accounts. Maître Reginald Thierry, dean of the church of Meung-sur-Yèvre and surgeon to the king, told how when St-Pierre-le-Moûtier was captured, Joan stopped the soldiers from ransacking the church so that nothing should be removed. Pierre Milet, clerk to the Electors of Paris, captures precisely the tone of her voice when he transcribed part of the letter to the English in her own French dialect: '*Messire vous mande que vous en aliez en vostre pays, car c'est son plaisir, ou sinon je vous feray ung tel hahay*' ('Our Lord wants you to go to your own country, as it's his pleasure, or if not I'll give you what for'). There is a more precise witness to her idiom: Seguin Seguin, Dominican Professor of Theology and Dean of the Faculty of Theology at Poitiers.

Seguin Seguin was the only surviving member of the distinguished group who had examined Joan in Poitiers. When asked why she had come, she replied 'in a grand manner', that 'there had come to her, while she was minding the animals, a voice, which told her that God had great compassion on the people of France, and that she must come into France'. On hearing the voice she began to weep; the voice then told her to go to Vaucouleurs, where she would find a captain who would conduct her safely into France and to the king, and that she must not be afraid. She had done what the voice had ordered, and had come to the king without meeting any obstacle. She was asked this question: 'You have said that a voice told you, God wanted to deliver the people of France from the calamity in which they now are; but, if God wills to deliver them, it is not necessary to have soldiers.' 'In God's Name!' Joan replied, 'the soldiers will fight, and God will give the victory' ('*En nom Dé, les gens d'armes batailleront et Dieu donnera victoire*'). Seguin then asked Joan what dialect the voice spoke in: 'A better one than yours,' was the reply. 'He,' said Seguin, referring to himself, 'spoke the Limousin dialect.' Joan spoke the dialect of Lorraine, strongly influenced by the proximity of Champagne, where 'j' or 'y' became 'ch', so that she pronounced '*joyeux*' as '*choyeux*' and used the typical Lorrainer expression *en nom Dé*, 'in God's name'.

Seguin found it harder to cope with her tone than her accent. He stated that 'God wills that you should not be believed unless there appear some sign to prove that you ought to be believed; and we shall not advise the king to trust in you, and to risk an army on your simple statement.' Joan replied: 'In God's Name! I am not come to Poitiers to show signs, but send me to Orléans, where I shall show you the signs for which I am sent!' She then asked to be given men in such numbers as may seem good, and went on to foretell four things that Seguin had seen occur: the siege of Orléans would be raised, the king would be crowned at Reims, Paris would return to its natural obedience, and the Duke of Orléans would be brought back from England.

The committee at Poitiers had then reported all this to the King's Council and given its view that in the existing extreme circumstances the king might as well send her to Orléans. They also made enquiries about her life and morals, found she was a good Christian, living as a Catholic, never idle, and arranged for her to live with women who were to keep the committee informed about her. 'As for me,' said Seguin, 'I believed she was sent from God, because at the time when she appeared the king and all the French people who supported him had lost hope: everyone thought the cause was lost.' He also remembered Joan was asked why she always marched with a banner in her hand: because she did not wish to use her sword or to kill anyone, she replied. Finally, Seguin, like so many others, testified to her hatred of swearing and to the way that she told the foul-mouthed La Hire to swear only by his staff; and in her presence he did so. 'The soldiers thought her holy,' said another witness.

Apart from Maître Thierry's reference to the capture of St-Pierre-le-Moûtier, nobody knew about the months between the check before Paris (in September 1429) and Joan's capture outside Compiègne (in May 1430); and the narrative resumes only when she was a prisoner. She was taken to Rouen Castle, where she was put in a prison opposite some fields. Raymond, Sieur de Macy, had much to say. The comte de Ligny, on whom Raymond attended, came to see her there. De Ligny also visited her with the earls of Warwick and Stafford, the comte's brother, Louis de Luxembourg, the English chancellor of France and bishop of Thérouanne, and Raymond himself. De Ligny said: 'Joan, I have come to ransom you, if you will promise never again to take up arms against us.' She replied: 'In God's Name [*En nom Dé*], you must be having me on, for I know well that you have neither the will nor the power,' and this she said over and over again, while the count persisted. She knew well, she ended by saying, that the English would have her killed, thinking that after her death they would gain the kingdom of France, but if there were a hundred thousand more '*godons*' than there are at present, they would not have the kingdom '*godons*' or '*goddams*' was the common French name for the English). The Earl of Stafford was so furious at these words that he began to draw his dagger to kill her, but the Earl of Warwick stopped him.

After this, while Macy was still in Rouen, Joan was taken to the place St-Ouen, where a sermon was preached to her by Maître Nicolas Midi – his memory tricked him, for the preacher's name was Erard – and this man said among other things: 'Joan, we have great pity on you; you ought to unsay what you have said, or we must give you up to the secular judges.' She answered that she had done no evil, that she believed in the twelve Articles of the Faith and the Ten Commandments, that she referred herself to the court of Rome and that she wished to believe all things in which Holy Church believed. All the same they pressed her to recant, to which she answered: 'You take great pains to seduce me,' and, to escape danger, she said at last that she was content to do all they required. Then the secretary of the King of England, Lawrence Calot, drew out of his pocket a little written schedule, which he handed to Joan to sign. She replied she could neither read nor write. Nevertheless, Secretary Calot handed her the schedule and a pen to sign it and for whatever motive – Macy thinks it was as a sign of contempt – she made a circular mark. Then Calot took her hand with the pen and caused her to make some sort of signature, probably a cross (Macy was not sure). Macy concluded: 'I believe her to be in Paradise.'

SIXTEEN

Witnesses to the Trial

The many witnesses who had come forward to share their memories of Joan twenty-five years or so after they had known her regarded her with a mixture of awe and admiration, not just because of her piety and purity, but also because of her competence, courage and kindness. Indirectly, the often long depositions by acquaintances, colleagues and friends revealed how shocking had been the bias of the judges who had condemned her. Her questioners had seen her as a deceiver, yet she was transparent; as a witch, yet she remained a virgin; as heretical, yet she was scrupulously Catholic; as a sorceress, yet she claimed no special powers. They had seen her decision to revert to male costume as the conclusive sign of her wickedness, yet those who had lived with her thought her merely sensible in her choice – they had not been shocked. Some of them knew she heard 'voices', but none of those who did found her experiences unusually preposterous or even interesting – they were plain matter-of-fact about them.

But Joan's new judges dealt in legal niceties rather than character assessment. As Macy realised, the key evidence concerned the trial; and what mattered most in the royal inquest and in the ecclesiastical inquests was the evidence of theologians and Church lawyers, for Joan, who could have been tried as a traitor to Henry VI and II, was tried for sorcery and heresy. Charles VII's royal lawyers did not restore Joan's good name because they could not: only a Church court could do that. Indeed, one royal official produced a witness who could have hindered Joan's case, for in 1450 the king's commissioner, Maître Guillaume Bouillé, secured the testimony of an unrepentant critic of Joan, who disappeared from history before he could speak to papal officials.

Maître Jean Beaupère, one of Joan's most implacable interrogators twenty years earlier and who had by now retired to Besançon, just happened to come to Rouen to collect dues from his canonry in Rouen Cathedral. He felt free to express a view of Joan not unlike that he had maintained in 1431. For a royal inquest of the mid-fifteenth century, Bouille's inquest proved to be remarkably fair. Beaupère himself still had no doubt that in many details his snide view of Joan had been sound. He believed Joan's 'apparitions' had natural and human rather than supernatural and divine causes, and he referred back to the evidence of the trial.[1]

Before she was taken to St-Ouen to be admonished on the following morning, Beaupère went alone, with permission, into Joan's prison, and warned her that she would soon be led to the scaffold to be preached to, telling her that, if she were a good Christian, she would say on the scaffold that she referred all her actions and words to the care of Holy Mother Church, and especially of the Church's judges. And this she said on the scaffold, having been asked to do so by Maître Nicolas Midi. On due consideration she was sent back to prison for a time, after abjuring, though some Englishmen accused Cauchon and the Parisian delegates of favouring her errors.

After her abjuration, and, after taking her woman's dress which she was given in prison, the judges were told the next Friday or Saturday that Joan had not repented of having put off a man's dress and had taken a woman's dress. For this reason,

> my Lord of Beauvais (Cauchon) . . . sent me and Maître Nicolas Midi to her, hoping we would speak to Joan and persuade her to persevere in the good intent she had on the scaffold and be careful not to relapse. But we could not find the keeper of the prison key, of the three keys to the prison, the Promoter had one, the Inquisitor a second and the Cardinal the third; and, while we were waiting for the prison guard, several Englishmen in the castle court-yard threatened, as Maître Nicolas Midi told me, that anyone throwing both of us into the water would be well occupied. We went back, when we had heard this. On the castle bridge, said Midi, other Englishmen said much the same. We were afraid and went away without speaking to Joan.

As for Joan's innocence, she showed a woman's subtlety, thought Beaupère. He did not understand from any of her words that she had been violated. As for her final penitence, he did not know what to say, for on the Monday after the abjuration (28 May) he left Rouen to go to Basel, as a delegate of the University of Paris. For this reason he had no news of the condemnation till he heard it mentioned at Lille in Flanders.

Careful though he had been to present himself favourably, Beaupère had not become an admirer of Joan's. He had, however, fashioned a way of becoming rich: in 1432 he was a canon of Besançon, Paris, Laon and Rouen and soon a canon of Autun as well; he was pro-English when he acquired his benefices, anti-papal when it paid him at Basel and pro-French when Charles VII reconquered his kingdom. He remained constant only in his mistrust of a woman who had dared to answer back to her betters.

Of the six other clerics interviewed who had taken part in the trial, four were Black Friars, or Dominicans – Jean Toutmouillé, Ysambard de La Pierre, Martin Ladvenu and Guillaume Duval – and two were secular priests – Guillaume Manchon, the notary, and Jean Massieu, clerk to Maître 'Jean Benedicite', the nickname of the Promoter, Estivet. They were willing to suggest that the proceedings of that trial had been vitiated by lies and intimidation. They had much to worry about, for if they supported Joan now, they knew that they had been too craven to support her then. In defending her in middle or old age, they had to confront the moral failures of their youth.

Jean Toutmouillé was cautious in judging the trial, which he had not attended, but he related the common view 'that they persecuted her from a desire of perverse revenge'. He says her enemies would put off besieging Louviers until she had been dealt with. Jean himself had been in the prison when Martin Ladvenu had to tell Joan she was to be burnt, which Ladvenu did 'most considerately and charitably', and he recalled how Joan had cried out in distress, saying that she would rather have her head cut off 'seven times than be burnt in this way'. Had she been kept in a Church prison instead of in the custody of her enemies, she was sure that she would not have been so miserably treated. 'I appeal to God, the Great Judge, over the great wrongs and injustices done me!' When Cauchon came, she told him, 'Bishop, I die through you.' Cauchon retorted that she had not kept to her promise, meaning her promise to wear women's clothes, and Joan reiterated her point about Church prisons and competent Church guards; and at this Toutmouillé left.

Brother Ysambard de La Pierre had been more intimately involved. At one stage he had urged Joan to submit to the Church, to which she replied she would submit to the Holy Father, and he had told her to submit to the Council of Basel. Joan had never heard of a general council, but when he explained that some people there were on her side and others on the English side – in fact most were pro-English – she cried out, 'If there are any of our side in that place, I am quite willing to give myself up and to submit to the Council of Basel.' This reply infuriated Cauchon. 'Shut up,' he said and told the notary to cut out any reference to her submission to the council. Brother Ysambard was also threatened by the English, who intimated that if he did not stay silent they would throw him into the Seine.

When Joan recanted and abjured and put on men's clothes again, 'I and many others were present when Joan excused herself for doing this.' She had told him 'that the English had tried violence on her, when she was wearing a woman's dress'; and he 'saw her weeping, her face covered with tears . . . so that he was full of pity'. She said publicly, after being declared an obstinate and relapsed heretic: 'If you, my Lords of the Church, had placed and kept me in your prisons, perhaps I should not have been in this state.'

After the end of this session and trial, Cauchon said to the English 'Farewell, be cheerful, it's done.' Brother Ysambard added that Joan had been asked 'such difficult, subtle, and crafty questions . . . that the great clerics and learned men present would have found it hard to reply'. He had been with the Bishop of Avranches, 'an aged and good cleric', who had been asked for his opinion of the case. The bishop said: 'He summoned me before him, and asked me what St Thomas [Thomas Aquinas] said about submitting to the Church. I sent him in writing the verdict of St Thomas: "In doubtful things, touching the Faith, recourse should always be had to the Pope or to a General Council."' The bishop agreed with this and seemed to be unhappy with the arguments put forward on this subject. His thoughts were written down but 'left out, maliciously'.

Even at the end of the whole process, the correct forms were not followed. When Joan had confessed and taken communion, she was declared a relapsed heretic, but the secular judge did not condemn her; instead, she was given immediately to the executioner, who was simply told to do his duty and burn her.

In her last moments, Joan was so contrite and so beautifully penitent that 'it was a thing to be admired, saying such pitiful, devout, and Catholic words, so that those who saw her in great numbers wept and . . . the Cardinal of England and many other English were forced to weep':

As I was near her at the end, the poor woman asked and humbly begged me to go to the Church nearby and bring her the Cross, to hold it up in front of her eyes until death came, so that the Cross on which God hung might be in life continually before her eyes. While in the flames, she did not stop calling out the Holy Name of Jesus in a loud voice, imploring and invoking continually the help of the Saints in Paradise; further, what is more, as she was dying and bending her head, she uttered the Name of Jesus as a sign that she fervently believed in God, exactly what we read of St Ignatius (of Antioch) and of several other Martyrs.

Brother Ysambard concludes: 'Immediately after the execution, the executioner came to me and to my companion, Brother Martin Ladvenu.' Overwhelmed by what he had just experienced and moved to feel sorrow for sin, he was 'quite desperate and afraid he would never receive God's pardon' for what he had done to this holy woman. 'And the executioner said and affirmed that, in spite of the oil, the sulphur, and the charcoal which he had applied to the entrails and heart of the said Joan, in no way could he burn them up, nor reduce to ashes either the entrails or the heart, which he found amazing, like an obvious miracle.'

Brother Martin agreed: 'Many of those who appeared in the court did so more from love of the English and the favourable feelings they had for them than because of their commitment to justice and to the Catholic Faith.' Cauchon, he thought, was an example of 'extreme prejudice', for which he suggested two proofs: his refusal to put her in a Church prison instead of an English prison; and, his delight at seeing that she had reverted to men's clothes, which he joked about with the Earl of Warwick, ' "Farewell! Farewell! It is done; be of good cheer!", or such-like words' (much the same words as those mentioned by Brother Ysambard). Cauchon was proud of his fluency in English.

Joan also told Brother Martin that in prison Joan had been abused by an English lord. He repeated the accounts relating that she had blamed Cauchon for her death and that before her execution she had not been condemned by the secular judges – a Dominican would have an eye for legal niceties – but had been handed over straightaway to the executioner. That this was all wrong was admitted in a later heresy case, when the judges pointedly said that this time, as had not happened in Joan's case, correct procedures must be followed. And the executioner himself said he had never been so afraid of carrying out a sentence, both because she was famous and because she had been so cruelly tied up that he could not hasten her death. Brother Martin also witnessed the way she called on the name of Jesus and on the saints while she was dying.

Guillaume Duval had been present at one session of the trial beside Ysambard de La Pierre. Alhough the two could find no room for themselves in the consistory, they sat at the middle of the table, near Joan. 'When she was questioned or examined, Brother Ysambard advised her what she should say, nudging her or making some other sign.' After the session was over, he and Brother Ysambard, with Maître Jean Delafontaine, were given the job of visiting her in prison that day after dinner and giving her advice, so they went together to Rouen Castle to do so. There they came across the Earl of Warwick, who was furious with Brother Ysambard and demanded to know why that morning he had nudged 'that wicked person' and made signs to her. 'If I see you again taking trouble to save her . . . I will have you thrown into the Seine.' He so terrified brothers Guillaume and Ysambard that they fled back to the priory. Brother Guillaume had no more to add, as he took no part in the trial.

As expert theologians and confessors, Dominicans may have been the clerical witnesses most sympathetic to Joan – in the 1450s they tried to show that they had been – but on the conduct of the trial Maître Guillaume Manchon, the trial notary, was the key witness. Of all the depositions his was the longest and the most damning. To him the proceedings were suspect, since he thought Cauchon and the Paris 'masters' acted out of 'hatred and anger over the cause of the King of France'. In the 1450s this was a view that anyone aware of the state of affairs was prudent to withhold.

First, Maître Nicolas Loiselleur, a friend of Cauchon's, pretended that he came from Joan's part of the country so that he could talk to her, be her confessor and use her words against her in the trial. When the trial began, Loiselleur secretly put Manchon, his assistant

Boisguillaume and other witnesses by a hole in an adjoining room to enable them to hear her and report what they had heard to him. Her comments were used as the basis of memoranda for questions in the trial, to find a means of catching her out.

When the process was under way, Maître Jean Lohier, a learned Church lawyer, came to Rouen, and was asked to give his opinion on what Cauchon had said. He asked for two or three days for research, but was told to give his opinion that afternoon. Lohier said the proceedings were invalid because they were not carried out in public where people were free to express their views, that the business concerned the honour of the King of France, as Joan supported him, but the king had not been called, there were none of the necessary legal documents available, and she had been given no counsel. Cauchon was wild with Lohier for saying this. 'This Lohier . . . would discredit everything, and says it is of no value. If we were to believe him, everything must be begun again, and all we have done would be worthless!' It was a Saturday afternoon in Lent, and on the following morning Manchon spoke to Lohier at the church of Notre-Dame at Rouen, and asked him what he thought of the trial and of Joan. Lohier told him that if Joan were to say 'It seems to me' instead of 'I know for certain' when she talked about her revelations, her judges would have no grounds for condemning her. He added, 'It seems they act more from hate than any other motive; and therefore I will not stay here, for I have no wish to be involved.' His views were not welcome in Rouen. He left and spent the rest of his life at the papal court, where his final job was to be the Dean of Appeals; and in Rome he died.

In the early stages of the process, as Manchon was busy for five or six days writing out Joan's answers and excuses, the judges, speaking in Latin, often tried to force him to change the words by altering their meaning. By Cauchon's order two men were put by a window near the judges' seat, hidden by a curtain, to write and report the charges against Joan, saying nothing about her excuses – this, Manchon thought, was Loiselleur's work. 'When a session was over, in the afternoon, when notes of what was written were compared, the others had a different version to mine, without any of the excuses, and Cauchon was wild with me.' Where Manchon wrote 'Nota' in the record – his minutes were eventually used in the 1455 retrial – there was disagreement, questions had to be asked, and, Manchon claims, 'it was found that what I had written was true'.

Often, says Manchon, Cauchon and the 'Masters' wanted to compel him to write what they imagined, not what he himself had heard. 'And when there was something that did not please them, they forbade it to be written down, saying that it was no use for the process; but he wrote only according to his hearing and knowledge.'

Joan had said that she wished to submit to 'our Holy Father the Pope and to the Holy Council'. The theological language made Cauchon suspicious, and he asked who had spoken with the Maid. The Guard said Maître Delafontaine, his lieutenant, and the two friars. As Delafontaine and the friars were absent, Cauchon was furious with Maître Jean Lemaître, the deputy inquisitor, and said he might do him an injury. When Delafontaine knew that he was threatened for this reason, he left Rouen, and did not return. As for the friars, they might have died but for Lemaître, who excused them and said that if they were harmed, he would stay away from the trial. From then onwards, the Earl of Warwick would not let anyone visit Joan, apart from Cauchon or those sent by him; and the deputy inquisitor could not go without him.

When the sermon at St-Ouen was over and Joan had abjured, Loiselleur said to her, 'Joan, you have done a good day's work, if it please God, and have saved your soul.' She then asked: 'Take me to a Church prison, so that I can be out of the hands of the English.' On Cauchon's instruction she was taken back to the castle. On the following Sunday, Trinity Sunday, the masters, notaries, and others involved in the trial were called. They stated that they were told that she was back in men's clothes and had relapsed. When they reached the castle, Cauchon was away and 80 to 100 English soldiers 'met us in the castle courtyard and said we clerics were all false, treacherous Armagnacs and false counsellors, so we found it hard to get out of the castle, and did nothing all day'. Manchon was summoned the next day and refused to go without a guarantee of safe passage, after the fright he had had the day before, and unless one of Warwick's followers acted as a surety. On these conditions he returned and took part in the rest of the trial, apart from the private examination of Joan, the account of which he would not sign, in spite of pressure from Cauchon.

Manchon saw Joan being led to the scaffold surrounded by 700 or 800 soldiers with swords and staves, and no one daring to speak to her except Brother Martin Ladvenu and Maître Jean Massieu. She listened patiently to the sermon right to the end, then said her 'thanksgiving, prayers and lamentations most notably and devoutly', so that the judges, prelates, and all present were in tears. Manchon had never wept so much over anything, and 'for a month after, he could not feel at peace'. For this reason, with part of the money he had received for his services he bought a missal, so that 'he could pray for her . . . As for final repentance, I never saw greater signs of a Christian.'

In his sermon at St-Ouen, Maître Guillaume Erard said: 'Ah! noble house of France, which had always been the protectress of the Faith, have you been so abused that you would adhere to a heretic and schismatic?' Joan replied by praising her king, calling him the best and wisest Christian in the world; Erard and Cauchon told Massieu to make her be silent.

Jean Massieu was the final cleric to testify. He said he was present at every moment of the trial as clerk to Maître Jean Benedicite, the nickname of the Promoter, Estivet. From what he saw, he was sure the proceedings were motivated by hatred and a wish to dishonour the King of France whom Joan served, and to take revenge and bring her to death, 'not according to reason and for the honour of God and of the Catholic Faith'. He said this because when Cauchon and the six clerics (Beaupère, Midi, Maurice, Touraine, Courcelles, and Feuillet, or someone else) interrogated her, before she could answer one of them, another would ask a different question, so that she was often rushed and anxious in her answers. And, besides, as he led Joan from her prison to the court, she would often ask if she could make her devotions in the castle chapel, which they passed. For granting her request he was often reproved by Estivet, who said, 'Traitor! What makes you so bold as to let this excommunicated slut pray without permission? I will have you put in a tower where you shall see neither sun nor moon for a month, if you do so again.' And when Estivet saw he was not obeyed, he stood in front of the chapel door, between Massieu and Joan, to stop her saying her prayers there and asked her expressly: 'Is this the Body of Christ?' When taking her back to prison on the fourth or fifth day, a priest called Maître Eustache Turquetil asked Massieu what he thought of her answers, if she would be burnt, what would happen. Massieu replied that so far he had seen only good and honour in her, but did not know what would happen; only God knew that. His answer was reported by Maître Eustache Turquetil to the 'King's' people, that is Henry VI's supporters, and he was said to be opposed to the king. For this reason Cauchon summoned him in the afternoon and told him to be careful to make no mistake, or he would be forced to drink more than was good for him. If the notary Manchon had not made excuses for him, he would not have escaped.

Massieu is one source that explains why Joan went back to wearing male costume. At the end of the sermon that Joan had to hear after abjuring her voices, Massieu advised her to ask to be taken to a Church prison, as it was the Church that had condemned her, but Cauchon said she should go back to the castle. After dinner that day, the Thursday or Friday after Pentecost, in the presence of the Church council she took off her man's dress and put on a woman's dress, as she was told, and 'the man's dress was put in a bag in the room where she was kept prisoner, while she remained guarded in this place by five Englishmen, three of whom stayed all night in the room, and two outside the door of the room'. Massieu was sure that at night she slept chained by the legs with two pairs of iron chains, and fastened closely to a chain going across the foot of her bed, held to a great piece of wood, five or six feet long, and closed with a key, so that she could not move from where she was. Next Sunday was Trinity Sunday, and she told Massieu that when it was time to rise she asked the English guards to take off the irons so that she could get up. Then they took away her women's clothes, emptied the bag with her men's clothes in it and told her to put her dress in the bag. She told them she was forbidden to wear male costume, but they would not give her the female costume, however much she begged them to do so. 'She told me all this next Tuesday before dinner, when the Promoter had left with the Earl of Warwick, and he [Massieu] was alone with her.'

Some prisoners summoned to the castle were driven back by the English soldiers with axes and swords. Before Joan left the castle on Wednesday, when she was condemned, the Body of Christ was borne to her without stole and lights, which upset Brother Martin, who had confessed her, so a stole and lights were sent for, and Brother Martin gave her communion. Massieu's version of her final acts is similar to Manchon's version. He emphasises the way she invoked 'the Blessed Trinity, the Blessed and Glorious Virgin Mary and all the Blessed Saints in Paradise', naming some of them, and asked to be forgiven by those she had harmed and forgave those who had harmed her – and this went on for about half an hour.

Massieu was with her until she died.

> With great devotion she asked to have a Cross: and, hearing this, an Englishman there made a little cross of wood with the ends of a stick, which he gave her, and devoutly she received and kissed it . . . crying and confessing God, Our Redeemer, Who suffered on the Cross for our Redemption, of Whose Cross she had the sign and representation; and she put the Cross in her bosom, between her body and her clothing. And, besides, she asked me humbly to get for her the Church Cross, so that she could see it continually till her death. And I got the Clerk of the Parish of St-Sauveur to bring it to her; which, being brought, she embraced closely and long, and kept it till she was fastened to the stake.

The English tried to make him hurry up, and as he tried to console her, asked him if they were going to dine there, so the executioner was told to do what he had to do. 'As she was dying, she cried, with a loud voice: "Jesus!"'

Testimonies collected in 1450 left no room for doubt that the 1431 trial had been a political trial masquerading as a religious inquest. Their accounts must have pleased Charles VII, but Pope Nicholas V was probably embarrassed. He wanted the French and the English to make peace in order to join forces against the Turks and so defend the capital of the Greek world. He could not know that in 1453, as the French drove the English from France, the Turks would finally capture Constantinople. By 1455 there was no hope of routing Sultan Mehmet III, and the new pope was less cautious than the old one, so the case to annul the condemnation could be resumed. On 7 November Isabelle Romée and her two sons came to the cathedral of Notre-Dame to demand justice for her daughter from judges who were the pope's representatives:

> She had a daughter born in legitimate marriage whom she had baptised and confirmed and brought up in the fear of God and respectful of the traditions of the Church so far as she could ensure, given the child's age and humble status. Growing up in fields and grazing land, she often went to Church and after going

to confession she would receive the sacrament of the Eucharist every month. Because the people were suffering so much, in her heart she had great pity on them and, though very young, she would fast and pray for them devoutly and fervently. She never thought, spoke or did a thing against the faith . . . Enemies had her arraigned in a religious trial. Despite her denials and appeals, both unspoken and spoken, and with no help in her defence, she was put through an unjust, violent, wicked and sinful trial. Judges condemned her falsely, damnably and illegally, and put her to death very cruelly by fire. To damn their souls and to atone for the notorious, infamous and irreparable loss to me, Isabelle, and mine . . . I demand her name be restored.

After this speech, however carefully rehearsed, Isabelle was so over-come that she had to be taken to the cathedral sacristy. The final nullification trial could begin.

During the 1452 inquiry, witnesses had been initially examined on twelve articles corresponding to the twelve articles of the original trial, but these were found not to correspond accurately to the actual way in which that trial had been conducted. Manchon, the notary, the two friars Martin Ladvenu and Ysambart de La Pierre testified, as did Pierre Miget, one of the original judges, and Pierre Cusquel, a Rouennais master mason. Those who had spoken at the 1450 inquiry usually elaborated what they said in the subsequent inquiries of 1452 and 1455.

Judicially, the notary Manchon's testimony was the most damning, since, as a man versed in canon law, he noticed points that were not strictly correct, such as Joan's incarceration in an English prison, the threat of torture, her prudential reasons for wearing men's clothes (she was guarded by soldiers), but most shocking of all, the way in which evidence was altered. 'I, as notary, wrote down Joan's answers and defence. Two or three writers, secretly hidden nearby, omitted from their writing everything in her favour. The judges urged me [Manchon] to do as they did, but I refused.' Manchon also pointed out that whereas Cauchon chose to take part, the Inquisitor was afraid of not taking part; the process was at English expense (in 1455 he mentioned the 1,000 crowns given for her surrender to the English and the 300 crowns given to the Burgundian soldier who had captured her), with the implication that the English wanted their money's worth;

and the assessors and theologians summoned dared not refuse to attend. Manchon wrote out what had been said in French, and believed it was subsequently translated into Latin. He also swore that 'the copy of the process that was shown to me is the true copy made' and he identified his own and his companion's signatures. 'One copy was given to the Inquisitor, one to the King of England, and one to the Bishop of Beauvais.' With Thomas de Courcelles he translated his version into Latin, 'long after the death and execution of Joan'. Because of the constant interruptions Joan had endured, some secretaries wrote down only what they wanted to record, without any record of the words that could have exonerated her. Manchon himself complained about such omissions, and when some said 'she had not replied as he had written', he 'wrote Nota at the top, so that the questions might be repeated and the difficulties removed'.[2]

Neither did Manchon recall the use of preliminary evidence, which should have been inserted in the trial record. He thought that Joan was tried not in Paris, but in Rouen, because that was where the King of England and leading members of his council were. He reiterated the view of Lohier that the trial could not be valid because it was held in a castle, not in a legal court. He reaffirmed the atmosphere of intimidation in which the trial had taken place, as when someone was advising Joan on the question of submission to the Church and Cauchon had cried out, 'Hold your tongue, in the devil's name!' Then there was another incident when the Earl of Stafford would have killed a person who had spoken up for Joan if he had not been told that they were in a place of sanctuary. Manchon added more on how Loiselleur ensured Joan's confession to him was overheard. He also claimed that the twelve articles of her indictment were not read to her, that she had not understood what she had abjured and that she believed in her visions to the end.

Brother Martin told how he was with Joan on the day of her death, until the very moment she died. When Joan saw the fire, she told him to go down and hold the cross of Christ high so that she could look at it. When the Bishop of Beauvais came to see her, she told him he was the reason for her death; he had promised to put her in the hands of the Church, but instead had given her up to her enemies. 'To the end of her life she maintained . . . that her voices came from God, and that what she had done had been by God's command.'

Other witnesses, less important to her, were still useful to the court. They could give details of the way she was treated in prison, knew that she was kept in chains, even in an iron cage, asserted that she had been tested for virginity and found to be still a virgin – a fact that the judges had carefully omitted to mention in 1431 – and confirmed the tales of persistent intimidation by Cauchon and the English. Massieu summed up the general sense of the 1431 proceedings, saying:

Many had a great hate against her, chiefly the English, who were very afraid of her: for, before she was captured, they did not dare to appear where they believed her to be. I heard it said that the Bishop of Beauvais did everything at the instigation of the King of England and his Council, who were then in Rouen . . . Some of them [the assessors] said she ought to be in the hands of the Church, but the Bishop [Cauchon] did not care, and sent her away to the English.

Among the clerical witnesses, none was as revealing as Thomas de Courcelles. Born in Amiens, trained in law as well as theology, he was appointed Rector of the University of Paris in 1430. As a representative of the university, he became a leading figure at the Council of Basel, where he argued alongside many against Pope Eugenius IV and promoted the cause of the anti-pope Felix V. He also revealed his political skills at the meeting in Arras where the treaty was signed between the Duke of Burgundy and the King of France that led ultimately to French victory in the Hundred Years War. There it was said of him that he spoke like an angel, moving many to tears as he talked of peace. In 1440 at Bourges he eloquently supported the Gallican case that saw the French Church as semi-independent of Rome; and in 1442 he preached on the end of conflicts between the king and the University of Paris. Later, he negotiated the abdication of Felix V and in time he became Dean of Notre-Dame and an archdeacon in Rome. Although highly articulate and a distinguished public speaker, few of those involved in Joan's 1431 trial or who testified on that trial in 1456 gave such imprecise testimony as de Courcelles.

He stated that he 'believed the Bishop of Beauvais accepted the task of trying Joan in a matter of the faith because he was a counsellor of the King of England and Bishop of Beauvais, in whose territory Joan had been taken captive. He had heard it said that money was given to the Inquisitor by a certain Surreau, receiver-general, but he did not know if the bishop was paid.'

He remembered Lohier's belief that the trial was illegal and he himself 'never held Joan to be a heretic except in her refusal to submit to the Church' and 'never positively gave an opinion that she was a heretic'. Nor did he give an opinion as to whether she should be tortured – a statement that contradicts the trial record. 'Many of the assessors . . . advised that Joan should be put . . . into a Church prison', but he 'did not remember' that this subject formed a part of his discussions.

Courcelles was clear that Joan was examined on the twelve articles that had been drawn up, but did not know if anyone had suggested they should be redrafted. He did know that Loiselleur had visited Joan in disguise and advised against it. He believed he heard Joan in confession. He stated that Joan had gone back to dressing in men's clothes 'because it seemed to her more suitable to wear man's clothing, being with men, than a woman's dress'. Finally, though he had been present at the last preaching made in the Vieux-Marché on the day she died, he had not watched her burn, since, 'after the sermon and the reading of the sentence, I went away'.

Ever the skilful lawyer, Thomas de Courcelles had said nothing incriminating: as a man famous for verbal fluency he had been extraordinarily reticent.

Laymen could afford to be freer in criticising the proceedings. One advocate in the civil courts, Laurence Guesdon, a burgher of Rouen, pointed out one lapse:

> . . . the sentence by which Joan was handed over to the civil authorities was read; and, as soon as it was pronounced, immediately . . . and before either the *Bailli* or himself [Guesdon], the witness, whose task it was, had given sentence, the executioner grabbed her and took her to the place where the stake was already prepared: and she was burned. And this he [Guesdon] held was an incorrect proceeding.

This view was confirmed by Jean Ricquier, chaplain of Rouen Cathedral, who was about twenty at the time. He knew that Joan was handed over by the Church authorities; he saw the English seize

her and lead her at once to the place of execution. He did not
observe any sentence read by the secular authorities. Both he and the
advocate knew this procedure to have been incorrect.

It was a visitor to the city, however, who saw clearly the flaws in
Joan's trial. Although originally from Viville, in Bassigny, not far
from Domremy, Jean Moreau came to settle in Rouen. He recalled
how 'a man of note from Lorraine came to the town' and how, as he
was from the same part of the country, they soon got to know one
another. The visitor came from the marches of Lorraine and had
been called to Rouen, 'having been commissioned to get information
in the native country of the said Joan and to hear what her
reputation was'. He had done as he was asked and reported to
Cauchon, expecting some reward for his trouble and expense.
Instead, Cauchon railed at him, called him a traitor and a bad man,
and said he had not done what he had been told to do.

> My compatriot complained that he could not get any wage from
> the bishop, who found his information useless. He told me that in
> what he had found out he had learnt nothing of Joan that he
> would not willingly have heard about his own sister, although he
> had made enquiries in five or six parishes near Domremy as well
> as in the village itself.

Cauchon had not wanted to know the truth. Moreau also noted
that Joan was said to be guilty of the crime of *lèse-majesté*, that is
treason, and to have led the people astray. She was condemned,
however, not for treason, but for heresy; and yet it is hard not to
believe that in her judges's eyes her offence was political rather than
religious. Having seen the volumes of evidence collected, a
commentator can be grateful to Moreau. At times it seems that the
new judges needed a hammer to bludgeon a nut. In a few sentences
Moreau said all that must be said: the original judges were dishonest
and the process dishonest.

In all, 150 witnesses related to the court their memories of Joan.
Much of what they said may have seemed irrelevant to questions of
heresy. Those who had known her as a child remembered Joan
before she was a figure of national renown. Her life alongside
French soldiers, about which Dunois, Alençon or Louis de Coutes
spoke, filled in details of her campaigns. There was virtually no

mention of the months when she campaigned in the upper Loire and few knew anything about her when she passed months in prison before coming to Rouen to be tried. For the trial itself there were abundant witnesses. Even if key figures at the trial, such as Cauchon and Estivet, did not testify, as they were no longer alive, it was amazing how many people had lived on into the 1450s. Beaupère appeared once, and, by extraordinary luck, the notaries who as young men had kept records of the trial were around in middle age to produce them or to verify them. A few priests had intimate knowledge of Joan's spiritual life: Father Jean Pasquerel for the period of her public career, several Dominican friars, notably Brothers Martin Ladvenu and Ysambard de La Pierre, for the period of the trial. There were women who had provided lodgings for her, men who had brief encounters with her, a relation, Laxart, and others who repeated what they had heard about her. Seguin Seguin had seen her in Poitiers.

One matter that had exercised the original judges, the fairies' tree at Domremy, interested only those who came from the area. The original judges had worried about her clothes, whereas the witnesses of the 1450s, except for Beaupère, were not so concerned. A third, most important concern, the nature and status of her visions, was hardly touched on in the 1450s. Only Joan could describe them, and at the original trial words sometimes failed her. In the later trials her visions were regarded as private unless they contradicted the teaching of the Church; and how they did so was difficult to prove. At the original trial any appeal to the pope was not allowed, if, as many of the later witnesses averred, Joan had appealed to him. In 1431 it was hard to say who was pope, for many doubted the position of Eugenius IV, but her judges would not allow even an appeal to the Council of Basel. As far as they were concerned, their court was the court beyond which there was no appeal.

One recent historian, François Neveux, has argued that in the ecclesiastical retrial the Inquisitor, Jean Bréhal, tried to blame Cauchon in order to preserve the good name of his own occupation, conducting inquests. The inquisitors had played an unenthusiastic part in Joan's original trial. This is a legalistic case. Neveux ignores all the evidence on Joan's character and behaviour provided by men like Alençon, the Bastard (now Dunois), de Coutes, d'Aulon and Father Pasquerel, let alone many obscure inhabitants of Domremy,

Orléans or Rouen; and yet, even in legalistic terms, it is hard not to conclude that the trial and condemnation of Joan in 1431 was a travesty of inquisitorial justice. That in the end was the verdict of the 1456 trial of nullification. The documents of the nullification trial were phrased dully, but their cumulative effect is devastating.

Time after time, best procedure in Joan's trial had been ignored. She could have been tried as a traitor to Henry VI and II, but she was not. Her heresy should have been notorious, a view that Charles VII's court and clergy had not noticed, but in fact, contrary to proper form, she was accused of heresy on the basis of cross-examination; and that should not have been the case. She should have been detained in a Church prison, but she was not. She should have been given counsel, but she was not until it was too late and then she was offered help only from the assessors in the court, who in view of their status could not give her unbiased advice. As her case was a concern of Charles VII's, he should have been represented in the case, but he was not. He should have informed the pope and asked the case to be tried in Rome, but he did not. She should not have been tried by her enemies, but she was. She should not have been guarded by men, let alone Englishmen, but she was. The salvation of her soul could not have depended on whether or not she was dressed like a man, but it did. If it did, she should not have been tricked into wearing men's clothes, but she was (or at least that is probably the case). After so many procedural errors, once condemned as a relapsed heretic, she should have been solemnly handed over to the secular power of Rouen, but she was not. There had been unjust ecclesiastical trials before, but Joan's was one of the most unjust trials ever undertaken in any ecclesiastical court.

SEVENTEEN

Verdict and Rehabilitation

The evidence that had been collected so painstakingly, first by the king's officials in 1450, then by Church officials in 1452, 1455 and 1456, was not collected for its own sake. The reason for gathering the information was to answer certain questions. At first the lawyers had thought that they could use the twelve articles of the 1431 trial, but soon they found out that they wished to discuss many other questions, so they redrafted and expanded the number of articles to twenty-seven.

These new articles were not just the old ones redressed; instead, they were a new set designed to respond to the evidence that could be found to nullify the verdict of the first trial. The first five refer to English hatred of Joan, based on her championing of Charles VII's cause and her victories over them (1, 2), a motive for taking her to Rouen and imprisoning her in the castle (3), for terrifying the judges, the advisers and the Promoter (4) and the notaries (5), so that the notaries did not dare record anything to favour her (6), so that she had no adequate advice or aid (7), was kept in chains in a secular prison (8). Joan was only nineteen or so, too young to defend herself (9). She was secretly visited so as to encourage her not to submit to the Church (10), she was interrogated in such a way that it was hard not to be trapped (11) and worn down (12), while she persistently said she submitted to the Church and the Holy Father (13), repeated that in court (14), but her words were not faithfully recorded (15) and if some thought that she would not submit to the Church (16), that was because she did not understand what was meant by the term 'Church Militant' or else because she thought that the Church was under English control (17). Besides, translations of the trial records from French into Latin were not always accurate (18). For all these reasons the trial sentence was unsafe (19), the trial documents untrustworthy (20) and its legal procedures incorrect (21). Joan could not defend herself properly (22) and, although a loyal communicating

Catholic, she was condemned as a heretic to appease the English (23), she was taken to be burnt without authorisation from the secular authorities (24), she died a saintly death (25), she had been harried by the English to discredit the Most Christian King (26). All these facts are well known both in Rouen and throughout France (27).[1]

It was hard to deny the truth of the case so outlined. The articles said nothing about matters that the first trial had raised: was it permissible for a woman to act a man's role; how far should a Catholic trust in private revelations; would God have sent a virgin soldier to fulfil a political plan; did God hate the English and the Burgundians? Those interrogated in the 1450s could not say much about Joan's intimate experiences, they were relaxed about her wearing of men's clothes and her months of fighting and by 1450 it must have seemed true, as it had not seemed twenty years before, that God intended Charles VII to be King of France and Henry VI to return to England.

On 18 June, Jean d'Arc and the Promoter, Chapitault, acting for the plaintiffs, appeared at the palace of the Bishop of Paris, and asked for a day to be fixed for the end of the case. The date was set for 1 July 1456, and notices were posted on the doors of Rouen Cathedral. On the following day it was announced that the final sentence should be delivered on Wednesday 7 July, and at eight o'clock that morning the rehabilitation was read by the archbishop. A procession and sermon was organised in place St-Ouen, and on 8 July a second sermon was preached in place du Vieux-Marché, where a cross was raised to perpetuate the memory of Joan's death. This cross was later replaced by a fountain, with a statue of Joan under an arcade surmounted by a cross. In 1756, in the tercentenary year of the rehabilitation, a new fountain was erected that remains there today.

What is striking about the processes of rehabilitation – or, technically, the nullification – from their beginnings in 1450 to their conclusion in 1456 is that they showed none of the signs of haste that had been characteristic of the process of condemnation. Not all the previous difficulties were solved: by the 1450s, the key witnesses of the 1431 trial had died. Cauchon had a heart attack while being bled, Nicolas Midi died a leper, Estivet died in a sewer; others, like de Courcelles, were anxious to excuse themselves or to blame those who could not answer back and no one was going to say that the Anglo-Burgundian case had raised objections to Joan's cause and conduct that were not always easy to contradict. And yet, from the start of the royal inquiry to the end of the papal inquiries, the witnesses speak with a freedom and liveliness that burst through the constraints of legal evidence. Attending to them, a student will find it hard to maintain that Joan was justly condemned. Accounts of her life that end with her death have missed out many of the most dramatic scenes in the drama of her story: the tales that in 1431 could not be told, the recollections of ageing men (and some ageing women) who had known her well. Some depositions may exaggerate, and, as only in some cases can their reliability be checked, the reader may not be sure which details to accept; but in the round and taken together they portray a Maid very unlike the Maid whom her judges had seen in 1431.

By 7 July 1456, when the court issued its decision, there could be no doubt what the decision would be. In the name of the Holy Trinity, acting on the authority of St Peter and his apostolic successors over the Church, the Archbishop of Reims, the Bishops of Paris and Coutances and the Dominican Jean Bréhal, professor of theology and one of the two inquisitors of France – all four judges being specially delegated representatives of the reigning pope – solemnly pronounced their sentence on the case brought by widow Isabelle Romée, mother, Pierre and Jean d'Arc, natural and legal brothers, of the deceased Joan of Arc, of good memory, commonly called the Maid, in the case brought against Cauchon the Bishop of Beauvais, Jean Lemaître, then vice-inquisitor of the diocese of Beauvais, and Jean d'Estivet, the Promoter. In the pompous terms beloved by lawyers anywhere and by churchmen everywhere, archbishop, bishops and Inquisitor declared the sentence on Joan was unsafe. They called the twelve articles 'iniquitous, false, prepared without reference to Joan's confessions in a lying manner', they thought with St Paul that private revelations should be referred to God alone and that the accusations against her were false in fact as well as in law, and so the case against her should be annulled. After a general procession and a public sermon, their decision was published in the square of St-Ouen, and again on the following day in place du Vieux-Marché, where Joan had died.

It has been urged that this decision, like the decision it reversed, was a political decision; and clearly Charles VII was exonerated for having believed in Joan's mission. His critics have excoriated him for not having tried to secure her release in 1431, but it is hard to see what he could have done then. He could do something only after Rouen had fallen to him and his servants could study the documents of the original trial; he could not have saved her life, but he could save her reputation. By 1450 it paid him to do so, but it became obvious that even if her first trial had been a political trial, in form it had been an ecclesiastical trial. Although he had worked hard to restrict papal control of the French Church, only a pope could override the original tribunal. In the end it needed a change of papacy to bring the final stage to a close. Pope Calixtus III, elected in 1455, tactfully appointed the Archbishop of Reims, the superior of the Bishop of Beauvais, a neighbouring Norman bishop, an inquisitor-theologian and finally the Bishop of Paris, since Parisian clerics had been all too willing to side with the Anglo-Burgundians against both Rome and the Valois King of France. The idea was to make the new judges credible representatives of the French Church. The judges' verdict pleased the French King, but was not therefore unjust. It pleased Joan's family, but did not decide if she was a saint.

In *c.* 1461, the most notorious poet of the age, François Villon, born in the year the Maid died, added Joan's name to the list of those whose passing he lamented: Thais, mistress to Alexander the Great, Héloïse, lover of the philosopher Peter Abélard, Queen Blanche of France and Dante's Beatrice, and:

> *Et Jehanne, la bonne Lorraine,*
> *Qu'Englois brulerent à Rouan. . . .*
> *Mais où sont les neiges d'autan?*[2]
> ('And Joan, the good Lorrainer,
> whom the English burnt at Rouen . . . But where are last year's snows?')

She was gone, and although Villon could not have known it, long after her death she would be more famous than she had ever been in a life so brutally curtailed.

PART THREE

The Cult of the Maid

EIGHTEEN

History, Legend and Myth

The verdict of 1456 should have settled Joan's reputation for good, but it did not. In contemporary England, which was soon exchanging the bitterness of defeat in a dynastic war overseas for the even more bitter experience of a dynastic war at home, there was no motive for anyone to study, let alone accept, the verdict. In France, apart from certain places associated with her life, such as Domremy and Orléans, there were not many signs of devotion to her memory. Joan belonged to history, she could become a figure of legend; only to a few was she a figure of myth.

History, legend and myth are various ways of coming to terms with the past. In narrative sections of the Old Testament it is possible to discover each of these kinds of explanation. The stories of Adam and Eve, Cain and Abel or Noah and his ark are properly myths. With the arrival of Abraham, the story moves on to legend. When exactly history begins is hard to establish. Some would say with Moses, others with David, others with the Babylonian captivity or the return of the Israelites to the Holy Land. What is worth noting is that some of the later figures in the narrative have been given mythic qualities: Moses is the man who gave Jews the Law, David the king who centred Israel on Jerusalem, Ezra the prophet who centred the lives of those returning from exile on the worship of the Temple and the observance of the law. These mythic qualities were later said to be incarnate in Jesus, as a new Moses, a new David and a new Ezra, lawgiver, king, priest and prophet. And in traditional Christian hagiography this or that characteristic of a figure in the Bible was thought to be evident in the life of a particular saint.

This is all remote from the case of Joan. The chief primary sources in her case are a series of carefully drafted historical documents, those connected with the 1431 trial and the inquiries of the 1450s, but she also appears in narrative accounts of the period; and there are even records of some of her expenses. Legends became attached to her name and she was also treated as a myth, but once the history was known the legends faded away and the myths were seen as attempts to focus on the inner reality of a known life.

If a myth is defined as an erroneous idea or a fictitious person, then Joan was not mythical in either of those senses. For a person of the fifteenth century some periods of her life are known in astonishing detail and the earliest records convey a vivid sense of a special person. Nor is Joan mythical in the sense that Adam and Eve are mythical: they stand for a collective reality, for all men and all women, whereas Joan was merely herself. In *Joan of Arc: the Image of Female Heroism*, Marina Warner has explored her myth by analysing Joan in terms of certain received categories of female heroism. Warner would probably admit that Joan eludes all such attempts at definition; indeed, what people have found difficult to comprehend has been her uniqueness.

But the techniques of ordinary biography do not elucidate all the available information about Joan. There is no easy way of making sense of what makes her unique – her voices. How can a biographer observe abnormal phenomena, when talk of phenomena is inaccurate, as the phenomena were not phenomenal? Joan remains elusive. She did not hear her voices in the way she heard the church bells that rang while she was listening to her voices, not did she see them in the way that she could see the priests who asked her to describe them. If she hallucinated, she did not have delusions in the same way as a schizophrenic or a thirsty man lost in the desert who sees a mirage of an oasis. The numinous quality in Joan puts her outside most classes of people, even spiritual people. Her judges, aware that she was unusual, put this distinctiveness down to the spirit of evil, but then they had not confronted the historic Joan, the girl who often prayed, went to confession and communion, was kind to her enemies – they did not want to know the Joan known to family, friends, colleagues and acquaintances. For this reason, efforts to consider her in purely political terms break down – her mission was political in its implications, but the mission, she asserted, was given her by God. Her critics understandably did not and do not agree.

Anyone who studies the story of Joan of Arc must be puzzled by three paradoxes. First, a girl tried and condemned in 1431 by a

French Church court was rehabilitated indirectly by the nullification of that verdict by another French Church court in 1452–6, and then, after a much longer process, in 1920 canonised as a saint of the Catholic Church. Secondly, in that year this belatedly canonised saint was also declared by the Church to be the patroness of France and given a public holiday by the secular French State, while at the same time she was widely admired in the English-speaking world, where in her lifetime she would have found her most determined enemies. Thirdly, whereas in the fifteenth century she had divided opinion, by the early twentieth century there was virtual unanimity in assessing her heroism, her patriotism, her goodness, since Allied victory in the First World War seemed to have implied a need to recognise her.

To those who realised how essential had been the contribution of women to the Allies' triumph in 1918, Joan was suddenly modern.[1] The English were Allies of the French; American soldiers fighting in Lorraine had paid their respects at Domremy; Allied propaganda made much of the German bombardment of Reims, where Joan had seen her king crowned,[2] and a popular French biography of Joan, written for children and beautifully illustrated by its author, had been translated into English and published in both England and America.[3] French and English speakers shared the conviction that Joan symbolised the values of freedom for which the victorious Allies believed they stood. Joan, a historical figure from the forgotten past, had become the subject of a modern myth.

The myth of Joan essentially involves spiritual realities or a spiritual way of looking at everyday realities. If not an evil person, as the nullification trial records testify, she may have been a good person who was simply misled – a spiritual simpleton. The spiritual side of Joan is hard to make sense of, and yet it was the most important part of her. The key to her lies outside the confines of normal history.

She was, however, a historical figure, not a legend. Famous people tend to attract those who find the mere truth boring. Some have maintained that Joan was in fact a member of the French royal family, that she did not really die at the stake in Rouen; and after her death at least one other woman claimed to be Joan of Arc. Such views do not merit serious discussion, for the numerous extant documents provide a firm basis for parts of her actual life and the whole of her actual death.

NINETEEN

Early Accounts, Partial Histories

Pierre Champion, one of the greatest experts on Valois France, has shown how manuscripts of the nullification trials were carefully kept in the collections of the king and of the Duke of Orléans, who both had a stake in Joan's good name. As for the documents of the 1431 trial, they were collated with great care after the event and deliberately diffused to as wide an audience as possible. The interrogations had been in French. The Rouen lawyer Guillaume Manchon and the Paris theologian Thomas de Courcelles were entrusted with the task of translating this French text into Latin, a task that gave de Courcelles the opportunity to remove his own name from the list of those who advocated torture. In the end there were no fewer than three official records of the documents, one for the Inquisitor, one for Cauchon, one for King Henry, and two other copies were made. This work of translation into Latin made the story of Joan's trial available to the learned; and the fact that many more clerics could read Latin than French may be a reason why the whole French text does not survive.

The documentation of the trials of 1431 and 1450–6 means that Joan as seen through the prism of legal inquiry can be better known than any other alleged heretic of her age, including even Gilles de Rais, her former companion, who was a great nobleman as well as a paedophile. The reason is that Joan's case mattered to rival claimants for the kingdom of France. But no legal inquiry can reveal all sides of a person. Joan is also mentioned by chroniclers, and although not one until eighty years after her death focuses specifically on her, insights into her story can be gained from early accounts, even if inevitably they are partial histories and sometimes legendary.

These early histories were not published collectively until they appeared in the fourth volume of the material on Joan collated by

Jules-Etienne-Joseph Quicherat from manuscripts in the Bibliothèque royale, now the Bibliothèque nationale, in the 1840s. The accounts are partial, because they were written down without knowledge of other contemporary sources.

Although an agitated English soldier who saw her die said he had burnt a saint, and although she may have been considered a saint by some who knew her well, such as her confessor Father Pasquerel, Joan was not written up as a saint. Anyone who reads the chronicles and commentaries of the day will notice, however, that she was a celebrity. Joan's public career had been so short and so strange that it was impossible to ignore her; and the nature of her achievements forced observers to make decisions about her private life. Was she deluded? Was she inspired by God? Was she misled by the devil?

The modern picture of a medieval chronicler is of an industrious monk bent over his parchment at his desk in the cloister. By the fifteenth century the time of such a man had passed. Most who wrote about Joan were gentlemen in the service of a king, a duke or a count, and wrote in French, English, German or Greek. A few clerics wrote for other clerics in medieval Latin. Some clerics wrote in the classical Latin that was fashionable in Italian cities. Manuscripts were illustrated by miniatures, new printed books by woodcuts, in both cases produced by professional lay craftsmen. In the fifteenth century, as in the nineteenth, the artwork rarely matches the literature about Joan in terms of quality – but then the writers had been set the more difficult challenge: how to come to terms with Joan. Artists could take refuge in fantasy, as in tales of the fierce prophetesses of the Old Testament, but they did not stray from conventional depictions. In most representations Joan wears a dress and her hair hangs long and loose in the style appropriate to a virgin, albeit a sword-wielding, horse-riding virgin. The texts, however, show that in her haircut as in her costume, Joan cultivated a masculine appearance, and in such matters the texts are right.

The texts are not all equally trustworthy: some depend on hearsay, some were composed later, and some conceal what the authors must have known. Joan may have been an astonishing person, but she was also an embarrassing one. She had embarrassed the king by insisting on the attack on Paris, by disappearing up the Loire and, worse, by coming back again, by trying to defend Compiègne, by inspiring his sacred coronation before being burnt as an enemy of the Church, heretic and sorceress. She embarrassed the Duke of Burgundy by being at a coronation in which he should have played a major role and yet the legitimacy of which, as from 1435, he had to admit. She embarrassed the English by outmanoeuvring them in 1430 and by predicting defeats that occurred in the 1440s and 1450s; and she embarrassed English patriots who went on claiming that their rulers were rightfully rulers of France.

Most of the chroniclers fall into obvious groups, pro-French, pro-Burgundian or pro-English, some with less immediate reasons of loyalty to one or other side yet take a strong line on Joan. Only one writes with something like a true historian's detachment. Enea Silvio Piccolomini stressed his accomplishments as a man of letters by calling himself Aeneas Sylvius. He was a cleric not yet ordained as a priest, a diplomat who had for long been in the service of the anti-pope Felix V who yet ended his life as Pope Pius II, a chameleon at ease in his rakish youth before turning gracefully into an austere old man. His *Commentaries* reveal him as the most astute observer of the age. He never met Joan, but he took the trouble to learn much about her. He may have spoken to Cauchon and some of Joan's other judges at the Council of Basel, but he shares none of their animosity towards her. He shows a special interest in the events surrounding the coronation and notes that the English had thought of removing the sacred oil from Reims before the French arrived, but failed to do so because 'they are thought to be have been frustrated by God's will'.[1] He has an improbable tale that Joan was captured outside Compiègne after charging at Duke Philip himself. And yet he demonstrates his innate shrewdness as he concludes: 'So died Joan, a wonderful, admirable virgin', before adding, 'whether her achievement was divine or human, I would find it hard to state.' Other writers found it much easier to make up their minds.

One of the most attractive of Joan's supporters, Perceval de Cagny, served the house of Alençon for forty-six years. He may not have been so much a witness of what he describes as the spokesman of his master's voice, but when he began to write in 1436 he was close to the events, and, since Alençon had known Joan better than any other member of the royal family and any other military leader, Cagny's own voice has a ring of authenticity. 'Before her arrival, neither the king nor the princes of the blood knew what advice to follow. And after by her aid and counsel things went from good to better to best.' There is a tone of mounting excitement as she encourages the people of Orléans, gives heart to the soldiers, helps win back the city and watches the English depart. Cagny conveys a sense of her manner of speaking, how she swore 'by my martin', how she called his master 'my fine Duke' (*mon beau duc*), how she could override all objections, for example to the march on Reims. He tells how, after taking a notable part in capturing the fortified towns of the Loire and winning the battle of Patay, she turned to Alençon to announce: 'Sound the trumpets, mount our horses! It's the moment to go to our gentle King Charles to put him on the route from his consecration at Reims.' Alençon stood in for the Duke of Burgundy at the ceremony, and Cagny does not mention what Joan did, for she played a unique, not a traditional part in the drama, before he and Joan resumed their military campaign. Her aim was simple: 'The Maid intended to restore suzerainty to the king and the kingdom to its obedience.' As the king seemed irresolute, while his mind sought out tortuous diplomatic paths, she eventually lost patience. 'By my martin,' she told Alençon, 'I want to see Paris from closer up than I have ever seen it.' The king's behaviour frustrated them both. For Cagny the withdrawal from Paris had a disastrous effect on morale: 'so the will of the Maid and the king's army was broken'. He was sure that the dominant royal councillors did not want the Maid and Alençon to be together. Her venture in the upper Loire confirmed her disillusion and led to her resolution to save Compiègne. Cagny did not trust her judges at Rouen, as they had used every ruse, he thought, to condemn her and have her burnt for heresy; and yet what angered him was the behaviour of the king, for Charles was reluctant to fight.

Charles VII himself was more inscrutable than his cousin; and the man charged with glorifying him had the harder task. Jean Chartier, a cantor from the royal abbey of St-Denis, was probably given the task of being royal chronicler just because it was traditional that a monk of St-Denis should hold that office. It is likely that he wrote about Joan in the 1440s, when the war had finally turned to French advantage. Again and again Chartier stresses the king's benevolent role. He tells how the king gave Joan the forces she needed, how after the relief of Orléans he provided extra forces to take the nearby Loire towns, how he raised a grand army to take him on his route for the coronation, how, when Joan wished to take Auxerre by force, the king arranged for the town to surrender peacefully. Chartier does not mention Joan's part in the coronation, and he kept the king firmly in the centre of the picture. The king decided to return to the Île de France, the heart of his dominions. At Senlis, just north of Paris, the English dared not confront him. Joan, not well informed about the moat protecting Paris, attacked it in vain. Chartier knows about St-Pierre-le-Moûtier – the king commanded her to go there – and does not admit that she was contravening the king's intention to surrender Compiègne when she was captured. He was certain that at the end she died a good Catholic – it would let the king down if she were not – then he ends the story with a surprising final remark. Once the sword she had received from Ste-Catherine-de-Fierbois was broken, she was never again so successful in war. Chartier is thinking back to the wonderful stories of chivalry, with their insistence on miraculous God-given swords, as in French stories about Charlemagne and Roland or British stories about Arthur. At heart he was a modern servant of a very modern king.

The two longest chronicles favourable to Joan have neither the fluency of Cagny nor the official air of Chartier; and they also date from later in the century. The longest of all, the so-called *Journal du siège d'Orléans et du voyage de Reims*, probably took much of its material from documents in Orléans that date from 1429, but it was not written down until some forty years afterwards. For the military historian it has a special value as it gives a blow-by-blow, shot-by-shot account of events; and for the general reader that is its greatest defect, since the facts are too much to absorb. The *Chronique de la Pucelle* derives from both Chartier and the *Journal du siège* and its author also knows what was said in the nullification trial of Joan, for instance by her page Louis de Coutes and by the Bastard of Orléans, now the Comte de Dunois. It starts with the accession of Charles VII in 1422 and goes down to the moment in 1429 when the king, having failed to take Paris, returned to his original base at Bourges. Like the *Journal du siège* it says nothing about Joan's capture, trial and death. Both these accounts are of local interest and they make no attempt to understand Joan's psychology.

Psychologically, some Burgundian courtiers were more sophisticated. The 'grand duke of the West', as Philip the Good of Burgundy was called, had his own pet advocate in his court chronicler Georges Chastellain, whose works in a nineteenth-century edition run to some eight volumes. Chastellain shared the duke's taste for flamboyant rhetoric and aims to be entertaining rather than accurate. On Joan, alas, he has little new to say.

Another Burgundian chronicler is especially important, because he became well known. Enguerrand or Enguerran de Monstrelet claimed he never bore arms, but documentary evidence suggests that he had once, in 1424. For Joan's story he had an advantage. Throughout his adult life he was a client of the house of Luxembourg, and so probably owed to Luxembourgeois favour the distinction of being awarded in about 1440 the post that marked the summit of his career, the provostship of Cambrai. The post gave him the leisure to write down what he remembered and so to repay his debt to the family. As a trusted follower of Jean de Luxembourg, comte de Ligny, he had had many opportunities to witness or hear of important events. The most famous example came in 1430, when he was with the Burgundian army outside Compiègne. He says he was present at the interview Duke Philip had with Joan after her capture, but adds, sadly for historians, 'I cannot recall his words.' He also knew that she was his master's prisoner for some time before being taken to Rouen to be tried and burnt, and he was able to quote part of the letter sent afterwards in the name of the King of England to the duke, but he does not mention anything about the process of the trial; nor does he say anything about the deal by which Jean de Luxembourg had sold Joan to the English. Monstrelet's forgetfulness begins to look a little too convenient.

His assertions are also not always sound. He states that Joan was a servant in an inn for a long time and that it was there she had learnt to ride and 'other things that young girls are not accustomed to do'. This fairy story had a long life and recurs in the eighteenth century. Monstrelet is perhaps ironic when he said Joan was divinely inspired and those who saw and heard her came to believe it too, but he does not grudge her a central role in the run of successes the French enjoyed in the summer of 1429. Writing in the 1440s, when the Burgundians were at least passive allies of the French, he has to approve the consecration of Charles VII at Reims, although he notices that many who should have been there, such as the Duke of Burgundy and the Bishop of Beauvais, were not. He does not indicate why they were absent, but is much clearer when citing the long letter Bedford sent in the name of his master, Henry, by the grace of God true, natural and legal King of France and England to the newly consecrated king – here called the Dauphin of Viennois. Joan is mentioned again when he tells the story of the siege of Paris, perhaps because she failed there and because Charles ordered a withdrawal, being greatly concerned about his own wounded soldiers. He also draws attention to Joan's willingness to have a captured Burgundian leader, Franquet d'Arras, executed. He thus subtly undermines her reputation.

As Monstrelet's style is clear and his tone placid, he has been regarded as impartial, but a close examination of what he says shows that, in the case of Joan, his version of events is often unfair. Another Burgundian sympathiser is much more unreliable.

The man known as the 'Bourgeois de Paris' was not in fact a burgess of that city; rather, he was a member of its university and his hatred of the Maid was all the more virulent. An intellectual with a bilious temperament, he scoffs at the likely tale that, at the time she was a child-shepherdess, birds came whenever she called them to feed from her hands. He becomes eloquent only when he comes to events with which he was familiar, those involving Paris, both Paris under siege and Paris as a place where people like himself approved of Joan's trial and condemnation.

The attackers, he says, were fighting 'for a creature like a woman among them, whom people called the Maid. What she was, God knows.' Naturally he mocks her assertions that she would take Paris. He was not impressed that the French had chosen the Nativity of Notre-Dame as the day for an attack. On 23 May 1430 'dame Joan, Maid of the Armagnacs' was eventually captured at Compiègne. Two women, the oldest of whom was Pierronne, from Bretagne *bretonnante* (that is, south Brittany, where people spoke Breton), testified in Paris that Joan, who was armed with the Armagnacs, was a good woman: Pierronne 'affirmed and swore that God often appeared to her in His humanity'. She went on to state that He also appeared to her in a white robe and she uttered other similar blasphemies; and that is why she came to be burnt.

The *Journal*'s entry for 30 May 1431 is lengthy, learned and venomous. Dame Joan, clad in male attire, had to listen to a long sermon, in which she was told about the great unhappy evils that through her had been brought to Christendom, especially in the kingdom of France, as everyone knows; and how on the feast of Our Lady's birthday she had come to bring fire and blood to Paris . . . and how at Senlis and elsewhere she had made simple folk idolise her, as, by her false hypocrisy they followed her as a holy Maid; as she had given them to understand that the glorious archangel Michael, saint Catherine and saint Margaret and several other saints appeared to her often, and spoke to her as one friend to another; and not as God has done sometimes to his friends by revelations, but physically and mouth to mouth, as one lover to another.

The mention of physical contact, which does not appear anywhere in the trial records, shows how strongly this 'journalist' felt. He is then ready to itemise her iniquities, paragraph by paragraph, remorselessly cataloguing her terrible errors, blasphemies, lies and heresies until it comes as a relief to the pious reader to know that such an appalling woman, who had worn the clothes of a man when she was as young as fourteen, who had left home in company with the devil, who was full of blood and fire until she was burnt – that when she called on her spirits to help her, none appeared. She was but one of the four women directed by the Dominican friar, Brother Richard (this was the man she had met at Troyes). The *Bourgeois* was glad that Pierronne and one other had been burnt in Paris and Joan in Rouen; and the fourth, who appeared in 1440, pretending to be Joan, was shown to be a fraud. The real Joan had not survived the stake and her ashes had been thrown into the river, so that no part of her body could be used for the purposes of sorcery. It was a thought from which one observer took comfort: the women had been seen as they were, as deceivers of mankind, and they were gone.

During the middle and late years of the fifteenth century there were no worthy successors to the English monastic chroniclers of the past, but then since the Black Death there were few men of wide experience in English cloisters; and lay writers to take their place had not yet been born. The first English printer, William Caxton, briefly records how the French revived under 'the Dolphin' (the English word for the Dauphin) and how one of their leaders was 'a mayde whiche they named *la pucelle de Dieu*'. Caxton knows a little about Joan's success and that with the help of 'syr John Luxemburgh' and many others 'the forsayd Pucelle was taken in the field, and there she was put in pryson, and there she was judged by the lawe to be brent'. One detail Caxton adds suggests what was to become an English obsession: 'And then she sayd that she was with childe; wher by she was respited a whyle; but in conclusyon, it was founde that she was not with chylde, and then she was brent in Roen.' English chroniclers liked to think that she was no maid. Joan was never 'the harlot of the Armagnacs'. Aristocratic women on the Anglo-Burgundian side were as sure as aristocratic women on the Armagnac side that Joan was a virgin. That was one reason why she could not be a witch. The 'English' view of Joan was simply wrong.

   What is more surprising is that in France, at a time when the Valois were in firm control, people were still confused by the different ways in which Joan was viewed. The anonymous author of the first biography of Joan of Arc, who claimed to be writing at the command of Louis XII (1498–1515) and of Louis de Graville, Admiral of France, pointed out that 'the chronicles dispute and differ' and yet he himself did not marshal his sources to give a convincing account of Joan from the Orleanist point of view that Louis XII, who had been Duke of Orléans before he became King of France, must have expected. He had read his Monstrelet and he was determined to vindicate Joan against the old enemies of France, the English. But he does give a clear version of the secret she revealed to privately to Charles VII. According to the anonymous biographer, this involved three requests the king had prayed for in the oratory of his chapel at Loches, and it was after Joan told him what the requests were that Charles had believed her. The biographer then summarises the triumphs of 1429, omits the failures and skips to Joan's capture at Compiègne and her transference to Rouen. He cites 'Anglo-Burgundian' letters, sent to and from Cauchon, involving the University of Paris, Jean de Luxembourg, Chancellor Nicolas Rolin, the child-king Henry VI and others, to justify Joan's condemnation.[2]

   This careful citing of some important sources has a curious result. The author wishes to show how wonderful his heroine was and how cruel her death, but most of the evidence he provides is hostile to her. The reason seems to be that as Graville was a Norman, the most accessible documents for his author came from Rouen, and they all dated from the time when the English held that city and master-minded the trial. The author therefore does not even discuss how the verdict of the Rouen trial was nullified in 1452–6, which means that he cannot have had access to the nullification records. Those records were kept by the people who had an interest in them: the king, the house of Orléans and the cathedral of Notre-Dame. The story of Joan's life and death was public knowledge. The grounds for thinking the initial verdict on Joan unjust remained private.

Joan's first biographer suffered from a fault shared by most historians down to 1850: he did not know the whole story. This is one of the reasons why by the start of the sixteenth century there were differing accounts of Joan that could not all be true; and yet there was little chance that anyone could have found out what was the truth. Contradictory chronicles were at the origins of differing traditions about Joan. One, that of Perceval de Cagny, fitted in with what was said at the nullification trial, but Cagny wrote for his master Alençon, a star witness at that trial. For a long time Monstrelet, who met Joan only once and who says he forgot what was said on that occasion, was much better known. English writers did not have the Burgundian problem of having to accept that the king their duke had repudiated in 1429 was indeed their king; they had no reason to wonder whether the Duke of Bedford, who demanded Joan's condemnation, and the Earl of Warwick, who supervised it, might have been mistaken. The way was open for many ideas about Joan that confused fiction with fact; and it was not until the mid-nineteenth century, when all the chronicles, all the records of Joan's life, above all the trial documents, were available that any sense could be made of that life. In the meantime, most people were guided by what they wanted to believe.

In the fifteenth century, history was largely an exercise in rhetoric, an attempt to persuade the reader to look at events from a particular angle. De Cagny put Alençon's view, Chartier that of Charles VII's court, Monstrelet that of the house of Luxembourg, the Bourgeois of Paris represented only himself but he wrote as an Anglo-Burgundian. Only in the 1840s did Quicherat make possible a careful comparison of the different texts. That process continues today. Two parts of Joan's life can be traced almost day by day: the period from 12 February 1429, when she told Robert de Baudricourt that the French had been defeated at the battle of the Herrings, to 21 September 1429, when her army was disbanded after the order to withdraw from Paris; and the period from

Thursday 9 January 1431, when her trial began, to Wednesday 30 May, when she died. Some portions of her early life can be inferred: it is possible to sketch in her activities from her dismissal in September 1429 to her capture on Tuesday 23 May 1430; and there is some knowledge of where she was imprisoned until the end of the year, including about four months at Beaurevoir, a stay over which historians have to be silent. By quarrying in the rich seams of Quicherat's documents, an ingenious modern historian, Kelly DeVries, has been able to write a detailed study, *Joan of Arc: a Military Leader*. Without knowledge of Quicherat's documents, Shakespeare and Voltaire, in a recent scholar's phrase, 'set fire to history',[3] in other words they had recourse to legend. At the same time, other writers, also with an uncertain grasp of her whole story, prepared the way for the development of her myth.

None of the early histories that mention Joan get to the root of her personality; and it was too early to write about her spirituality. The Church was not yet ready to understand her, kings of France may have been content just that their title to the throne was not invalid because she had encouraged Charles VII to believe in it; and English kings were too embroiled in their own dynastic quarrels to reassert their ancestral claim to France. What kept Joan in people's minds was chiefly popular devotion. Nobody, not even the most pedantic of scholars or the dullest of poets would be concerned about the legends or the myths if they were not reminded that Joan has remained famous. Her name was preserved by popular piety, especially as demonstrated at Orléans.

TWENTY

Reinventing the Maid

SHAKESPEARE'S PUZEL

One of the first notable attempts to make sense of Joan came from England and dates from the 1590s. Whoever started the fashion, whether Shakespeare himself, Marlowe or a lesser playwright, one way to fill theatres in Southwark was to dramatise recent English history. At the time, England was fighting Spain: in the past England had fought France. For audiences, tales of derring-do on land against the French resonated with overtones of the battles against the Spaniards at sea. In any case, it was still easier for English writers to think of England's occasional ally, France, as the country's traditional foe.

The immediate narrative source of Shakespeare's (or, as some believe, Shakespeare and friends') *Henry VI* Part I, was Holinshed's chronicle (1587), but that in turn was indebted to Hall's 'Union of (the) Families of York and Lancaster' (1548). Holinshed has the more favourable view of Joan, mentioning her physical dexterity, her apparent chastity and her devotion, and describes her as a 'person raised up by power divine, only for to succour to the French estate then deeply in distress'.[1] Hall was much more severe. She rode horses in an unmaidenly way and kept her virginity because she was ugly.[2] 'I marvel much that wise men did believe her . . .'[3] Hall gives Joan little credit for the raising of the siege of Orléans or the crowning of Charles VII at Reims, and after recounting how at 'Roan', after a long inquest, 'she was brent to ashes', he comments condescendingly, 'this witch or manly woman (called the maid of GOD) the Frenchmen greatly glorified and highly extolled . . . this woman was not inspired by the Holy Ghost, nor sent from God (as the Frenchmen believe) but an enchantress, an organ of the devil, sent from Satan, to blind the people and bring them to unbelief.'[4] To this version Holinshed adds a detail of his own, that she had lovers, while admitting that at her trial she was found to be a virgin. With such accounts before his eyes, an English playwright was bound to treat Joan as a deceiver. Besides, no such man then was going to admit that the Hundred Years War had ended in decisive French victory.

The play's structure turns on a struggle between England (represented by Talbot) and France (represented by Joan Puzel), so it has to ignore the actual sequence of events, for Talbot's career lasted from 1419 to 1453, whereas hers occupies only just over two years (1429–31). Besides, the playwright is uncertain what to make of Joan 'Puzel' (the Elizabethan term for '*pucelle*'). She starts off as a holy woman, turns into a witch and ends as a character from farce as she tries to save her skin by claiming to be pregnant.

AN EPIC HEROINE

Shakespeare's plays were initially ephemeral, played today, forgotten tomorrow. Any writer who wished lasting stories wrote narrative poems. Elizabeth I may have laughed at Falstaff so much that she asked Shakespeare to write her a play about Falstaff in love, but she was presented with a copy of the first part of Spenser's *Faery Queene*, a poem whose central theme was the love between Gloriana, representing Elizabeth herself, and Arthur, who stood for Britain. Spenser's heroic romance used a hybrid literary form, combining something of the medieval romances of chivalry with the spirit of classical epic. Unluckily for Spenser, Elizabeth, in spite of her literary skills, took more pleasure from the music written to celebrate her everlasting virginity than his poem.

Of the countries in Europe with a noble literary tradition, only France lacked poets who had developed heroic romance to a fine art. Jean Chapelain wanted to make up for French neglect of the genre. In Joan of Arc he found a subject as worthy of patriotic fervour as the subject chosen by Spenser. Born in 1595, Chapelain grew up while the late sixteenth-century civil wars were coming to an end. In 1656, when he published the first part of *La Pucelle, ou La France delivrée*, France had virtually won its conflict with Spain. It was a moment that a proud Frenchman could savour: France was rescued from a foe as formidable as the English had been when Joan was a child. Chapelain had his chance, but without the ability to create a masterpiece he became the butt of the tragedian Racine and the satirist Boileau. An anonymous member of their circle mocked him in a spoof play, *Chapelain Décoiffé* ('Chapelain dewigged'), in which 'Chapelain' even offers to make the supreme sacrifice: to give up his *Pucelle* in return for his wig. Boileau mocked him over and over again.

> *La Pucelle est encore une oeuvre galante,*
> *Mais je ne sais pourquoi je bâille en la lisant.*[5]
> ('Although the Pucelle is a polite work,
> I don't know why I yawn as I read it.')

Boileau also parodied him in one of his *Epigrams*:

> *Maudit soit l'auteur dur, dont l'âpre et rude verve,*
> *Son cerveau tenaillant, rima malgré Minerve;*
> *Et, de son lourd marteau martellant le bon sens,*
> *A fait de méchans vers douze fois douze cens.*[6]

('Cursed be the hard author, whose harsh, unpolished effort,/ mastering his brain, rhymed in spite of Wisdom,/and with his heavy hammer hammering good sense,/has made of nasty verses twelve times twelve hundred.')

Unknown to his tormentor, Chapelain had written twice as many lines, but then Chapelain was a courtier, whose poem was meant for His Highness Henri d'Orléans Duc de Longueville et d'Estouteville, Peer of France, Sovereign Prince of Neuchâtel, Comte de Dunois, de Saint-Pol, de Chaumont, etc., etc., etc., Governor on behalf of the King and Hereditary Constable of Normandy, who just happened to be descended from Joan's Bastard of Orléans (and was also a collateral relation of the Estoutevilles of the nullification process). Indeed, Chapelain confessed that his real hero was the Bastard, who was later given the title of Count of Dunois, and that Joan was to Dunois as Pallas to Ulysses, a 'divine' guide to the person at the centre of the epic. Although his recurrent epithet for Joan was 'saint',[7] Chapelain failed to win converts to her cause. In de luxe editions of his book there were fine illustrations by Vignon engraved by Abraham Bosse, in which Joan was depicted in an appropriately heroic style, with gleaming armour, flowing locks and a helmet bedecked with plumes – this Joan looked the part for an operatic heroine, but the thump of Chapelain's six-foot lines muffled in tedium all sound of her greatness.

Some scholars, especially in Lorraine, published their research into Joan's story, but their enthusiasm was exceptional. Until the final years of Louis XIV it seemed self-evident that stability in French life came from its absolute monarchy; official historians lauded Charles VII the Victorious. Joan came into her own only in a more individualistic age, when a new type of historian began to write for the general reader.

One of the first to discuss her story was a Huguenot or French Protestant. Paul Rapin de Thoyras had lost the right to practise his religion in France when Louis XIV prohibited Protestant religious practice. Most Huguenots left for Holland, Prussia or England. In Holland Rapin wrote the lengthy *History of England* that in 1728–32 was translated into English in twelve volumes. Volume five, on the reigns of the three Lancastrian Kings, concludes with a section called 'A dissertation on the Maid of Orleans'.

Rapin had read Monstrelet and repeats some of Monstrelet's mistakes. Joan was 'a good while servant in an inn, and had the courage to ride the horses to water, and likewise to perform other feats which young girls are not wont to do'.[8] She was twenty when 'she hired herself at Neufchatel to a woman that kept an inn called Larousse', and twenty-nine at the time of her public career, so becoming a fifteenth-century Annie Oakley. Rapin also takes a 'Burgundian' line on Joan's supposed subtlety: 'I conclude from the examination I have made, that a man may reasonably suppose that Joan's pretended inspiration was all a contrivance to revise the courage of the dismayed Frenchmen.' But Rapin also takes a sympathetic view of Joan's fate and fame. He is indignant: 'I cannot but help reflecting on the barbarous usage Joan met with'; he himself knew all about religious persecution. He is also shrewd on the sentences of the two trials, the one that condemned her and the one that set aside the condemnation. 'The former was passed by her enemies, whose interest it was to defame her; and the latter by her Friends, to whose Glory and Advantage it turned to make her innocent.'[9] He anticipates a view common among modern historians who are sceptical about Joan.

Not until the mid-eighteenth century was there a British version of English history to rival Rapin's. David Hume is now considered the leading sceptical philosopher of the Scottish Enlightenment, but he made his name and his money as a popular historian. His fluent style, which contemporaries thought slightly French, makes him so pleasant to read that his ideological message is almost concealed. But the man who thought miracles impossible was sure that he knew what could not happen. Joan's 'unexperienced mind, working night and day, on this favourite subject', how to save her king, 'mistook the impulsions of her passion for heavenly inspiration; and she fancied that she saw visions and heard voices, exhorting her to re-establish the throne of France, and to expel the foreign invaders'.[10] He continues, 'It is the business of history to distinguish between the miraculous and the marvellous, to reject the former in all narrations merely profane and human, to sample the second . . . and to receive as little of it as is consistent with the known facts and circumstances.' Hume was able to say confidently that it cannot have been true that Joan recognised Charles at Chinon, that she told him she was sent to raise the siege of Orléans, to take him to Reims to be crowned and anointed, to ask for a particular sword (he means the sword at Ste-Catherine-de-Fierbois) – he knows better than anyone there at the time that none of these stories could have been true. He also pours scorn on those who made Joan out to be a shepherdess in her late teens, for it was ridiculous not to believe that she had worked in an inn and there learnt to ride a horse and that she was in her late twenties when she came into prominence. Hume relies on Hall, Holinshed and Monstrelet, but he is not above a sly dig at medieval piety to reinforce his credentials as a doubter. 'The ceremony of coronation was here performed with the holy oil, which a pigeon had brought to King Clovis, on the first establishment of the French monarchy.' Hume's pigeon was other people's dove, but then a dove was a symbol of the Holy Spirit and symbolism was alien to Hume. What he could understand was common humanity, and he ends his account of Joan with a moving peroration. 'This admirable heroine, to whom the most generous of the antients would have erected altars, was, on pretence of heresy and magic, delivered over alive to the flames, and expiated by that dreadful punishment the signal services, which she had rendered to her prince and to her native country.'[11]

Among the group of 'philosophical historians' to which Hume belonged, none was so prolific, amusing or admired as Voltaire. Inevitably, a man who waxed eloquent on credulity and cruelty was drawn to the topic of Joan. Voltaire already knew of Joan when he praised her in his epic on Henry IV as

> *. . . brave amazone,*
> *La honte des anglais, et le soutien du trône.*[12]
> ('brave amazon,
> the shame of the English and the support of the throne'.)

His view of the achievement of Charles VII, elaborated in his *Essai sur les moeurs* ('Essay on customs'), which despite its title deals largely with French history, depended on Monstrelet. He seems to endorse Joan's view of her role when he writes 'she talks to the soldiers from the point of view of God',[13] but he makes clear his own view when of her unjust trial he writes that this 'heroine' was 'worthy of the miracle that she had feigned'.[14] He admired her but did not believe in her. Eventually he lost patience with the exalted emotions her coming inspired. Joan became an excuse to have fun.

Voltaire's sense of humour often let him down. In 1730 the topic of the now forgotten epic by Chapelain came up in conversation with friends and by 1735 Voltaire had finished ten cantos of his riposte; over the years he added and amended the poem, he endured the arrival of a series of pirated editions until at last, in 1762, an approved edition was published. He went on revising the text throughout the rest of his life. It amused the immense circle of his correspondents and a generation after his death it gave his Romantic enemies a reason to detest him.

Chapelain annoyed Voltaire for choosing a 'saint' as his protagonist. Voltaire's Joan was more worldly. She was

> a servant at an inn, born in the village of Domremy on the Meuse, who, finding a strength in her body and a temerity beyond her sex, was used by the Comte de Dunois to restore the situation of Charles VII. She was taken in a sortie from Compiègne in 1430, taken to Rouen, judged to be a sorceress by an ecclesiastical court that was equally ignorant and barbarous and burnt by the English who should have honoured her for her courage.[15]

Not altogether accurate nor altogether adequate, this account is different enough from what is in his poem to make it clear that, had he wanted to do so, he could have been reliable. He preferred to enjoy himself. He joked that, unlike Chapelain, he was not meant to write hagiography:

Je ne suis pas né pour célébrer les saints.
Ma voix est faible, et même un peu profane.
('I've not been born to celebrate the saints.
My voice is feeble and even a little profane.')

But with a shrug of his shoulders he must do his best:

Il faut pourtant vous chanter cette Jeanne
Qui fit, dit-on, des prodiges divins.
('Needs must I sing about this Joan,
who accomplished, so they say, holy marvels.')

With her maidenly hands, he says, she strengthened the French stem of the fleur-de-lis, saved the king from English fury and at the high altar in Reims had him anointed. In just four lines he recapitulates what she achieved. His true subject is announced in the lines that follow. He would have liked a beautiful heroine as gentle as a lamb rather than Joan with the heart of a lion, but she caused consternation by acting as she did; and what he most admired about her was that she kept her virginity for a whole year. And so, after a few swipes at Chapelain, he was off: his theme would be the losing of virginity. The variations on the theme kept him and his readers enthralled for twenty-one books and over 8,000 lines. As he explains in a note correcting Boileau's epigram, at least unlike Chapelain he had not written twelve times twenty-four cantos, nor, unlike Chapelain, had he been rewarded with a pension of 12,000 *livres tournois* by the Longuevilles, a sum that could have been better employed. Voltaire did not add that his own writing had made him rich.

Chapelain was only an excuse. Soon, without a nod to chronology, Voltaire was expatiating on the physical charms of Charles VII's mistress Agnès Sorel. She would be the comic foil to Joan, ever liking the idea of being faithful to her royal lover, but sadly fragile whenever a handsome young man came near her. The king's love-making worries St Denis, patron of France, who, admitting that he has an instinctive dislike of the *race bretonne*, justifies it on the grounds that his people, the French, will stay good Catholics while the English will become heretics; and for this reason St Denis puts his trust in the arrival of a *pucelle*. The presence of St Denis on one side and St George on the other enables Voltaire to guy Milton's warfare in heaven in *Paradise Lost*. He admits that in the end the saints must make peace, but enjoys the opportunity to have a go at one of his pet obsessions, as St George speaks for the Old Testament – Voltaire never failed to point out how savage was the Israelite idea of God – while St Denis replies for the New Testament:

> *Il a chanté le Dieu de la vengeance,*
> *Je vais bénir le Dieu de la clémence . . .*
> ('He [St George] has sung the God of revenge,
> I am going to bless the God of mercy'.)

But if religion is never far from Voltaire's mind, he focuses on chastity. Joan has to be constantly rescued from ever more bizarre temptations. Of all his masters in heroic romance Voltaire is closest to the Italian Ariosto, only more ridiculous, for instead of the Italian's hippogriff, a horse with wings, the Frenchman elects for a winged donkey. So he stresses the gentle absurdity of his tale, as it moves to a fitting conclusion. Orléans will be saved and Joan will lose her virginity to the man who truly loves her, Dunois.

For all his intelligence, Voltaire's mind was closed. He had little appreciation of traditional France, which survived happily in the provinces, where the year was still marked by the festivals of the Church, where great numbers of priests, canons, monks and nuns occupied large areas of every town and where during the quiet prosperity of the eighteenth century there was a new sense of ease and contentment. Joan's adopted town of Orléans did well out of its close connection with the royal family and also its exploitation of international trade – its factories refined much of France's valuable Caribbean sugar – and it fondly remembered Joan.[16]

CELEBRATING THE MAID OF ORLEANS

For centuries Orléans was devoted to Joan. As early as 1430 money was paid for candles to be lit to commemorate the lifting of the siege the year before; and from 1435, even while Joan's memory was blackened by her condemnation as a sorceress and heretic, the Orléannais celebrated her goodness to them with songs, floats and lights. The habit lasted for centuries.

One of the most extravagant of the early entertainments was the very first, staged at his own cost by Marshal Gilles de Rais in spring 1435; or so an archivist told an historian.[17] The documents recording the events have vanished but the story is plausible, for that year de Rais sold off as much of his extensive property as he could. Only foolhardy expenditure can explain his behaviour, and nothing in the fifteenth century, except being ransomed, could cost as much as organising a pageant. The point of the liquidation of his assets seems to have been his determination to give the Orléannais an experience they would never forget.

Le Mystère du Siège d'Orléans eventually became enormously long, with speaking parts for 140 people and walk-on parts for 500 extras. The venues for the action, as was common with a medieval mystery play, were dotted about the city, scenery was carved and decorated, costumes magnificent. No extant account tells how the citizens reacted to this show, but the *Mystère du Siège d'Orléans* was put on until about 1470, while it grew with each performance. No later production can have been quite like the first, but then Gilles de Rais could not sustain his moment of glory. Already the man who rode a Barbary horse covered in rich blue cloth (his *'barbe bleu'*) was being changed into the fairy-tale Bluebeard (*'barbe bleue'*), who murdered many wives. The facts are more grotesque than the fiction. Gilles de Rais was already indulging his perverse taste for abusing and killing children that led to his death just twelve years after he was enthralled by the high-spirited girl with and for whom he had fought and in whose presence, briefly, his life had had some meaning.

Gilles de Rais was forgotten: in their adopted city the memory of Joan and her family survived. Isabelle Romée, her mother, and Pierre, her brother, came to live there; and there the people heard that Joan's trial for heresy was being reinvestigated and that its verdict had been nullified. Once this process had been completed, Cardinal d'Estouteville encouraged participation in the celebrations of 8 May; and his practice was followed by other eminent ecclesiastics. When the *Mystère* was no longer played, new pageants took its place. From the time of Charles VIII (1483–98), grandson of Joan's Charles VII, or of Louis XII (1498–1515), son of Joan's Duke of Orléans, dates a motet honouring Joan sung at the Porte Dunoise (named after Dunois, Joan's beloved Bastard):

Noble cité de moult grant renomée . . .
Rejouy toi à icelle journée,
Peuple vaillant et très loyal français . . .
A la doulce prière
Vint la Pucelle bergière
Qui pour nous guerroye . . .
Chantez, o le clergé et messieurs les bourgeois[18]

('Noble city of great fame,/rejoice on this day,/valiant and very loyal French people . . ./At the sweet prayer comes the Maid shepherdess/who fights for us . . ./Sing, Clerics and citizens . . .')

Members of Joan's family came to Orléans. Pierre, elevated as Pierre du Lys to the ranks of a gentleman entitled to bear arms, was welcomed in 1436; the city supported Joan's mother between 1440 and 1458, the year she died; and on his marriage Pierre's son received a handsome gift from the city. The family was favoured by Charles VII, by Charles d'Orléans, by Louis XI. In the annual procession to commemorate the relief of the city, Pierre's son would walk behind a huge wax candle on which was carved a picture of his aunt. He died in 1502, but as late as 1550 he was still fondly remembered by one of his former domestics.

With devotion to Joan and her family Orléans coupled devotion to the king and the royal family, and the kings of France reciprocated this love. Francis I came there in 1515 and from his reign dates the curious custom of having Joan's role played by a virginal boy, the *Puceau*, a practice that lasted until 1912. Other changes caused problems. The citizens asked for a ruling from the next king, Henry II: could a bishop with a beard preside? The answer was yes. Three years later Henry was dead, killed in a tournament by a Huguenot nobleman, and so his three weakly sons became kings in turn. The lack of a decisive king left the way open to those powerful enough exploit the growth of religious dissent. Jean Calvin, the leading French Protestant, had studied in Orléans before taking refuge in Geneva; and nearby Saumur, now famous for its light wines, became a centre of Huguenot theology. The Loire valley was full of Huguenots, whose leaders, once religious war broke out, tried to take it from the king.

In 1568 the fiery Prince de Condé, uncle of the future Henry IV, made Orléans a Protestant base; and his troops set about attacking the cathedral. Condé intended it for Protestant worship (*un beau temple calviniste plutôt qu'une ruine papiste*)[19] but could not prevent his men blowing up the central tower and much of the nave. Meanwhile, city magistrates took to plundering Catholic property and to having Catholics hanged. Four years later Catholics exacted revenge after the marriage of Henry, then the new King of Navarre, to his royal cousin. Instead of the intended religious reconciliation, the queen mother's botched assassination of one leading Protestant led to a general massacre of Protestants throughout France. In the bloodshed Joan was forgotten; and not until after 1589, when Henry of Navarre as a beneficiary of the Salic Law became King Henry IV, could the Orléannais celebrate their heroine again.

For the next two centuries Orléans enjoyed royal and ducal favour. In 1601 Henry IV spent April in the city. The restoration of the cathedral by his grandson Louis XIV confirmed the strong bond between Orléans and France's kings. Joan's feast was still being celebrated in 1650. A hundred years or so later, work on the cathedral was virtually finished in a second lengthy reign, that of Louis XV, and, as Orléans cathedral recovered, so did devotion to the Maid.

From the time of Louis XIV's brother Philippe, Duke d'Orléans, one duke of Orléans placidly succeeded another; and the commemoration of Joan continued under the joint patronage of city and duke. On one occasion the *Puceau* was splendidly arrayed in sixteenth-century costume in the city's gold and red colours, with a scarlet hat on his head sporting two plumes. Late in the century the old bridge, where Les Tourelles had been sited, was replaced by the Pont Royal; and in rue Royale leading off it there was soon a new bronze monument to Joan. In 1786 the *Puceau*, chosen as always by the city council, was joined by a girl, *la Rosière*, the 'rose' of her village, chosen for her outstanding virtue. This role was invented by the duke and duchess, who declared that they wished to mark the feast of 8 May by the marriage of a poor, virtuous girl from the city, to whom they offered a dowry of 1,200 *livres*.

On 14 July 1789 a mob in Paris sacked the Bastille; and in 1792 France was declared a republic. In the steady downfall of Louis XVI (1774–92) the Duke of Orléans, Philippe 'Egalité' took the principle of equality so far as to vote for the execution of his distant cousin 'Louis Capet', the former king, perhaps hoping to be king himself;

but in April 1793 he was arrested, imprisoned and guillotined. The feast in Orléans stopped.

The French Revolution swept away its royal family in the year that it swept away the cult of Joan; and soon French armies were marching all over Europe in order to sweep away the old order wherever it survived in neighbouring countries. As revolutionary France took on all the unregenerate monarchies of Europe, the bronze monument to Joan in Orléans was melted down to be a cannon, since Joan of Arc seemed tied irrevocably to France's past. No one expected that the Maid of Orléans could belong to France's future; a modern scholar has even claimed that 'Joan of Arc was the creation of nineteenth-century historians.'[20]

TWENTY-ONE

Reviving Joan

ROMANTIC AND REVOLUTIONARY JOAN

Voltaire died in Paris in 1778, less than a decade before the collapse of the French *Ancien Régime*. As France moved with a seemingly inexorable logic towards a revolution in the affairs of State and Church, abolishing privilege in favour of unitary social order, Voltaire was regarded as a luminary of the age. He would have hated this description. The very thought of heroism would have alarmed him, but heroism was the order of the day.

Joan had been a medieval, Catholic, royalist heroine. The new heroine of revolutionary France was the classical, half-naked Marianne. Joan found admirers in the land of the old enemy, England, and in Weimar, arguably the seat of the most civilised court in Europe.

The age of revolution was also the age when the movement called Romanticism began. Young writers became fascinated by the medieval past. One of Joan's first advocates was the Englishman Robert Southey, now the least known of the Lake poets. At this stage Southey, not yet Wordsworth, was close to Coleridge. With Coleridge Southey had planned to apply the principles of 'Pantisocracy' in a commune on the banks of the Susquehanna river in New England. Coleridge married Southey's wife's sister; and he cooperated with Southey in the production of a poem about Joan.

Traditionally, the writing of an epic was a task for middle or old age, but Southey wrote an epic poem before he was twenty. In six weeks he dashed off twelve cantos, the same number as in Virgil's *Aeneid*, a friend then suggested revisions, so several lines and two cantos were cut. For the second canto Coleridge added 450 lines. Southey, the chief author, was rewriting when the manuscript was at the printers. In 1796 the poem was published in Bristol.

In his preface Southey expatiated on the merits and defects of his Italian and Portuguese predecessors Ariosto, Tasso and Camões and he discussed Spenser, 'the favourite of my childhood', and 'the singular excellence of Milton', whom a whole troop of English poets had imitated during the eighteenth century. With easy fluency Southey used Milton's curious inversions, lengthy constructions, Latinate diction and rolling blank verse. He troubled to do some research. He knew of Voltaire's poem, while admitting he had not read it, and through Boileau he knew of Chapelain. He knew English views of Joan from Holinshed, Shakespeare's main source, he knew Hume's *History of England* and he quoted from Monstrelet and Rapin. As a young radical he willingly admitted Henry V's cruelty at Agincourt, when the English king had ordered the killing of many prisoners by having their throats cut. He chose to side with his French heroine.

Southey wrote quickly and can be read quickly. Dunois played a major part in his narrative, as most of his story focused on the relief of Orléans. He was less sure of touch in delineating Joan, who is made to declare, like a Lakeland peasant:

> In forest shade my infant years train'd up
> Knew not devotion's forms. The chaunted mass,
> The silver altar and religious robe,
> The mystic wafer and the hallowed cup,
> Gods priest-created, are to me unknown.

And

> For sins confest
> To holy priest and absolution given
> I knew them not; for ignorant of sin
> Why should I seek forgiveness?[1]

Eventually, the English army's defeat at Patay clears the way to Reims, where

> The Mission'd Maid
> Then placed on Charles's brow the Crown of France.[2]

And so the Maid

Redeem'd her country. Ever may the ALL-JUST
Give to the arms of FREEDOM such success.[3]

Southey later became an anti-French Tory journalist, and from
1813 until his death in 1843 he was poet laureate. The one book of
his readily available is the *Life of Nelson* (1813), his encomium on
one of the most anti-French of English heroes.

Meanwhile, in 1801 a version of Joan's life was staged at Weimar
by one of the most formidable of European Romantics, Friedrich
von Schiller. *Die Jungfrau von Orleans* (*The Maid of Orléans*) was
but one of many plays in which Schiller re-examined the past of
many European countries. Schiller took pains to gain a sound
knowledge of history; he probably first came across Joan in Hume's
History of England and he knew Shakespeare and Voltaire. Joan to
him was a woman given a national destiny. Like Wilhelm Tell, she
stood for liberty, but as he explained, he had 'overcome the
historical facts'. Schiller's Joan was important in legend. As facts
about her did not matter, he could decide what the facts should be.
Without Voltaire's wicked sense of humour, his story is full of love
interest. Joan and her two sisters, called Margot and Louison, each
have suitors, Dunois falls in love with Joan and she falls in love with
an English knight, Lionel, whose life she spares, with the result that
her failure to remain free of sexual feeling brings about her fall, a
Romantic variant on the Shakespearean slur that she was a
seductress. Historical dilemmas did not interest Schiller. In the
prologue, Joan seizes a helmet, because she must fight, and she dies
in battle, since that is her destiny.

NAPOLEON'S JOAN

Within ten years of the execution of Louis XVI, Joan's fortunes
revived in France. After the tumults of the 1790s the youthful
General Napoleon Bonaparte seized power and as First Consul
became Head of State of the French Republic. Since 1789 France
had been divided chiefly by religion and royalism, and so Bonaparte
planned to woo natural conservatives by offering them a sort of
monarchy, and to woo Catholics by assuring them that they could
practise their faith without the protection of a king.

The Concordat Bonaparte signed with the pope in 1803 gave
him some control over the French Church. Operating under the

Concordat system, the Bishop of Orléans wrote to the Minister of the Interior, Chaptal, to beg permission to revive the festival of Joan of Arc. Chaptal consulted Napoleon, who, with his eagle eye for propaganda, responded in the official paper, *Le Moniteur*:

> The deliberation of the city council is very pleasing to me. The illustrious Joan of Arc has proved that there is no miracle that French genius cannot achieve when national independence is threatened. United, the French nation has never been vanquished, but our neighbours, abusing the openness and loyalty of our character, constantly sowed in us the dissension from which came the calamities of the period in which the French heroine lived, and all the disasters our history recalls.[4]

To mark the resumption of the feast the city acquired a statue by Etienne Gois showing Joan as an Amazonian maid, wounded in the shoulder by an arrow, grabbing hold of her sword and rolling up an English flag.

Napoleon's intervention had a lasting effect on the cult of Joan. Before 1789 France had been a kingdom and all French people were subjects of the king. After 1789 France was a nation and all French people were citizens. Between 1799 and 1870 monarchical power remained the norm, as First Consul Bonaparte gave way to Emperor Napoleon I, then two senior and one junior Bourbon king, Louis XVIIII, Charles X and Louis-Philippe and finally Emperor Napoleon III. If dynasties changed, there was a constant search for heroes and heroines from the nation's past.

From 1803 Joan steadily became better known. Scenes from her life were themes for paintings or sculptures in the Salons, the biennial State-sponsored exhibitions held in Paris; it was in the Salon of 1802 that Gois first showed his statue of Joan. The new interest in Joan was initially just a sign of the new vogue for medieval history; and the new school of painting that cultivated the so-called troubadour style was much loved by Napoleon's first wife, the Empress Joséphine. There was something glamorous in the sheen of a coat of armour and the fantastic hats and long trains beloved by high-born ladies in the fifteenth century, and Joan, an elegant girl in male costume, had an air of becoming grace.

THE END OF LEGEND

Joan came from an era when the kings of France were anointed with the oil of St Remigius and crowned in Reims Cathedral. The ceremony she regarded as the supreme triumph of her mission was re-enacted for the last time in 1825, to honour Louis XVI's youngest brother, Charles X. Fervent royalists longed for the reunion of throne and altar, which Joan took for granted.

At the base of Gois's statue of Joan, four scenes were sculpted in relief: the battle of Orléans; Joan receiving a sword from the hands of Charles VII; the coronation of Charles VII in Reims Cathedral; the reading of the death sentence and the carrying out of the sentence in Rouen. This Napoleonic statue was itself a neoclassical concoction, with no trace of medieval reality, but after 1815 artists began to aim at authenticity. The department of the Vosges bought Joan's family house in Domremy, and once the building was refurbished, its new status was commemorated in lithographs. Some pupils of Napoleon's first painter, David, wrote to their former master, now in exile in Brussels, to inform him of the recent revival of interest in Joan. They told him that there were 'crowds of Maids at the Salon; there have never been so many in all classes' (of works of art). 'Joan of Arc is represented in the principal situations of her too-short career, and her life, almost in its entirety, is set before people's eyes.'5 Some of the painters were committed royalists, notably Pierre-Henri Révoil, whose painting of Joan of Arc in prison at Rouen, now in the city's museum, demonstrated meticulous research into the clothes of the time. Others discovered a lifelong vocation for historical painting. Paul Delaroche achieved fame in 1824 with his treatment of Joan's interrogation in prison by Cardinal Beaufort. This picture, also in Rouen, illustrates a fictional scene. Its realism is psychological rather than historical. The fierce Bishop of Winchester in his blood-red cardinal's robe points down to hell while a sick Joan raises her eyes heavenwards. In this painting too, the painter is keen to render the costume in authentic detail.

Although Charles X fell in the glorious revolution of 1830, medievalism survived; and with it the artistic obsession with Joan. The July Monarchy set up after the mob had done its work, under the junior Bourbon, Louis-Philippe, Duke of Orléans, took a paradoxical view of Joan. The new ruling classes were by instinct anticlerical; for a time the festivities in Orléans were suspended; and yet in a reign when sceptics and republicans set the tone of society, scholars took pains to gather the materials the past had left behind. This coincided with a private concern of King Louis-Philippe to make Versailles a museum of all French history, royalist, republican and Napoleonic. One picture chosen for permanent exhibition was Auguste Vinchon's *The Consecration of Charles VII at Reims, 17 July, 1429*, in which Joan occupies the geometric centre of the painting. Also in Versailles is a fine sculpture by Louis-Philippe's own daughter, Marie d'Orléans, who sculpted several statues of Joan. A copy of the Versailles *Joan* now stands in front of the town hall in Orléans. The royal sculptress managed to express what few contemporaries were able to portray in any visual form – Joan's inner life.

In the 1840s Jules-Etienne-Joseph Quicherat set to work on the task of editing the manuscripts relating to Joan in the royal library. The scholarly and literary achievement of the age had an enduring effect on the cult of Joan. Her life and death were finally subjected to honest, scrupulous evaluation.

Using the techniques of the Ecole de chartes (the school of charters), an institution founded by Louis XVIII, Quicherat edited all the texts he could find relevant to her story. Between 1841 and 1849 he produced a great work in five volumes, *Procès de condamnation et de réhabilitation de Jeanne d'Arc dite la Pucelle . . . suivis de tous les documents historiques qu'on a pu réunir et accompagnées de notes et d'éclaircissements* ('The process of condemnation and rehabilitation of Joan of Arc, called the Pucelle . . . followed by all the historical documents that can be found together with notes and explanations'). The first volume contained transcriptions of the trial of 1431, the second and third volumes those of the nullification trials, the fourth the 'chronicles, reminiscences and impressions by contemporaries', the fifth consisted of 'literary extracts, contemporary poetry' and an index. Quicherat enabled scholarly historians to study not just the relatively familiar trial of 1431 (most accounts of Joan stopped with her death), but also the duller form, in which the memories of those who had known, loved and admired her were preserved. He also freed historians from dependence on a chronicler like Monstrelet, who could not recall anything that was said on the one occasion when he said he met Joan and who forgot that his patron had sold her to the English. Quicherat made researchers aware of the cult of Joan since 1456, down to the moment when the Orléans festival was revived in 1803. His work has lasted. Only recently have modern editions of the trials of 1431 and 1450–6 replaced his first three volumes, and even in the twenty-first century no publication has yet has made his fourth and fifth volumes obsolete.

Quicherat's sound erudition has in the long term done more to restore the reputation of Joan than any great writer's most exalted flight of fantasy, but it could hardly make her popular, even when in the 1860s his collection of medieval Latin and French texts was translated into modern French. What was required was the verve of a master of the hard art that the French call *haute vulgarisation* (sophisticated popularisation), and in 1830 such a man emerged into prominence when Jules Michelet, a Parisian university professor, lectured on medieval history. His original account of Joan formed part of his course on the history of fifteenth-century France, but in 1853 it was printed as an independent work. This was a lucky accident. By writing so much Michelet became prolix: what makes his life of Joan a pleasure to read is that for once he was concise, a rare achievement for anyone writing about Joan. Indeed, concision gives his little book its air of authority. When he has pronounced, it seems as if there is nothing more to say.

Michelet saw in Joan a visionary who noticed problems only in order as to solve them. 'She declared in the name of God that Charles was the heir; she reassured him about his legitimacy which he doubted. This legitimacy she sanctified, by leading her king straight to Reims and gaining over the English the decisive advantage of the consecration.'[6] His view of her was based on common sense: 'it was not rare to see women take up arms'. 'The originality of the Pucelle did not consist in her visions. In the Middle Ages who did not have them?' 'The court of Charles VII was far from being unanimously in favour of the Pucelle . . . Everyone was curious to see the sorceress or the inspired woman.' At Poitiers the clergy decided: 'this girl is the messenger of God'. It was not that France did not have enough able soldiers to win back Orléans, but they were not used to obeying the king; this was the age when men obeyed the Virgin rather than Christ; they needed a virgin come down to earth, a virgin 'popular, young, lovely, kind, brave'.

Michelet's chapter headings are terse; 'Childhood and vocation', 'Joan delivers Orléans and has the king consecrated at Reims', and

'Joan is betrayed and surrendered' is followed by 'The trial – Joan refuses to submit to the Church', 'Temptation' and 'Death'. Michelet is careful to show his sources in footnotes that reveal he knows the chroniclers, Monstrelet, the Bourgeois de Paris, the author of the *Chronique de la Pucelle*; and he quotes from the records of the 1431 trial and the trials of 1452–6 as well as from other archival material.

Michelet rightly claims that the consecration of Charles VII in Reims Cathedral marked the apogee of Joan's mission. 'Everyone who saw her' at the moment when she knelt to thank God (here he cites the words of the *Chronique de la Pucelle*) 'believed more than ever that this happening was the work of God'. His use of this comment shows how well he could enter into the mentality of the age, since the only comparable occasion during Michelet's own life, the last consecration of a French king, Charles X, in Reims (in 1825), was greeted with derision by all except devout royalists. Michelet was a man of the Left, however, who became first a liberal, then a republican; and his view of Joan endorsed Napoleon's assertion that she was a French heroine. In Michelet's narrative she had perhaps changed from a saint to a captain, from one who took up the sword reluctantly to one who enjoyed wielding a sword. Once captured, she was a political tool. Her king did nothing for her and the Duke of Burgundy, who surrendered her, was more concerned with Anglo-Flemish trade than justice; and so in January 1431 the Anglophile Bishop Cauchon opened the case against her. There must be only one result: her death. 'If the fire was lacking, the iron remained.'

While she wavered, the English, secure in their pride, never did. 'Never were the Jews so vehemently opposed to Jesus as they were to the Pucelle.' Under pressure she gave up her sole protection in the world in which she moved, her male attire. When she resumed men's clothes, she was doomed and the English made sure there would be no escape. 'As she died, a secretary of the King of England called out, "We are lost, we have burnt a saint"' But Michelet is clear they had also burnt a French woman. 'This last figure from the past was also the first figure of the future. In her appeared at the same time the Virgin . . . and already the Nation.' Joan stood for a stable national destiny. France was given to frequent regime change between 1814 and 1870, but all the while the French nation persisted; and Joan symbolised the nation at its best.

By the time Michelet's work was published, the pear-shaped citizen-king Louis-Philippe had died in exile in England, there had been a new revolution and a new republic and then the Second Empire. For a time Napoleon III toyed with the idea of being crowned. One of the first artistic commissions of his Minister of Art was to ask the painter Ingres to finish the picture *Joan of Arc at the Coronation of Charles VII at Reims* (1854). The emphasis in the painting is not on Charles VII but on Joan, standing at the composition's still centre, her soft flesh set against the hard, gleaming armour, her lustrous eyes cast up to heaven, standing with one hand on the altar, the other holding her standard, in front of a tonsured cleric and a page both on their knees, some way in front of a standing nobleman. In the end Napoleon was not consecrated and no other French ruler has ever been crowned. The idea of sacred monarchy was dead.

Even without a consecrated monarch Joan was central to the story of France. In the preface to the historical novel *Joan of Arc* (1842), Alexandre Dumas (the father) called her the 'Christ of France', who has 'redeemed the crimes of the monarchy', and for him a scholar wrote an extended appendix outlining the sources available before the publication of Quicherat's volumes.

The first and one of the most scholarly Englishman to discuss Joan's case was John Lingard (1771–1851), who was born a year after Wordsworth and who died the year after him. A Catholic priest with unrivalled knowledge of Continental archives, Lingard was conscious of intending to refute popular misconceptions about English history by the dispassionate presentation of the evidence; and this method he applied in his discussion of Joan. His account of Joan, like that of Dumas, is based on a reading of those texts available before Quicherat's studies. In it he practises the methods he thought historians should use, methods essentially sceptical and open-minded.

Lingard wondered why she 'mistook for realities the workings of her own imagination'. She was marvellously successful, he said, in the two important enterprises for which she claimed divine inspiration, the relief of Orléans and the conducting of the Dauphin Charles to his consecration at Reims, and then she wanted to return to her simple life, but was persuaded by Charles to continue in his service. When she was captured, 'the unfortunate maid was treated with neglect by her friends, with cruelty by her enemies'. The Bishop of Beauvais, who was devoted to the English interest and in whose diocese she had been taken, 'claimed the right of trying her in his court on the accusation of sorcery and imposture'. After various attempts had been made 'to save her from the punishment of death, by inducing her to make a frank and explicit confession' and after one abjuration which she quickly recanted, she was finally burnt at the stake 'embracing a crucifix and calling on Christ for mercy'.

At the start of his account of Joan, Lingard comments: 'The wonderful revolution which she accomplished by means apparently supernatural, will justify an endeavour to trace the origin of the enthusiasm which, while it deluded, yet nerved and elevated the mind of this young and interesting female.' Towards the end of his discussion, he states: 'An impartial observer would have pitied and respected the mental delusion with which she was afflicted; the credulity of her judges condemned her, on the charge of having relapsed into her former errors . . . This cruel and unjustifiable tragedy was acted in the market-place of Rouen, before an immense concourse of spectators, about twelve months after her capture.'[7] Lingard reserved for a mere footnote a reference to the nullification of her trial. In not discussing her extraordinary psychology, he is typical of people who never go beyond the facts in dealing with Joan.

A younger Englishman, Thomas De Quincey, was more partisan. His essay on Joan was an unashamedly Francophile response to Michelet. Best known now as a writer on opium addiction, he also left his *Recollections of the Lake Poets*, a group he had cultivated assiduously. In commenting, then, on Michelet's first thoughts on Joan in the *History of France*, De Quincey had the advantage of knowing Southey. 'Twenty years after, talking with Southey, I was surprised to find him still owning a secret bias in favour of Joan, founded on her detection of the Dauphin.'[8] Thanks to Michelet, De Quincey was better informed. Rightly he divides her public career into two parts, but is drawn to the sequel when 'what remained was – to suffer.'

De Quincy points out astutely that the one way the English undid the psychological effect of Charles VII's coronation was to 'taint' it 'as the work of a witch'. He is astute too in pointing out that Cauchon's ambition made him not the only Frenchman to be 'an instrument of the English', but adds 'even at this day, France exhibits the horrid spectacle of judges examining the prisoner against himself'. He ends by rebuking English historians in general for bias against Joan.

Enmity was put on one side when in the Crimean war England and France became allies.

REVIVAL IN ORLEANS

It was supremely important for the cult of Joan of Arc that in 1849 one of the most gifted French bishops of the nineteenth century, Félix Dupanloup, a man of letters and member of the French Academy, became Bishop of Orléans. His career in the Church was defined by the fact that his 29-year episcopate coincided with the pontificate of Pius IX, Pio Nono (1846–78). Dupanloup remained in the see of Orléans until the year of his death, the year in which the pope died also.

Before Dupanloup's episcopate, devotion to Joan was largely a local cult. The Orléannais had never forgotten that Joan had raised the siege; in the 1840s, however, even while a former Duke of Orléans ruled, the annual festivities had stopped. Dupanloup made sure they would not stop again. Gois's statue, now unloved, was moved to the bridge where the Tourelles had once stood, and Foyatier's dignified equestrian statue of Joan was put up in the main city square, place du Martroi. Dupanloup reorganised the festivities himself and on the first occasion that the new rite was observed (in 1855) he preached her cause. He also pronounced the panegyric for the 1869 festival.

'In her I find everything that moves me,' he announced, 'including the name of Orléans, that has become mine since God called me to be the bishop of your souls; I like the peasant simplicity in her origins, the chastity in her heart, her courage in battle, her love for the land of France, but above all the holiness in her life and death.' [9] He described his visit to Domremy, which reinforced his opinion that she was remarkable in the way she combined love of France with love of God. 'Do not think . . . you must chose between the duties of a Christian and those of a Frenchman . . . Religion points its finger towards the sky, but it does not make us forget our dear country down here.'

Dupanloup had read Quicherat, for he reminded the congregation how Dunois, her captain, and d'Aulon, her steward, both said they had never met a woman more chaste than Joan. Faced with such virtue, now that feelings of the past had calmed, the bishop was not surprised that almost daily he heard some Englishman express his admiration for Joan:

> In spite of English Protestantism a descendant of one she defeated said only yesterday: 'Such a person sustains our faith and brings splendour to the human spirit and her rightful setting is a church.' . . . I promise you that you cannot approach her and read, as I have just done, the pages of her story in the processes of the two trials, in which she seems to live on still and even, I would dare say, to be full of vitality, without having the irresistible conviction that in her you are face to face with a heroic saint, a messenger of God . . . She is a saint: God was in her.

On that same day, 8 May, the anniversary of the relief of Orléans, Dupanloup sent off a petition to Rome to open Joan's cause as a saint.

TWENTY-TWO

Holy Patriot

THE MAID OF DOMREMY

The early 1870s was a period of decisive change in the history of France, of the Catholic Church and of the cult of Joan.

France's defeat in the Franco-Prussian war destroyed for ever its reputation as the leading Continental power. The crowning of the King of Prussia as German Kaiser in the Hall of Mirrors at Versailles symbolised France's national humiliation, and the siege of Paris brought misery to a capital to which the Emperor Napoleon III had given its majestic layout. The ensuing civil war between the left-wing supporters of the Paris Commune and the Versailles government fuelled lasting class hatred, but nothing hurt so much as the wresting away from France of German-speaking Alsace, which had been French since the reign of Louis XIV, and still more the industrial parts of French-speaking Lorraine, French since the reign of Louis XV.

The threat of war had led France to withdraw troops that for a generation had protected the pope in Rome and the patrimony of St Peter (which corresponds approximately to the modern Lazio). As Prussia's ally, the new kingdom of Italy was free to invade papal territory and to take control of most of Rome. Pope Pius IX, a 'prisoner in the Vatican', would have nothing to do with the anti-clerical regime based in his own city. At the Vatican Council that met just before war broke out, he had been declared infallible when, speaking as successor of St Peter for the whole Church, he pronounced on matters of faith and morals. This doctrine would have surprised fifteenth-century conciliarists such as Gerson, who thought that the ultimate authority of the Church lay in a General Council; and indeed a minority at the Vatican Council, including Dupanloup, thought the timing of the pope's declaration inopportune.

Defeat in the Franco-Prussian war transformed the role of Joan in France. The new borders meant that, as in Joan's time, Domremy was situated at the edge of France; and now all Frenchmen were united by a desire for revenge. France set out to train all its young men to fight; and the spread of primary schooling inculcated a sense of national identity.

As an act of reparation for the sins that had brought disaster, a conservative government voted for the building of a church dedicated to the Sacred Heart of Jesus. The Sacré Coeur, perched high on the hill of Montmartre, may look like the sugary confection of some architectural cake-maker, but it implied France's Catholic destiny and, when a huge picture of the Triumph of the Sacred Heart was eventually designed for the church, Joan of Arc was the one Frenchwoman among the group who worship Christ.

By the time church and the picture were ready, Joan was on the point of being made a saint. The process had been halted by warfare, but in 1874 Dupanloup resumed his project of supervising preliminary enquiries in Orléans. By then he knew that France's failure against Prussia in 1870–1 meant that France was a republic. The Bonapartist cause was in defeat a lost cause, and so the alternative was a Bourbon king, who could be one of two princes: Henri, comte de Chambord, grandson of Charles X, last Bourbon of the senior line to be king, or the comte de Paris, grandson of Louis-Philippe of the junior line who had supplanted Charles. To make matters easy the comte de Paris was heir to the childless comte de Chambord, but Henri 'V' made matters harder. He had not set foot in France since he was a child and gauging the country's mood was beyond his imagination to grasp. It would be an affront to his honour, he announced, to accept the tricolour as the national flag instead of the fleur-de-lis, 'the flag of Henry IV, of Francis I, of Joan of Arc'.[1] He went into exile, where he remained until he died. His behaviour made clear that the royalist restoration Dupanloup hoped for would never take place. Others, like Louis Veuillot, a rabid right-wing journalist, supported the stand taken by the comte de Paris, although the royal heir had left France for ever, and looked forward to an ideal king who would rescue France from atheists, socialists, radicals and Catholic liberals like Dupanluoup, all of whom might accept a republic, if they disagreed about what sort of republic France should have. Royalist sentiment survived, but did not unite the French. And yet while the lilies of the French crown withered, the demand to proclaim Joan's sanctity grew.

At the same time, however, many on the republican, anticlerical Left in France also developed a devotion to Joan, seeing her as the simple peasant abandoned by her king and her Church; and outside France, above all in the English-speaking world, she was admired.

THE GIRL ON A GOLDEN HORSE

A fine gilt statue of Joan of Arc on horseback holding her banner in place des Pyramides is one of four statues of Joan in Paris. The statue of Emmanuel Fremiet evokes the strongest emotions. It was erected in an area where, and at a time when, the statue mattered. The site is near the heart of Napoleonic Paris, not far from place Vendôme, home to the column Napoleon put up in honour of the army that triumphed at Austerlitz in 1805. This was a part of Paris that was devastated in 1871. On the defeat of French troops in the Franco-Prussian war a mob hacked down the Vendôme column and burnt down the Tuileries Palace, the principal residence of France's rulers from 1799 to 1871. The erection of Fremiet's statue in 1874 seemed to reaffirm faith in an older, more permanent France.

The statue was a call to arms. Glistening in the sun, it would inspire the nation to recapture Lorraine, and, if Joan could not yet be called a saint, she was the heroine who would ride out to inspire the soldiers of France. All over France similar statues of Joan were put up, in churches, in squares, even in remote landscapes. In French Lorraine alone there were said to be some 1,000 statues of Joan. From 1871 to 1914 the aim of winning back Alsace-Lorraine was the policy from which no politician dared dissent. Every young conscript was taught the story of Joan. Domremy, her village, was again a frontier village, but now a frontier village in what became a 75-year war against the Germans. As in the fifteenth century, in a period of national humiliation, Joan's hour had come. The republican Anatole France noted that after the Franco-Prussian war, under the influence of patriotic feeling and the revival of Catholic belief among the middle classes, 'the cult of the Maid redoubled in fervour'.[2] A 1883 life by the republican historian Fabre called her the 'Libératrice de France'; and in 1912 the quincentenary of her birth was celebrated throughout France.

She was born a peasant. In the late nineteenth century French rural society was in process of modernising; and as it did so the cult of Joan spread. Eugen Weber, who has studied the transformation of rural society in this period, insists that ignorance about Joan among French schoolteachers had become unacceptable by the 1880s. In five years in the 1870s the number of signatures in the visitors' book at Joan's house in Domremy jumped from about 1,300 to over 2,000. Visitors were largely either from neighbouring departments or from Paris. Other than soldiers, they were for the most part lesser nobility and elegant townsfolk. Travel was still a pastime for the rich and only slowly did Domremy turn into a popular shrine. In 1881 work began on building the huge basilica of Bois-Chenu in Joan's honour. The basilica was given a function when Domremy became an official place of pilgrimage; and artists vied to decorate its walls. Two statues were made for the village: *Joan Hearing her Voices* and *France Arming Joan*. Visitors to Domremy now came from every class and many came from much further away. It is not hard to account for the increasing numbers. The popularity of miniature encyclopaedias like the Petit Lavisse had inexorably spread knowledge of Joan. In 1907 *Le Figaro*, the Paris-based newspaper for the well-educated Right, indignantly noted that of the previous year's recruits to the army, almost half had never heard of Joan. They soon would. The young men in the barracks were not allowed to speak Breton or Basque or any local patois such as the Lorraine dialect Joan had used. Better educated than her in that they were semi-literate in French, they were more aware of their common identity than any young Frenchmen before them; and devotion to her person bolstered their sense of being French.

Popular writers, artists and illustrators also spread her fame. Henri Wallon, Catholic, republican and sometime Minister of Education, wrote a life of Joan for the Catholic middle classes that remained unopened on the shelves of many private libraries. A more overtly political life by Joseph Fabre became much better known. It was priced low to widen circulation, and with patriotic fervour the author donated his profits to the construction of thousands of monuments to Joan all over the country. As a result, as Anatole France put it, 'people saw in amazing abundance Joan praying, Joan armed and skirmishing, Joan the captive, Joan the martyr'.[3]

Among illustrations of Joan's story, one book written for young people is striking.

Louis-Maurice Boutet de Monvel had fought in the war of 1870–1. He wanted to give future French men the conviction to fight another war in the hope of victory. He decorated his text with pictures of an unequalled intensity, directness and clarity of design. Pure colour reinforces his message. 'Open this book, dear children, with devotion in memory of this humble peasant girl who is patron of France, who is the country's saint as she is the country's martyr. Her story will tell you that to conquer you must have faith in victory. Remember her on the day when your land will need all your courage.'[4]

In central Paris, the national shrine, the Panthéon, became home to Lenepveu's series of paintings on the life of Joan, which were copied into history books for generations. No work of art, however, is quite as startling as Leroy's *The Saint of the Frontier*, ominously shown at the Salon of 1914, which sets an ethereal armoured saint holding her banner inscribed Jesus and Mary in the midst of a party of dragoons. They relax like coiled springs. She has only to give the word, then they will mount their horses and charge.

This was a country where industrialisation was casting its grim shadows in the department of the Nord and in the east, in St-Etienne, where trains belching smoke and coal dust chugged into remote hamlets. Paradoxically, in this country whose ruling middle class worried about its shares and workers' strikes and ambitious businessmen invested in an ever expanding colonial and commercial empire, the nation clung to a figure from a society that had been overwhelmingly rural and dominated by a privileged caste of nobles. Intellectuals knew that many of their families had been recently uprooted from peasant life; and in retrospect the life of one devout peasant girl seemed marvellous.

LISTENING WITH JOAN

Joan had been a listener. One of the most moving nineteenth-century statues of Joan is by Rude, the sculptor famous for the clamorous relief sculpture of *La Marseillaise* on the Arc de Triomphe. Rude's Joan is a girl who stands calmly with one ear cocked. In another attempt to capture this side of her character, the artist Bastien Lepage had placed her in front of her home at Domremy with Sts Margaret, Catherine and Michael festooned like wreaths on the house. Both sculptor and painter wished to convey the same truth, but Rude's omission of any ghostly saints is more effective. His work implies as well as any work of visual art can that Joan was in touch with an invisible world known only to her. She could never adequately convey what she heard or what she saw.

A moving example of the new devotion to Joan is found ironically in Lisieux, in whose cathedral is buried its former bishop, Pierre Cauchon. On 27 January 1894 Pope Leo XIII had permitted the introduction of Joan of Arc's cause for beatification, after which she was given the title of Venerable; and in the National Assembly Henri Wallon proposed a national holiday of patriotism on 8 May to honour her. Although the editor of the Lisieux paper *Le Normandy* thought the idea a plot to secularise her, on 8 May 1894 a flag of the 'glorious Liberatrix' was placed in Cauchon's chapel. This was the chapel where the editor's pious nieces had attended daily Mass; and the youngest of them, Thérèse Martin, was to be a powerful advocate of the cause of Joan, although in 1894, with two older sisters, she was a nun in the local Carmelite convent.

At this stage, Céline, the sister closest to Thérèse, was the only daughter at home in the Martin household, where she cared for their ageing father. In the course of the year Monsieur Martin died and Céline was free to become a Carmelite too. She brought into the convent one precious possession that kept up the link with her previous way of living, as she was allowed to bring her camera. One of her first photographs in the convent shows a smiling Thérèse – in 1894 it was still hard for a photographer to snap people smiling – with hair over her shoulders, a banner and sword in her hands, acting the protagonist in her own play on Joan of Arc.

Since childhood Thérèse had been drawn to the figure of Joan. In her autobiography, *The Story of a Soul*, first published in 1898, the year after her death, she speaks of her early devotion to Joan. 'In reading the tales of the patriotic actions of French heroines, in particular those of the venerable Joan of Arc, I had a great desire to imitate them.'[5] Now as Sister Thérèse of the Child Jesus and the Holy Face, she could write about Joan, whom she thought of as a shepherdess – in this Thérèse was mistaken, but then shepherdesses were in vogue – for she was convinced that her own role in life, like Joan's, was to emphasise the value of obscure origins. In the convent she was told to write and to act. She produced two plays about Joan, *The Mission of Joan of Arc* (or *The Shepherdess of Domremy Hearing her Voices*) acted on 21 January 1894, and *Joan of Arc Fulfilling her Mission*, performed on 21 January 1895.[6] The facts came from Henri Wallon. What fired the fiction was its theme – vocation. Thérèse emphasised the way in which Joan had been called from a remote village to follow a calling that would make her famous throughout the world. It was a theme that matched Thérèse's own destiny, although in her case she did not live to see that destiny fulfilled.[7]

Sister Thérèse's view of Joan mirrored that of the pious milieu in which she lived. Her writings reveal attitudes typical of French conservatives of the 1890s who strove to avoid making a noise in national life. But the nineties was a clamorous decade; and the conservatives who became prominent were those who took their battles into the streets.

MARCHING AS TO WAR

In the 1890s most French Catholics, while like the Martins still instinctively royalist, were less spiritually minded than Sister Thérèse because they were stirred chiefly by religious politics. French society was polarised in 1894 by the unjust conviction of the Jewish officer Alfred Dreyfus for spying. What kept the Right together, Catholic or unbelieving, was not republicanism but admiration for the Army. The Army's verdict had been challenged, but the Army could do no wrong. Among the most vociferous on the Right was the group of able journalists of Action Française, an organisation that, regardless of truth, would stand up for 'true' anti-Dreyfusard, anti-Jewish France. Their magnetic leader Charles Maurras made a powerful impact on the elegant young men of the Right who rejoiced in the nickname of hawkers of the king, the 'Camelots du Roi' who sold the paper, called *Action Française* like the movement. In 1908 *Action Française* became a daily paper. It was never widely read, but its writers were widely influential. Even more influential in the long run was the behaviour of the Camelots, who set a pattern of street fighting followed only too often in the last century. In 1905, in the aftermath of the Dreyfus affair, an anticlerical government transformed France into a secular State and banned religious processions. This prohibition made the Camelots all the keener to process in honour of their heroine, Joan.

The most notorious example of their mob violence occurred in the winter of 1908/9. Thalamas, a professeur at the Lycée Condorcet in Paris, called Joan of Arc a witch who had deserved to be punished. For this he was exiled to the provinces. It was then announced that on Wednesday 5 December he would give a free lecture on history at the Sorbonne. The Camelots made ready for him, greeted him with jeers and rotten eggs and, when he tried to leave, he was slapped in the face by Maxime Réal de Sarte, a young man with a future. Such behaviour became a weekly affair. On the *mercredis de Thalamas* the Sorbonne was in a state of siege and Thalamas could lecture only with the help of a military guard; and twice a supporter of Action Française took over a room to give his own course on la Pucelle. At his last talk Camelots got hold of Thalamas and beat him up. Republicans resisted such right-wing efforts to define Joan as a proto-nationalist by reminding Catholics that she had been burnt by the Church and royalists that she had been deserted by the king. Action Française countered by urging that the well-being of France demanded faith in the Army, of which the warrior maiden Joan was heavenly patroness; and only by military victory could France recover Lorraine.

Maurras believed in France, not in God; what mattered to him on Joan's banner was the fleur-de-lis, not the names of Jesus and Mary, and yet many of his followers were devout. Both non-believers and believers considered Joan their patron, but the Right would not accept that the Left could venerate her honestly; she belonged only to them, as they alone believed that France should have a king.

Early in the new century such a view of Joan was acceptable to some on the Left. If she belonged to the Right, then let them have her, for she had done little, deceived many, including herself. This case was argued in 1908 when one of France's best novelists, Anatole France, published his *Life of Joan of Arc*. Since he was friendly with Maurras, he was not beaten up.

Intending to write a well-researched biography acceptable to most contemporary readers, Anatole France solicited the help of a youthful researcher, Pierre Champion. The preface to France's *Life of Joan of Arc* shows that, if he had paid careful attention to primary sources, he also mistrusted many of them. Joan's perpetual hallucinations made it hard for her to distinguish between truth and falsehood. Chroniclers wrote to please their patrons. Of even less value was the witness in Joan's rehabilitation, for they had grown old and forgetful. If Alençon asserted Joan knew how to place guns he must have been out of his mind – by the 1450s, like many who had supported her, he had gone to the bad. Even in her lifetime, knowledge of Joan was based on legend. Surprisingly, after this sceptical introduction,

Anatole France yet managed to write a large book on a person about whom there was little trustworthy information.

He was more of an amateur than he indicated; the true scholar was his assistant, Champion, future editor and translator of the texts of the nullification trial. France was right to emphasise that the most important contemporary sources were written by clerics; but this applied to the trial documents, not to the chronicles. France's Joan was manipulated by the clergy, who encouraged, condemned, killed and exonerated her, so that she was, as it were, a clerical construct. But then if clerics could be so manipulative, the Joan of the records was not afraid of contradicting them in ways that were fearless, direct and honest.

Her sense of conviction, for Anatole France, came from belief in her voices, and for this reason he inserted an appendix by a distinguished psychologist, Docteur Dumas, whom he had consulted. Dumas said that at the age of thirteen, the age when puberty normally starts, Joan had unilateral hallucinations (from the right only) affecting her sight and hearing. Charcot, who at one time had influenced Freud, thought these sorts of experiences common among hysterics, but Dumas stated that Charcot's view was no longer widely accepted. Joan, he wrote, had not expected her voices and they gave her orders, but later she had disobeyed them or summoned them at will. They seemed as real to her as her normal life. In some ways she was like an hysteric, but in other ways not, for she was far from passive. If she were hysterical, the function of the hysteria was to release her secret feelings – it let what she called God come into her life, so that she strengthened her faith and gained a sense of her mission; and yet her character remained holy and upright and, if there was a neurotic element in her, neurosis had not affected her whole personality. Dumas was careful to hedge his bets. Anatole France, however, was a man with a mission: 'We must finish our liberal monument, before the priests have her placed on their altars.'[8] The *Life of Joan of Arc* was quickly translated into English; and in France it has remained in print. His sentiments were shared by French anticlericals, but he had reckoned without Joan's Anglophone admirers.

UNITING BEHIND JOAN

In the course of the nineteenth century Joan acquired more friends in the English-speaking world. She attracted the attention of Pre-

Raphaelite painters, notably Dante Gabriel Rossetti and Edward Burne-Jones, and of the fairy-tale illustrator Charles Ricketts.[9] No less a person than Queen Victoria saw a play about Joan by the French dramatist Jules Barbier set to music by Gounod and pronounced it 'lovely'.[10] The French firm Hachette published in London and Boston an abbreviated version of a life of Joan by the French poet Alphonse de Lamartine, complete with a scholarly introduction and a glossary at the back.[11] English and American students of French therefore could learn the language by learning about Joan.

A wider public was reached in the 1890s when a great American novelist restated the case for Joan by depicting her as the heroine of a romance. For Mark Twain Joan was a sort of female Huck, a boyish girl who did not want to be 'sivilised' and whose simplicity was an unconscious rebuke to scheming courtiers and devious clerics; she was almost a fifteenth-century democrat. He began writing in 1892. By including Michelet, Quicherat and Henri Wallon in his bibliography he showed that he had consulted French as well as English authorities. He gave his narrator, sieur Louis de Conte, his own initials, S.L.C., Samuel L. Clemens; and he said he felt a tender affection for his, that is 'de Conte's' *Recollections of Joan of Arc*. The legendary Conte, whose name bears a suspicious likeness to the historical de Coutes, is said to have been Joan's secretary. Two years her senior, he had grown up with her in Domremy and had stayed with her to the end of her life. Twain signals to the reader that de Conte, writing in 1492, exactly 400 years before Twain, was alive when Columbus sailed to America. The memorialist is thus a modern as well as a medieval man, a mediator between Joan's age and ours.

Few would assert that Twain's novel is a great work of fiction, but it can give much pleasure in idle moments, as the Joan de Conte recalled was physically as well as morally attractive. For his courage and fidelity de Conte almost deserved to be an American. In finding a pretty girl both heroic and wholesome, de Conte anticipated Twain himself. His American outlook is summed up in a conclusion that Michelet would have liked. With Joan of Arc, love of country was more than a sentiment – it was a passion. She was the 'Genius of Patriotism' – she was Patriotism embodied, made flesh, palpable to the touch and visible to the eye.[12] Twain had made Joan accessible in the land of the free.

Just before the First World War, a Scot, irritated by the translation of Anatole France's *Life* into English, took up the cudgels for Joan. Andrew Lang was a Scots critic, poet, translator and historian, in love with Homer, myths, legends, border ballads, French medieval love poems and the house of Stuart. He had already written a historical romance about a real monk of Dunfermline who commented from Scotland on the story of Joan of Arc. He boasted that 'the Scots stood for her always, with pen as with sword', and he counted a fellow Scot as one of his predecessors, the empirical philosopher David Hume, whose *History of Britain* 'recognised the nobility of her character'.[13]

Before Lang's writing, no British life had been based on Quicherat, and nobody had been so well briefed. While carrying on a polemic against Anatole France in his preface and footnotes, Lang provided a well-written account of Joan, in which his own tendency to whimsy was kept under control. *The Maid of France* appeared in 1908, and in 1912 its author died.

It was, however, a native of Orléans who put into verses sentiments that are the poetic equivalent of the pictures of de Monvel and Lenepveu. Charles Péguy was tormented by doubt; and he worked through his doubts in relation to his persistent love of Joan. In 1895–7, while studying in Paris, he wrote his first book, a trilogy of plays on Joan, but few people took any notice of his writing, much of it left-wing journalism, until he returned to the topic of Joan's vocation with *Le Mystère de la Charité de Jeanne d'Arc* in 1910. He claimed that his earlier work had been about 'the history of her inner life', but it was in truth his own problems he focused on rather than hers, for in becoming a socialist he had ceased to be a believing Catholic. By the time he wrote the second work, however, he had recovered his faith and it was as an individualistic Christian that he prepared for the quincentenary of his heroine's birth in 1912. He had shifted from viewing Joan as a class heroine to the conviction that her religious calling was one of the most remarkable there had ever been. He believed her to be one of the greatest of saints, only a little lower in heaven than Mary mother of Christ. He made a new claim for Joan: it was her charity that raised her so high. What fascinated him was Domremy, the place where Joan found her vocation, rather than the sites of her later victories or defeats.

Le Mystère de la Charité de Jeanne d'Arc does not attempt to be a drama. Set in Domremy in 1425, at the time when Joan first claimed to hear her voices, it focuses on how she came to realise and accept the role she was to play. Péguy sticks to just three characters, Joan, Hauviette and Madame Gervaise. Much of the writing is in prose, until it bursts into a free verse that can be as sonorous as the Psalms or clipped, even harsh. Madame Gervaise talks the most, as she exhibits the piety of the conventionally religious (she is a young nun), whereas Joan is called to a life out of the ordinary. At the end of the play Madame Gervaise prays that Christ will save Joan's soul and Joan says Amen to that and adds the words 'Orléans, which is in the country of the Loire', for her vocation calls her to action.

Once this poem made his poetry well known, Péguy, who always regarded himself as a man of the Left, came to be cherished by those on the Right who saw in Joan the standard bearer to lead them. In the circumstances of 1910 the popularity of Péguy's poem showed that the cause of Joan was a cause believed in by both the French nation and the French Church.

THE MAKING OF SAINT JOAN[14]

In 1909 Joan was declared Blessed by the Catholic Church. Bishop Coullié, successor to Dupanloup, continued with enquiries in 1885 and 1887–8, which led to Joan's cause being submitted to the Sacred Congregation of Rites in Rome. In 1892 and 1898–1902 Joan was subjected to new enquiries, more searching than any since the fifteenth century. In 1452–6 her first trial had been nullified, but its verdict had been grudging. What her supporters hoped for was an enthusiastic endorsement of her life as one of heroic virtue. Those who acted successively as the *Promotor Fidei* (Promoter of the Faith), better known as the devil's advocate, outlined the case against her. They were energetic in carrying out their task. The first, Augustine Caprara, found no difficulty in 1456 in admitting that she deserved to be rehabilitated, and he admitted that she was an outstanding figure in fifteenth-century history, a person with an impact on her age analogous to that of Christopher Columbus, whose candidacy for canonisation had been mooted only to be rejected. Like Columbus, he said, she was admired for political not religious virtues. Caprara took seriously many of the points made against her at the 1431 trial. He trusted the records of the condemnation process more than the records of the nullification process; and he maintained that before her capture she was admired chiefly as a soldier, not so much as a saint, for he doubted her modesty; he was also worried that the Duke of Alençon had seen her beautiful breasts several times. Caprara could not see how she could be a martyr for the faith, he was not sure if she had submitted her visions to the judgement of the Church. He conceded that in recent time there had been a growth in devotion to her. He also conceded that if she were added to the ranks of the blessed, she would deserve extremely well not only of France but also of all Christendom. In short she could be a Catholic saint. He admitted her cause might triumph.

Against Caprara's arguments, set out in 55 pages of arguments and 47 pages of documents, the defender of Joan's cause replied in 170 pages. The defender was delighted with his opponent's conclusion, but indignant at the slurs on Joan's character. The judges decided that at this stage there was no insuperable obstacle to her cause; in 1894 it was announced that the case could go further – this was the moment when Pope Leo XIII declared her Venerable.

Joan's sanctity was put to the test on two subsequent occasions: in 1898–9 and in 1903. In 1898–9 the Promoter, Joseph Baptist Lugari, argued that, like the original trial, her rehabilitation 'trial' was a political act. He also questioned her virtues. She did not practise faith, hope and charity heroically, nor prudence and justice, while her courage was shaky; she took too much pleasure in finery and her own chastity to be truly temperate. He did not like the fact that she was always glad to be tested for virginity, not having given sufficient weight to the fact that in the fifteenth century, as a witch was considered to be always promiscuous, so a virgin could not be a witch. His chief worry concerned her reliance on private revelations, in other words her voices, and a secondary worry was her lack of deference to her judges. As a cleric himself, he did not like the fact that she had rebuked a bishop. The precise grounds on which the Promoter's views are based are not recorded. All that is known is that once more they were not held to be grave enough to impede the progress of the cause.

There is more information about the final stage of the process. This time, whereas Alexander Verde, the last devil's advocate, presented his ideas in 24 pages, the reply takes up 367; and this was followed by 198 pages exposing Joan's virtues. The opponent's chief concern was the suspicion of hysteria and a secondary one, whether her stand for France was inspired by God; the defenders also worried about the passage of time since the records dated back to the fifteenth century. On the first point her defender replied that she did not exhibit the normal symptoms of hysteria. On the second point the Promoter had already conceded that she may be 'praised to the stars as the liberator of France whose deeds had been inspired by God Himself'.[15] On the third point he defender also thought the documents were in the main reliable.[16]

In her lifetime Joan probably did not perform any miracles. Had she done so, contemporaries might have found it harder to discount the views of those moved by her goodness, just as her carefully guarded virginity prevented the charge of witchcraft from being pressed home. To promote her canonisation, however, those directing her cause in the early twentieth century had to prove that from heaven she could perform four miracles, of which two at least were 'of the first class'. Two were needed for beatification, two more for canonisation. The pope might dispense with one miracle if the candidate had founded a religious order. Joan was let off one for having saved France.

Three miracles of the first class were produced. One nun had been cured of leg ulcers, a second of a cancerous ulcer of her left breast, a third of cancer of the stomach.[17] These cures were attributed to Joan since they had been preceded by invocation to her in prayer. Pope Pius X solemnly accepted the three miracles as authentic on 13 December 1908. He declared: 'Joan of Arc has shone like a new star destined to be the glory not only of France but of the Universal Church as well.' For heroic virtue she was declared Blessed on 18 April 1909. There was nothing to prevent Joan from being canonised, except the coming of war.

By the end of 1918, as Austria–Hungary disintegrated, there was no longer a major Catholic power in Europe. France and Italy were officially secular, and Spain was politically powerless. In 1919, in the Hall of Mirrors at Versailles, the weak German republic was forced to cede the territorial gains of 1871 back to France. Since the French once more had possession of all Lorraine, they were glad to have a Lorrainer as their national heroine. The First World War briefly united Frenchmen; and national unity was briefly symbolised by Joan.

In the trenches of the Western Front soldiers were painfully aware of their lack of women. They wanted women for every need. They made an industry of prostitution. *Poilus* became a new nickname for the 'hairy' private soldiers who enjoyed cheeky *chansons* about the barmaid Madelon they met in a café, but above all they sought to be consoled. The cult of Joan had been given the approval of State and Church. *Poilus* carried pictures of Joan in their pockets. Joan had saved them, nurtured them and made them victorious. Once peace came, it would have been unthinkable for Benedict XV, pope since 1914, not to have declared Joan a saint. In May 1920 the French bishops came to Rome to see her canonised; and that year the French National Assembly at last announced the national holiday in her honour. Quarrels between the French Church and the French State were forgotten. The national feast of Joan was fixed for the Sunday after 8 May, a date that has kept its place in the celebrations of Joan's triumphs and is still a national holiday. The Church reserved 30 May, the day of her death, for her feast day, not as a martyr, for she had not died for the faith, but as a virgin, a woman who was pure until death. The trials of Joan were finally over.

TWENTY-THREE

The Cult of St Joan

In 1920 France was united by Joan. At the same time France was on good terms with the countries it chose to call Anglo-Saxon. The war had improved French relations with English-speaking countries. The Entente Cordiale of 1904 had survived the stresses of an alliance in wartime, and as for the USA, the sympathy that many American intellectuals felt with France had been transformed in 1917 when the nation joined that alliance. The American President needed to persuade the American people that Liberty (as sculpted by Eiffel) should be preserved in the home of Eiffel's Tower, and when American troops arrived in France, General Pershing recalled France's aid in the American Revolution with the words, *Lafayette, Nous voici*. But, when it came to persuading the troops to leave home, the American government found one of the best ways to stir up support for France was to invoke the name of Joan.

One poster read: 'Joan of Arc saved France. Women of America save your country. Buy war stamps.' One painting shows Allied soldiers being led by the spirits of Washington, St George and Joan. Another, for Henry Van Dyke's book *The Broken Soldier and the Maid of France* has the inscription, 'They were also pilgrims drawn by the love of Jeanne d'Arc to Domremy'. A photograph was taken of American soldiers standing by the high altar in the nearby basilica of Bois-Chenu. A popular song, 'Joan of Arc They are Calling You', opens with the invocation:

> While you are sleeping, Your France is weeping,
> Wake from your dreams, Maid of France,
> Her heart is bleeding: Are you unheeding
> Come with the flame in your glance.

Two members of the Air Ambulance posed before the statue of Joan in front of Reims Cathedral. A popular French picture emphasised the key importance of the site where Joan's king was anointed and crowned, for, while in the background the cathedral burns, Joan herself waves her banner and confronts the Kaiser. Against him Joan was fighting at Verdun, for Lorraine, for Alsace.[1]

English speakers were Joan's friends. Once canonised, Joan became a topic so fascinating that whatever their beliefs, dramatists wished to retell her tale. Outside France the best-known versions of this story are by non-Catholics; and in one case the writing of a play about St Joan in English revived the reputation of an ageing playwright.

George Bernard Shaw's *Saint Joan* was staged in 1924, first in New York and then in London. *Saint Joan* was soon thought the masterpiece of a writer who had long said he was 'the second Shakespeare', and in this case at least he excelled his rival. Shaw's Joan is no witch, no heroine, no martyr, just a stubborn, spirited young woman, condemned by well-intentioned judges; and this Joan made Shaw once more the darling of the theatre-going public.

An English translation of the text of Joan's trial in 1431 and of the rehabilitation in 1456 appeared in 1902: T. Douglas Murray's *Jeanne d'Arc, Maid of Orleans, 1429-1431*. Shaw was fascinated by the story of the trial, which had never been treated in a play before. The drama was, as it were, ready-made. All he had to do was to disclose it.

Saint Joan consists of six scenes and an epilogue, to which Shaw, as was his custom, later appended a preface. The preface provided him with an opportunity to argue the case for his interpretation of his heroine. In his survey of previous authors, Shaw was both witty and judicious. After noting the curious degeneration in the Joan of Shakespeare or 'pseudo-Shakespeare', he sees Schiller's Joan as 'drowned in a cauldron of raging romance' and is sensible in maintaining that Voltaire's aim was not so much to denigrate Joan as 'to kill with ridicule everything' he 'righteously hated in the institutions of his own day'.[2] He noted that Quicherat's work marked the turning point in imaginative depictions of Joan, for the availability of transcripts of the trial and rehabilitation had also given credibility to Mark Twain's romance, which Shaw disliked for its gentility, and to the rival lives of Anatole France and Andrew Lang.

As a playwright of ideas, Shaw was attracted to the debates over the person and importance of Joan; for him she was a proto-nationalist and a proto-Protestant. But, if his preface is fascinating, it is the variety of styles within the play, its humour, its rapid dialogue that makes it such a convincing play on stage. At the climax of the play he condenses all the interrogations of Joan into one grand enquiry that sets Joan against the court; and the dialogue leads up to a magnificent speech by the Inquisitor, not Cauchon, in which he expounds the terrifying consequences of not condemning the girl he calls a Protestant. What Shaw wished to emphasise was the sweet reasonableness with which Joan was sentenced for being a 'Protestant'. As theatre his idea is a superb invention, as history an invention. His correspondent, the abbess of the Catholic convent of Stanbrook, pointed out, 'Joan more than once appealed from the court to Rome and a Council.' She added graciously: 'There are gifts of wit and wisdom everywhere . . .'[3]

For generations now, some English-speaking theatregoers have known Joan through Shaw's play, but most English speakers, like most French speakers, know her from the cinema. By the First World War Hollywood already ruled the world of film. One of the first films about Joan came in 1897 from the pioneer of silent films Georges Meliès, but the first brash director to see the potential of the subject was Cecil B. de Mille, the man of biblical epics, who adapted Schiller's play for the screen in 1917.

Joan's public life was divided into two parts, the first centring on her time at the French court, at sieges and on the field of battle, the second centring on her imprisonment, trial and death. The first involved external conflicts, the second inner ones. As in Shaw, it is her passion and her death at the stake that have elicited the most impressive work of art-house film directors drawn to Joan's story, the best of whom have worked in France. The greatest of all Johannic films was made in the 1920s by a Dane from a Lutheran background, Carl Theodore Dreyer. For *La Passion de Jeanne d'Arc* (1927–8), Dreyer developed a minimalist technique, not just by concentrating the whole story into the final stages of the trial at Rouen, by using almost no furniture and by eschewing glamorous costumes, but above all by restricting the action largely to the expressions on people's faces. The silence of a silent film is turned into this film's strength. There is just enough dialogue to make sense of the action, and the action is emotional reaction. The heads, with cunning or confused expressions, could come from an etching by Rembrandt; and at the film's heart is the extraordinary acting of the protagonist. Maria Falconetti, the actress who played Joan in her only film role, conveys only a small range of feeling – rapt attention, deep suffering, quiet resignation – but each with almost unbearable intensity. Her judges rail and smirk. At the close, with flames flickering over her body, Joan's face is shown for the last time, her arms clutching a cross, until her face is destroyed by fire.

Dreyer's historical adviser was Pierre Champion, the man who had helped Anatole France. His scholarship, Dreyer's direction and Falconetti's acting set a standard no other early film could approach. At the time it was not a commercial success but with time it has been recognised as a great work of art. In 1995, on the centenary of the invention of cinema, a journalist for the papal paper *Osservatore Romano* named it one of the ten best religious films of all time.

Joan of Arc had become a heroine with universal appeal, accessible to those from Protestant as well as Catholic backgrounds. The papacy, however, although won over to the view of the French Church that Joan was a saint, was unhappy about those who regarded her purely as a political symbol. Pius XI used his training as a librarian and soon had a study full of books by Action Française writers. Of Jacques Bainville, the historian of France, he noted that the chapters on Joan of Arc and the Crusades were inadequate from a religious point of view. Of Maurras himself he said, 'he has a fine mind, one of the finest of our age . . . but he is only a mind. Christ is alien to him . . . [he sees] the Church from outside, not from inside'.[4] His conclusion was that the movement valued politics above religion; and this made its influence insidious. In 1927 he placed the movement under the ban of the Church and its paper on the Index of forbidden reading matter. When, on the national holiday in honour of Joan, Action Française staged its procession, Monseigneur, later Cardinal, Baudrillart, Rector of the Institut Catholique in Paris (one of the most prestigious Catholic institutions of higher learning in France), found it impossible to prevent his students from joining in and so thought of resigning. Soon, however, he had the chance to put forward his own views on Joan. Just before the quincentenary of Joan's execution in Rouen in May 1931, he was one of nine members of the Académie française, along with Marshal Foch, who wrote an essay in a volume called in its 1930 English version *For Joan of Arc*. Baudrillart focused on Joan the Saint.

Baudrillart is impressive on the issue that made Shaw think Joan was a Protestant, her condemnation for seeming to oppose her own, private revelations to the authority of the Church as represented by one ecclesiastical court. Baudrillart counters: 'It suffices that these revelations contain nothing contrary to Catholic doctrine or unworthy of true wisdom. The soul thus favoured, after being sufficiently enlightened, is bound to give them the assent of faith.'[5] He adds that, if normally the Christian ought to consult his or her confessor, it is not an obligation so to do if the Christian soul is morally certain that it is inspired by the Holy Sprit. The Rouen judges had no right to condemn Joan, for her voices commanded nothing against faith, saying only that 'Charles VII's cause was right', nor against morals, since male costume was 'a practical matter, not a rule of conduct'.[6] Finally, if her opinions involved doctrine, Cauchon should have allowed an appeal to the pope.

England and France were now at peace over Joan: it was only the French who quarrelled about her. On the 500th anniversary of Joan of Arc's death in Rouen, on 30 May 1931 the Archbishop of Westminster, head of the English Catholic Church, went to the city to express his great admiration of her virtues. Hilaire Belloc, the leading literary historian among English Catholics, had written a moving life of Joan for English readers that could have been written for his French relations. From 1931 dates an eirenic lecture by an Anglophile French scholar Louis Cazamian, who was asked to deliver the Andrew Lang lecture at St Andrews University. Cazamian was at pains to emphasise the involvement of both nations and their institutions in Joan's fate. 'England and France join in the guilt; they are at one in the homage of admiration and regret. I may be excused if I claim here as a burden of solidarity what is otherwise an honour, membership of the University of Paris: the Sorbonne took the lead among the abettors of the crime, and showed itself, as Andrew Lang puts it, *"capable de tout"*.'[7]

In the same year Maurras gave to his followers an Action Française version of Joan's life. Maurras was correct to stress Joan's loyalty to her king, which he admired, but he downplayed her faith, which he did not share. He was also unrepentant in rejecting the papal view of Joan. His essay on Joan for the 'Association of Young Royalist Ladies' aimed to be political and divisive.

'This heroine of the Nation,' he insisted, 'is not the heroine of Democracy. Was she just a daughter of the people in the sense that she was ignorant and ill educated? Joan stood for three ideas held by the common people of France: the land saved; the country saved; both

saved by royalty re-established.'[8] Maurras contends that these truths
of French politics were part of the story of Joan of Arc, but generally
they were ignored at every feast day of Joan of Arc. Her essential
mission was to save the nation by the office of kingship. She was not
ungrateful to the founding dynasty, whereas those now claiming to be
devoted to her are ungrateful. At the moment the authorities exclude
from her career its political element, the cinema starts to leave out of
her story its religious element. Soldiers admired her fighting capacity.
The principles of her conduct were religious, but her aim was
patriotic. Had circumstances been different, she might have been a
pure republican, but as it was she acted at a time when kings ruled,
when it was important to know who was the true heir of the
Capetians. As a patriot she was a legitimist, and so also the heroine of
the dynasty. She spoke of the sacred rights of the crown and of holy
warfare, she stood above all for the king. She was a soldier in her
reactions, not a liberal, nor a democrat. 'The example of Joan of Arc
leads us to ask for a king who reigns and who governs.'[9]

Maurras was right to maintain that Joan had believed in the
divine authority of her king, but this was a normal belief at the time.
By 1931, however, the regime she took for granted was irrelevant to
France's situation. Joan could not have believed in the Third
Republic, just as she could not have understood what a modern
scholar might tell her, that there is no reliable reason for believing
that 'saints' Margaret and Catherine ever existed. Maurras and
other members of Action Française lived in the past.

Another more profound voice saw in Joan a good reason for not
conforming. If any thought Joan staid in her virtue, then Georges
Bernanos, novelist and polemicist, invoked a fiery heroine. In 1908,
during the heady days of Action Française, Bernanos had taken part in
the scuffles of the Camelots du Roi but, having left the movement, he
made a point of showing how awkward Joan had been. He wrote a
brilliant pamphlet that could be read as a defence of Action Française
against Pius XI's ban but should be read as a defence of nonconformity.

Jeanne, relapse et sainte (1929) takes as its subject the woman,
Joan, who was condemned for heresy, submitted, retracted her
submission, was condemned again as a 'relapsed' heretic and is yet a
saint. Bernanos enjoyed upsetting people; he found it easier to quarrel
than to make up. His tract hammers home one simple message: with
ruthless logic he exposes the evasions of both Joan's enemies and her

friends. After the unjust trial nobody dared to defend her until it was safe to do so. Then, over and over again, he says: 'Our church is the church of saints.'[10] The subtext is, 'but our church also condemns saints' – Bernanos found the idea of being a conventional Catholic unappealing. While in Majorca in 1936, he witnessed the beginning of the Spanish Civil War and he saw how anti-Christian was the behaviour of Catholic nationalists towards their political enemies.

In the same year, the anti-Semitism that had flourished during the Dreyfus affair set on a new target in France, since the new Prime Minister, Léon Blum, was a Jew. The Right saw evidence of a Jewish conspiracy. In Orléans, Joan's city, some leading officials were Jews, so a cruel cartoonist pictured a stained-glass window filled with stars of David.

In 1938, just before the Second World War, there was a remarkable marriage of text and sound when the Swiss composer Arthur Honegger, most serious-minded of the group called Les Six, set words by Paul Claudel to create the oratorio *Jeanne d'Arc au bûcher* ('Joan of Arc at the stake'). Claudel, a devout Catholic, found his ideal match in a Protestant musician; and Honegger called on various Christian traditions in music.

At times in the oratorio, words are spoken, notably by Joan and by Brother Dominic, Joan's chief interlocutor, the same Dominic who had founded the order of Friars Preacher, to which some who had taken part in Joan's trial belonged. This device was taken from Protestant oratorio, as was the use of choral tunes by one part set against elaborate melodies for the other parts (as for example in Bach's Advent cantata *Wachet Auf*, or *Sleepers Wake*). Honegger also uses monastic plainchant, sometimes given to a priest, sometimes to a choir of children, just as Claudel uses dignified liturgical Latin. Dramatist and composer also liked jokes. The variety the two men aimed for may be one reason why the piece is still performed.

Jeanne d'Arc au bûcher is a sort of popular medieval entertainment, a synthesis of spectacle and speech. Like Claudel himself, it is other-worldly, belonging to a world remote from the political concerns of the age; but then Claudel, a former ambassador, with diplomatic flexibility praised Pétain, who accepted defeat in 1940, and de Gaulle, who resisted it; and in this sense his Joan is apolitical. But in the war that followed the figure of Joan became more political than ever before.

TWENTY-FOUR

Vive la France! Vive Jeanne d'Arc!

The spirit of reconciliation that St Joan had brought about in France in 1920 was remarkable, but there were vociferous groups in France that did not want to be reconciled. As French armies were brushed aside in May 1940, many on the French Right assumed that it alone stood for Joan's vision of France. The collapse of the forces of the atheistic republic before the onslaught of Panzers and Stuka bombers proved that if France recovered, that recovery would be thanks to an ageing marshal, Joan's true representative.

The Vichy government over which Pétain presided and which Laval tended to run was meant to stand for French values distinct from those of the republic it had replaced. In the place of the internationalist and universal *Liberté, Egalité et Fraternité* Vichy's motto was the cosy *Travail, Famille, Patrie* (work, home, country). Before the war Pétain approved of conservative movements that defended the family; and like many on the Right he linked attachment to the family with attachment to the soil. When Rouen celebrated Joan's fifth centenary in 1931, he wrote: 'Joan of Arc incarnates patriotism in its most complete sense.' Her great lesson to her own and his fellow countrymen was 'unity in the service of a country'.[1] In 1940 his role would be to foster such unity.

The ethos of the Vichy government opposed the economic, political and social results of modernity. It admired folk song, folk dance, quaint customs, local patois, regional writers. Joan's feast at Orléans was an excuse to praise the Marshal. The preacher in 1941 called Pétain's arrival in the city 'an unexpected joy', as the people cried '*Vive la France! Vive le Maréchal! Vive Jeanne d'Arc!*'

In the First World War Joan's image had been used pictorially and politically to attack the Germans for bombarding Reims and damaging the cathedral where Charles VII had been crowned King of France. In the Second World War the bombing of Rouen was marked by a poster in which a huge figure of Joan wrings her hands over the city where the English had betrayed her twice. On 13 May 1944 a series of posters and stickers appeared with the text: '*Pour que la France vive il faut comme Jeanne d'Arc bouter les Anglais hors d'Europe*' ('So that France may live, like Joan of Arc we must kick the English out of Europe'). When D-Day came, the Marshal spoke of an invasion of the country; and the Free French who joined in the invasion were cast in the role of modern Burgundians. Pétain was too senile to note the paradox that Vichy's Joan was the saint-as-collaborator.

Throughout the war, to lay a wreath at the feet of a statue of Joan of Arc could be seen as an act of patriotic defiance. The annual commemorations of Joan in Chinon always cited her struggles against the English but were construed by some as covert signals of anti-German sentiment. The national festival of Joan of Arc on the Sunday after 8 May might be an excuse for pulling down a swastika flag. As France was progressively freed, former supporters of Vichy took refuge in silence; and the only acceptable idea of Joan became the idea of her held by de Gaulle.

As late as 1942 Jacques Maritain, a French intellectual who took refuge in the United States, told an audience bent on raising money to help the French that 'France ardently desires another Joan of Arc, and she has nobody.'[2] De Gaulle may not have agreed. He was a staunch believer rather than a devout one, but he was sure that in French history he would occupy a special place. Brought up in a royalist family in the north, he was a republican, even if a critic of the republic. In 1940 he fled to England, where with the help of Churchill he broadcast to his fellow countrymen, urging them to resist. At first ignored, he gradually gained sympathy for the cause of the Free French, so that by the time of the D-Day landings he was the only possible leader of a liberated France. Although he never said as much, Joan became the patron saint of resistance.

For de Gaulle the key to France was the love of liberty. Revering the Lorrainer Joan, he chose the cross of Lorraine as his symbol. Family legend had it that Sieur Jehan de Gaulle fought at Agincourt, accompanied Charles VII to Bourges and was one of six men-at-arms who went with Joan to Chinon. De Gaulle's views on the French past were normal for a man born in 1890, but he also had the literary panache to expound these ideas with a fervour that recalls French pulpit oratory. His favourite poet was Charles Péguy, who had spent sixteen years writing about Joan. In exile at the Connaught Hotel in London, de Gaulle received visitors sitting under portraits of Joan and Napoleon. At his first meeting with Roosevelt, he gave the American President a lecture on his vision of French history, describing inspiring people since Charlemagne who had come to the nation's rescue, such as Joan of Arc, Napoleon and Clemenceau (a list which might have included himself). This convinced Roosevelt that de Gaulle was a megalomaniac. He joked that de Gaulle believed that he himself was Joan, a joke the general did not find amusing and never forgave.

It was not only because of a portrait that de Gaulle kept Joan in mind in London. He also referred to her in many of his speeches from London. On 2 July 1940 she was one of that dauntless band who 'would never have agreed to surrender all the arms of France to their enemies so that their enemies could use them against her Allies'. This was a theme he returned to over and over again in the early years of the war. In 1940 the crisis of 1429 had returned. France will recover its sense of national unity as 'in the age of Joan of Arc and in the age of the Revolution'. De Gaulle saved for 10 May 1942, the eve of Joan of Arc's feast, a speech devoted exclusively to her:

> Our meeting is the proof of our hope. We all think today that, if five hundred years ago France discovered in herself, at Joan of Arc's call, the flame needed for her salvation, today she can also rediscover the same flame . . . We wish only to join together our minds and our hearts in unshakeable confidence in the destiny of eternal France.[3]

De Gaulle's Joan of Arc was the Joan both of Michelet and of Péguy. While he venerated her, he had no nostalgia for a purely peasant society. He wanted France to modernise: Joan had used cannon – she had wanted to modernise too. On 25 August 1944 de Gaulle re-entered Paris before the Allies and at once walked through bullets to Notre-Dame to thank God for national deliverance. In his *Memoirs* he noted that the statues of Joan of Arc were still standing.

De Gaulle was a man of the Right, but never of the far Right. When in power from 1944 to 1946 he allowed Maurras to live and was content that Pétain dragged out his last days in a remote gaol. One writer, however, he refused to pardon: in 1941 Robert Brasillach had revised a play on Joan's trial that owes its air of authenticity to a close reading of the actual words Joan had spoken in her French dialect. The first words in his preface to *Le Procès de Jeanne d'Arc* set out his theme:

> The most moving and purest great work of art in the French language has not been written by a man of letters. It is born of the horrid, sad collaboration of a young girl aged 19, visited by angels, and some priests transformed, for the moment, into torturers. Timid legal clerks wrote to dictation, and it is in this way that this stupendous dialogue between Holiness, Cruelty and Weakness, that, while easily surpassing them, brings to life and in the end encapsulates all the fictitious dialogues the allegorical genius of the middle ages had produced . . . Compared with the simplest words of Joan, the most illustrious saints seem like chatter-boxes elaborating on Cicero.[4]

There is no need to discuss the play in detail, for its details were fixed by the documents. All Brasillach had to do was to re-present them. What makes reading his play a sad experience today is the knowledge that the writer was a Nazi supporter, who in the 1930s had been intoxicated by nostalgic dreams of France's past and by an idea of athletic Aryans seen in films patronised by a tiny clever man with a club foot, Josef Goebbels, and most seductively by the beautiful Leni Riefenstahl in *The Triumph of the Will*, her documentary of the 1934 Nuremberg rally. Brasillach was so carried away by his devotion to Joan that he carried with him a picture of an actress playing her, and at the same time he advocated the purging of France's Jews. He had tricked himself into supporting the acceptance of torture he had abhorred in the trial of Joan, so that the man who wrote of the charm of innocence with beguiling fervour fell for a false Messiah. He was sentenced not for anti-Semitism but for treason, and although a petition circulated among writers was signed by both the Catholic Mauriac and the existentialist Camus, de Gaulle refused a pardon and early in 1945 Brasillach was shot. His mother told him he was playing the role of Joan of Arc.

Another artistic figure of the Right lived on to die in peace in 1954. In 1908 the fanatical young monarchist Maxime Réal del Sarte came to prominence by taking part in the attacks on Thalamas and by openly challenging the pardon that had been granted to Dreyfus. He had been trained as a sculptor, and after the First World

War, which left him without a left arm, he became celebrated for a series of public monuments to the dead erected all over France. He also produced several statues of Joan: *Joan of Arc at the Stake*, for place du Vieux-Marché in Rouen (1929); *Joan of Arc Prisoner*, for Arras (1930); *Joan of Arc*, for Domremy (1940). The emphasis on the suffering Joan rather than the triumphant Joan fitted the sombre mood of interwar France. For his work he was given the Légion d'honneur in 1940. Like Brasillach, he has a place of honour in the pantheon of those who inspire the modern far Right.

On 8 May 1945, Joan's French national feast day and the day Europe celebrated VE Day, de Gaulle visited the tomb of a French hero – but it was the tomb of Georges Clemenceau, the Prime Minister who had led France to victory at the end of the First World War.

France had found two saviours, first Marshal Pétain, then General de Gaulle. A clever young boy, with Turkish immigrants parents, was puzzled. Why should his new home have two saviours? Both were soldiers, but one did not want to fight on and the other did – and yet both with equal confidence but not with equal plausibility invoked the blessing of Joan of Arc. Even before the war was over, the boy, Edouard Balladur, was sure that de Gaulle was right and Pétain wrong. It took the appalling experience of subjection to the Nazis for most of the French nation to see too that de Gaulle had been right all along, and at least two generations before most French people have been able to come to terms with the betrayal of quintessentially French ideals that collaboration with the Nazis entailed.

As a boy, Edouard Balladur was astonished that his compatriots held mutually exclusive views of Joan. Now in his seventies, an ex-Prime Minister (1993–5), much respected by the moderate Right, Balladur has tried to explain why the memory of Joan, so vivid in his childhood, has slowly slipped away from national consciousness. For too long, he thinks, France has relied on a myth of the saviour; and the saviour of the nation has often been cast in the mould of Joan. Mature people, however, are self-reliant, and a mature nation too needs to solve its problems itself. In the past France has been both too arrogant and too insecure.

Balladur may be right that Joan has fulfilled her role in French history, and in a period when the French are preoccupied with how to treat their Muslim fellow citizens, how to provide pensions for an ageing population, how to base foreign policy around their relations with Germany, how to preserve French culture, the French language and French cuisine, how to cleanse some local governments of corruption, Joan's call to heroic action may seem irrelevant.

The one party to stick by Joan is the party of the far Right, the Front National (FN), led by Jean-Marie Le Pen. Le Pen is no thug like the leaders of the British National Party. He is versed in the tradition he stands for: his website refers to Maurras, Brasillach and Réal del Sarte; he is a demagogue, with honed rhetorical skills, at turns noble, sarcastic and grandiloquent. Every 1 May members of the FN meet in front of Fremiet's girl-warrior in place des Pyramides, to be harangued by Le Pen. These meetings are the only political rallies in modern France that invoke the spirit of St Joan. Le Pen's addresses begin with an evocation of Joan's remarkable life before he launches into an attack on the euro, the European Union, immigration, the erosion of French sovereignty – and he is contemptuous of President Chirac. At the last presidential election Le Pen was the alternative candidate to Chirac in the final round of voting, and he gained about 20 per cent of the vote, which probably represents the support he can expect from a worried electorate.

For Le Pen Joan is the emblem of a finer France, when first the non-French, then the English, recently the Jews and now the Muslims are booted out back to their own country, while society is stable, jobs secure, France free. To some this is a seductive ideal.

TWENTY-FIVE

St Joan: A Modern Heroine?

THE LATE FRENCH CATHOLIC REVIVAL
In 1961 a French lay philosopher and theologian subjected Joan to a rigorous analysis. His slim book is a reminder that Joan took to politics because of her faith.

According to Jean Guitton, Joan presents the enquirer into her life with a 'problem' and a 'mystery'. If the trouble with Michelet, Guitton says, is that he reduces Joan to a myth, the weakness of Anatole France is that he reduces her to a nonentity, so that there is no need to ask how her success is related to her faith. For Guitton the essential problem with the story of Joan is that historical method as such is inadequate for the task of evaluating her: no scanning of sources, for example, provides adequate material to answer the question 'were her voices true?' Guitton claims that for Joan the voices were true, but that no one who shares her belief can explain why someone who does not believe in them is wrong; on the other hand, the sceptic cannot prove that one who believes in them is wrong; and for the sceptic there is the additional problem that often what her voices told her was no illusion. She did save Orléans, she did bring about the coronation of her Dauphin as king at Reims before she was tried, and after her trial her Duke of Orléans and France were freed from the English. Joan is a historical figure who exists beyond history. Part of her 'mystery' is that she did not view her voices with detachment. To her the experience was clear. What muddled her was the attempt of her judges to make her experience comprehensible to them. But her voices were not akin to the experiences described by later mystical theologians such as Teresa of Avila and John of the Cross, since what they describe was remote from Joan's sense of persistent contact with angels and saints. Her voices did not tell her sublime truths, but simply what to do or not to do, and what would happen; and sometimes what she thought they said turned out to be wrong or misleading. She seems to have been convinced that she would be saved from prison, but she was not. She faltered in her belief in her voices; and yet in the end she died for believing in them.

There is an additional problem about the voices that Guitton touches on. Even Joan's admirers like Michelet and Lang had not known what to make of them; and those assessing her during the process of canonisation had wondered whether she was hysterical. Today hallucinations are normally regarded as signs of schizophrenia. The problem, Guitton notes, is that psychiatrists relate psychological phenomena such as the hearing of voices to the onset of psychosis. But Joan was remarkably sane; and nobody has a theory of how a sane person can hallucinate. For modern scientists Joan's voices are a problem; for the student of Joan, they are a mystery.

One trait that separates her from the standard spirituality of her day is that she thought of her religion in terms appropriate only to a lay person; her mission involved civic duty and a political programme; almost everything written on Christian devotion, however, was predicated on a life that was essentially monastic. Joan lived, it is true, at a moment of cultural change. She was at the beginning of adult feminine life. As discovered again and again, she remained a virgin; and it is as a virgin that she is ranked among the saints of the Catholic Church. Joan was not without faults. She was too fond of martial glamour; she could be manic; she could be hectoring.

Guitton asserts that, just as Aristotle became more important in the thirteenth century AD than he was in the fourth century BC, so Joan has become more important in the twentieth century than she was in the fifteenth. In her own lifetime her case forced the Church to look at its inquisitorial processes and the king to ponder the justification of his authority. Now it forces the French to redefine their sense of national destiny and the Church to re-examine its ideas on sanctity. In 1963, soon after Guitton wrote his book, a personal friend succeeded John XXIII as Pope Paul VI, and so Guitton had a semi-official position within the Church.

In the early years of the new pontificate an even more eminent lay philosophical theologian, Jacques Maritain, was able to write with greater freedom than had been possible about the historical record of the Catholic Church. His book *The Church of Christ* (1970) has a long section confronting difficulties from the past: the Crusades; the treatment of the Jews; the role of the Inquisition; and finally two test cases, the condemnation of Galileo and the condemnation of Joan. His verdict on Joan is that her story is 'the most extraordinary of Christian times'. Her mission is universal. 'I think,' he adds at the end, 'that Joan of Arc . . . is *par excellence* the saint and the patron of the temporal mission of the Christian, in other words the saint and patron of the Christian laity.'[1]

Guitton and Maritain were among the last of their kind. They were writing towards the end of the Catholic revival in France, which had embraced intellectuals and artists of all kinds. Maritain, for example, championed Modernist Christian art as evident in Georges Rouault, whose tiny *Notre Jeanne* (1940–8) expresses in stark design and rich colours the isolation of a saint. Joan, defined with thick lines that recall the outlines of stained glass, dominates a desolate landscape whose only notable feature is a distant church. Oblivious to what surrounds her, with head raised to look at her banner and surrounded by a ring of light like a halo, she rides towards her unknown destiny.

If Rouault's Joan was aloof, detachment was the way of one of France's finest film directors. Robert Bresson emphasised the religious meaning of Joan's story in *Le Procès de Jeanne d'Arc* (*The Trial of Joan of Arc*, 1962). Obsessed with the workings of God's grace, a preacher of a self-effacing kind, he indicated a story's meaning in its unfolding. Long after colour film had become the norm, he stuck to black and white camera work because that technique uses subtlety of tone instead of a kaleidoscope of colours. He reduced his plot to essentials, for like Dreyer he understood the advantages of classical drama unified by action, time and place. Scrupulously accurate, he based his screenplay on fifteenth-century documents. His Joan of Arc is sharper in her replies than Dreyer's Joan and more remote. Spied at through keyholes, she is watched relentlessly in one long act of voyeurism. For this reason the spectator too is detached, so that Joan (played by Florence Carrez, now a well-known writer) is a model to be admired rather than pitied – that is, until the body is burnt to nothing and her chains of imprisonment are left hanging from the stake; and then and then only, is she free.

Shaw exaggerated when he argued that Joan was a proto-Protestant. In the fifteenth century, Europe defined as a Latinate, clerical, international order was beginning to die. By the twenty-first century that order is virtually moribund. It is noticeable how many from

Protestant backgrounds, such as Shaw himself, Dreyer and Honegger have found Joan an inspiration to their art. Even the Catholics Bernanos and Bresson were so keen to draw attention to the workings of God's grace that they seemed more sympathetic than many fellow Catholics to the views of Luther and Calvin. In the light of the Second Vatican Council it is possibly to maintain that Joan has taught many Catholics the truths dear to Protestants. Religious wars are over.

Joan's Church claimed to be universal, but to say that she can be a patron of freedom for all would have seemed extraordinary before the 1960s. After the Second World War, first the United Nations, then European countries, then the Catholic Church affirmed the concept of universal human rights. By 1970 the Catholic Maritain stated that Joan's role has a universal meaning. For most French people, however, Joan is still primarily a symbol of their common national destiny, but as the memory of war recedes, her kind of patriotic appeal wanes. In the festivities at Orléans she has been honoured by presidents of Left and Right, by believing and non-believing presidents. In this sense she does not belong to any one faction. In an address at Orléans, Michel Rocard, Prime Minister from 1988 to 1991 and at one time the most popular socialist in France, compared Joan to famous figures like Mother Teresa, Lech Walesa or Nelson Mandela. But Joan has steadily drifted from the forefront of French minds. In 1948 11 per cent of those asked put her in a list of famous French men and women; in 1980 that figure was 2 per cent, in 1989 zero per cent. She is no longer the model for enterprising and modern girls. Marie Curie, a physicist who won two Nobel prizes and was an atheist, is now regarded as a more inspiring figure from the past, and her past is more recent. Thanks in part to André Malraux, the novelist and art historian who became de Gaulle's Minister of Culture, the Centre Jeanne d'Arc was founded in Orléans as an international centre of Johannic studies; and partly thanks to such official approval, French Johannic scholarship operates at the highest level. The French people in general, however, take Joan for granted, and the young scarcely know her. An ironic result is that Joan has become relatively more important in the English-speaking world, partly because English (usually American-English) preoccupations dominate popular culture. 'Anglo-Saxon' Joan is known through films and through university departments of women's studies.

JOAN IN HOLLYWOOD

In the 1930s, Joan intrigued English literary historians such as Vita Sackville-West. While taking care to consult the Jesuit scholar Father Thurston, who had written about Joan thirty years earlier, Sackville-West tried to understand Joan, if she shared none of Joan's Catholic assumptions. The same may be said of Edward Lucie-Smith in recent times. English professional historians who specialise in fifteenth-century studies tend to view Joan sceptically.

None of these writers has had any influence comparable to that exercised by popular drama. Jean Anouilh's delightful *L'Alouette* (*The Lark*, 1953) certainly set up some cultural ripples. As an artistic construct the play makes clever use of flashbacks, but as history it is flawed since Anouilh followed Voltaire in introducing Charles's mistress Agnès Sorel into the story. Besides, whimsically he allows Joan to be put on trial but not to be burnt, as 'the story of Joan of Arc is a story that ends well'.[2] Films, the more populist dramatic form, are made of sterner stuff.

The great years of blockbuster Joans came soon after 1945. For fifteen years, costume epic flourished, until the rising costs of extras and the competition of television, with its leaning towards intimate drama, forced studios to cut back on sumptuous productions. In this golden age of 'Medieval' Joan, Ingrid Bergman played Joan twice, once with Victor Fleming in 1948 (based on a Maxwell Anderson play in which she had played in New York), and once with her lover Roberto Rossellini in 1954 (based on Claudel). Bergman was too majestic, and yet in the end Fleming's is still the most successful Hollywood version of the Maid, and Bergman remains Hollywood's Joan; if the film shows how limited is the genre when treating a spiritual theme, then the audience did not object. *Joan of Arc* won Oscars for costume and photography; a special award went to the producer Walter Wanger for adding to the industry's 'moral stature in the world'; and Jose Ferrer (who played the Dauphin) and Bergman won Oscar nominations. As for Fleming, he owes lasting fame to *Gone with the Wind* and *The Wizard of Oz*, rather than to his last film, *Joan of Arc*.

Not until 1957 was a boyish Joan shown in film. In that year Otto Preminger asked Graham Greene to revise Shaw's text (with, in French, subtitles by Anouilh). Preminger looked for the perfect Joan and came up with an amateur actress, the *gamine* Jean Seberg, who sadly lacked the appropriate personality. 'I always wanted to make a picture of it,' Preminger told Bogdanovich, the film critic and director. 'I loved the play so much that I didn't analyse it. I realised only later that the play is actually a very intellectual, analytical rendition of the story of St Joan. It's not an emotional story, and it just wasn't moving enough to get the masses to follow. Even the play, as I found out later, was never a big popular success.'[3] Joan had been portrayed as a new woman, but did not fit into the New Wave, the movement in French film direction that began in the late 1950s.

Authenticity inspired a very late New Wave account of Joan's career, trial and death in Jacques Rivette's 1994 *Jeanne la Pucelle*, a version of the life that opted for comprehensiveness. Like many attracted to Joan of Arc, Rivette had read Péguy and saw that the real events of her life were so dramatic that there was no need to invent. His chief actress Sandrine Bonnaire was no mere amateur. Those with time to spare for a six-hour, two-part film may find her riveting. Some like their films cut, and *Joan the Maid* makes Luc Besson's long-winded *The Messenger* (1999) seem short.

Besson has emigrated from France to Hollywood, and in *The Messenger* he brought Hollywood to France – and French audiences loved it. The film won eight nominations from the French Academy of Cinema and took the prize for cinema photography. It aimed to replace Joan the saint with Joan the soldier, but it was not only the restricted range of Milla Jovovich that damns the film: despite its international cast, Besson's view of Joan is chauvinistic. The film starts with a scene of rape in Domremy that leads to the murder of Joan's sister by an English soldier, while historically, the 'foreigners' who went to Domremy were Burgundians. Besson glosses over the truth that Joan's captors and all her judges were French; and so he gives the English actor Timothy West the part of Cauchon. One overt nationalist, Le Pen, admits that the film misleads. Even in fiction Joan deserves the truth.

At least Besson has shown that Joan can be commercial. He also saw the potential of playing on the morbid fascination of unhealthy psychology. His Joan is hysterical, not just when she is having visions but also when arguing or fighting or encouraging others to fight. A century earlier the great actress Sarah Bernhardt, who attended Charcot's public lectures, had studied photos of hysterics before performing in a play on Joan at Domremy by Jules Barbier.

Even Sybil Thorndike, Shaw's first Joan, thought that because she did not menstruate, Joan must have been an hysteric. Poor d'Aulon has never known what trouble his single sentence has caused.

JOAN AND HER SISTERS

Joan challenges the way in which women are perceived. Not until 1912, in the annual festival at Orléans, did a girl play the role of Joan. The First World War gave women a sense of freedom, and since 1945 women have become more prominent in public life, above all in the United States. Not only teenage girls in Orléans compete for the thrill of being Joan, actresses from Bernhardt to Bergman and women politicians feel compelled to play the part, for Joan opened a new way for women to act.

If 'new women' were boyish, then Joan's boyishness became easier to understand: her cropped hairdo was 'sensible', her male clothes fashionable – so much more practical than the dresses with long trains worn by the ladies at court – and presumably she never rode side-saddle. Shaw put a modern girl on stage and cinema heroines set a new style.

Views of Joan have changed as views of women have changed. It is tempting to think of Joan as fitting a feminist archetype, as a young woman who, like some redoubtable actresses who have played her, enjoyed wearing trousers. And yet since her canonisation, the world has changed more slowly than some commentators think. The emancipation Joan stood for was never freedom from Christian morality, only freedom from foreign rule. This is not to deny that in the context of the fifteenth century she defied ordinary conventions of female behaviour in dress and behaviour.

Joan's contemporaries were familiar with prophetesses like Catherine of Siena, with women who wielded power as royal consorts or as mothers of kings and, if rarely, in their own name or even, as in the case of Christine de Pisan, as educated writers; but a woman warrior, familiar to fiction, was unfamiliar in fact. Nobody's interpretation of Joan is fixed in stone. Shaw asserts in his preface that Anatole France was 'a Parisian of the art world' who did not know any of the 'hard-headed, hard-handed' women who run business Paris and provincial France.[4] Shaw was perhaps unkind, but his wit was acute.

Another, more subtle error was committed by suffragettes who saw Christabel Pankhurst in the line of Joan, and much the same error is committed by Bertold Brecht in his play *Joan Darc* (*Saint Joan of the Stockyards*, 1932), where Joan Dark is transmuted into a Salvation Army girl fighting injustice in Chicago meat factories. In each case Joan is just the outspoken woman who demands to exercise a function, as voter or union agitator, conventionally allotted to men. This Joan was a fearless woman in pursuit of a moral goal. But the real Joan was much more. She was a girl-woman following a mission she was believed was God-given.

Radical changes in the status of women during the nineteenth and twentieth centuries have meant that Joan, exceptional in her own day, is easier to understand in our own. At universities, above all in America, the academic discipline of Women's Studies has developed in the context of the feminist movement. Medievalists are familiar with the singing nun Hildegard of Bingen as well as the travails of those accused of witchcraft, most of whom were women. Female mystics achieved a new influence in the fourteenth and fifteenth centuries, but Joan was exceptional. Kelly DeVries has shown that at the time there were no other noted female soldiers; and yet Joan was no Amazon in either the ancient or the modern sense.

The word 'extraordinary' needs to be emphasised. Joan's clerical judges in Rouen had probably never met a woman who wore men's clothes. They expected a man to wear clothing that indicated his status in society, his occupation, his wealth and, not having ever met a female soldier, they assumed that Joan was either the sort of girl who likes to be with soldiers, or else a freak, like a witch or a sorceress, which meant that she was by definition unnatural – and so in either case offensive to God and the Church. Was she a freak of nature? Some have thought that d'Aulon's one remark about not knowing the malady of women meant that she was, in a biological sense, not truly female; and yet any view about her femininity is a guess.

Few at present would deny that in the past, history has been viewed in terms of the deeds of men. Furthermore, most historical documents have been written by men for men to read. Women's activities have therefore been seen as ancillary. Such assertions have always been part of the truth, but never the whole of the truth, and in fifteenth-century France, when the literate were mostly men except perhaps in noble households, most political power was held by men, men fought the battles that decided the fate of their nations or at least of their lords, men drew up the charters that recorded rights and men alone went to universities, then it might seem that the role of women scarcely mattered. But Joan challenged normal expectations, those of her father, who expected her to stay at home until she was married, those of Robert de Baudricourt, who wanted her to return home, those of courtiers who took it for granted that they alone should run the affairs of the kingdom, those of priests who thought they alone should interpret the will of God. She elicited some sympathy from ladies of the court, just as she elicited some from the good bourgeois of Orléans or from noble ladies when a captive. What might surprise us is that she found men who believed in her mission – her page, her steward, her chaplain, her companions in arms, notably the Bastard of Orléans and the Duke of Alençon – and she was able to convince the theologians of Poitiers and even the suspicious Charles VII that she might be trustworthy.

What would surprise her is that over 550 years since the nullification processes she has been taken up by learned people drawn from her own sex, that she is now a figure of universal significance as a feminist model, if not a model feminist. As joint editor (with a man) of an academic discussion of Joan of Arc, one in a series of books on the Middle Ages that deals with 'women's history and feminist and gender analyses', Bonnie Wheeler states that: 'Joan proves that self-confidence and independent judgement are qualities so rare and suspect, especially in women, that they are sure to be punished, sometimes by death.'[5] The most intelligent of recent English studies of Joan, by Marina Warner, is subtitled 'the image of female heroism'. Most, but not all, Bonnie Wheeler's research has centred on women, for instance on Eleanor of Aquitaine, wife of a king of France and of a king of England, on Héloise, nun and ex-lover of the theologian Abélard, on women in Arthurian literature, on medieval mothering, on representations of the feminine, on Muslim women. So, too, Marina Warner has written with elegance and erudition on the Virgin Mary, on fairy-tale women and on *Monuments and Maidens*. Such female scholars may well have insights and qualities rare in male professors; if only for this reason their verdicts on Joan of Arc would deserve respect, were it not that they also compete with men on equal terms. And yet it is possible for a male author to say that Bonnie Wheeler is wrong in saying Joan died because she was forceful.

Joan was punished because she asserted she was told by saintly and angelic voices that she must instruct the King of France to take back his lands from the King of England, who was to return to his own land, and that to fulfil this heavenly mission she was to dress in men's clothing, usually armour, since her role as a leader of men was singular. In her society it was men she led, men who tried her; and, while some condemned and some doubted her, others were her enthusiastic devotees.

EPILOGUE

St Joan in Orléans

Debates continue; women's studies in the United States will be ever more refined; but whoever wishes to understand the continuing appeal of Joan of Arc must make for Orléans.

On the evening of the first or occasionally the second Friday in May, a crowd converges on the cathedral of Ste-Croix. Although there have been continuous festivities of some sort since the end of April – when a girl chosen in alternate years from a Catholic college and a secular lycée rides into the city – serious enjoyment has only just begun. Bands of young people clad in coats of many colours from all over Europe play outside the fine Renaissance hotel that is the Hôtel de Ville, at whose entrance stands a bronze replica of the quiet, meditative statue of Joan carved by Marie d'Orléans, daughter of the citizen-king Louis-Philippe. At the end comes the band of the stolid folk of Orléans, with comfortable bellies on which to rest their little, high-pitched drums.

This concert is the *entrée*. The *chef d'oeuvre* is a *son et lumière* spectacle, a style of show the French have made their own. As night falls, sonorous speeches by Monsieur le Maire and Monseigneur l'Evêque are lost in the wind, but as their public rhetoric gives way to professional singing and an actor's commentary, an amazing sequence of pictures are projected onto the façade of the cathedral and all present crane their necks upwards to watch the familiar story re-presented and to learn yet again how a teenage girl had inspired the city's relief. Darkness returns and Orléans has just begun to celebrate the 570th and something anniversary of the singular triumph of Orléans's own Maid.

On the morning of the official 8 May national holiday, the principal event is High Mass in the cathedral. In the nave hang the escutcheons of Joan's companions, among them the arms of Gilles de Rais (who was nicknamed either *Barbe bleu* or *Barbe bleue*),

Etienne de Vignolles, known as La Hire, Poton de Xaintrailles, the obscure Florent d'Illiers and, chief of all, those of royal blood: the Duke and the Bastard of Orléans and Joan's *beau duc*, the Duke of Alençon. After Mass, the first of the processions due that day file past, the procession of the provinces of France. In the afternoon, the armed forces and the dignitaries go on longer circuits, which like the morning's parade also lead to place du Martroi, centred on Foyatier's statue. That occasion is more serious, for behind the fighting men in uniform on foot and in motorised transport come robed figures of the administration, the law, the university and the clergy – France is a country that loves to honour the professions – and fittingly the place of honour is taken not by an ecclesiastical figure but by a political grandee, though none was as grand as President Mitterrand, who came twice, in this way symbolising secular and republican reconciliation with France's Catholic and royalist past. Elsewhere in the city, medieval banquets, markets, dances and jousts, jugglers and minstrels bring excitement to the Sunday. Since the Second World War, presidents, prime ministers and, recently, distinguished women such as Bernadette Chirac or Régine Pernoud, have led the celebrations. The wily Le Pen has harangued his followers on 1 May in place des Pyramides in Paris, beside Fremiet's statue of Joan; and on 30 May the Church will venerate Joan's death in Rouen. The events in Orléans, however, are meant to unite not to divide: all the French, all nations are welcome; and, radiant in the rain, a seventeen-year-old girl with two pages beside her reminds everyone that there is no honour equal to that of playing Joan.

Orléans always has been the place where Joan is most cherished. Shortly after the festivities a producer may put on the plays about Joan by Ste Thérèse of Lisieux. During the festivities guides at the Maison de Jeanne d'Arc – not really her house, which was destroyed in the last war – greet visitors in medieval dress. A few metres' stroll on foot would take the idle tourist to the Musée Charles Péguy, devoted to Orléans's finest poet, who worked out his religious, political and ethical convictions by writing about her.

In the grand street of rue Jeanne d'Arc, which leads up to the cathedral, the closed doors of the Collège Bailly conceal the entrance to the Centre Jeanne d'Arc, which has the best collection anywhere of material related to Joan, based on the extensive holdings of

Régine Pernoud, doyenne of Johannic studies. Prominent in the cathedral are the tombs of Bishop Dupanloup and Cardinal Touchet, the men chiefly responsible for the first and the last steps in her canonisation; in the south aisle a series of fine stained-glass windows just over a hundred years old make her tale shine in the light; and in the old *quartier* to the south, the deconsecrated church of St-Pierre-le-Puellier, once the church dear to Joan's mother in her old age, has been used to mount a retrospective exhibition of the modern pageants. The oddest poster was printed in anticipation of an event that never occurred, when in 1946 de Gaulle was invited to come to Orléans. He did not turn up until 1959, after receiving a second invitation. In the 1946 picture the silhouette of his great nose and massive body dwarfs the figure that stands in for Joan – but in reality, Joan made even that great man feel small.

The celebrant at Mass in 2004, the Archbishop of Tours, metropolitan of central France, preached on the theme of national reconciliation brought to France by Joan's canonisation, and as the Mass was introduced in five European languages care was taken to stress her international role. In 2005 the celebrant was the Archbishop of Barcelona. In such ways, somewhat incongruously, Joan has become a symbol of reconciliation in Europe – but then a myth is nothing if not adaptable. And as a myth 'Joan' stands for virtues that were too long neglected in past struggles between European nations. In 2005, 8 May was also the sixtieth anniversary of the ending of the Second World War in Europe. 2004 was the centenary of the Entente Cordiale, 2005 the centenary of the French secular State. Such events are reminders that however much historians dispute her importance in her lifetime or however much she has puzzled theologians and psychologists – or however hard it is to identify a just cause for warfare – Joan has come into her own only in a world she could not have imagined, where there is no chance that France will ever have a king again, where France and England still quarrel, but only over how much each contributes to a common budget or how close each country should be to the United States, not over who has a right to rule France. Joan of Arc still matters, since in her story Church and country, myth and history intersect.

GENEALOGICAL TABLES

1. Valois and Plantagenet

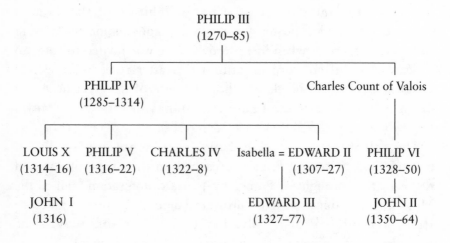

PHILIP III
(1270–85)

PHILIP IV
(1285–1314)

Charles Count of Valois

LOUIS X   PHILIP V   CHARLES IV   Isabella = EDWARD II   PHILIP VI
(1314–16)   (1316–22)   (1322–8)   (1307–27)   (1328–50)

JOHN I   EDWARD III   JOHN II
(1316)   (1327–77)   (1350–64)

2. *Descendants of Edward III*

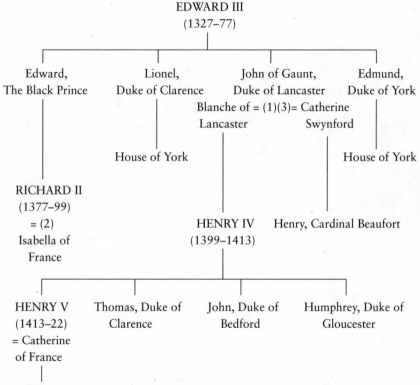

EDWARD III
(1327–77)

Edward,
The Black Prince

Lionel,
Duke of Clarence

John of Gaunt,
Duke of Lancaster

Edmund,
Duke of York

Blanche of = (1)(3)= Catherine
Lancaster   Swynford

House of York

House of York

RICHARD II
(1377–99)
= (2)
Isabella of
France

HENRY IV
(1399–1413)

Henry, Cardinal Beaufort

HENRY V
(1413–22)
= Catherine
of France

Thomas, Duke of
Clarence

John, Duke of
Bedford

Humphrey, Duke of
Gloucester

HENRY VI = Margaret of Anjou

3. Descendants of John II

JOHN II
(1350–64)

CHARLES V
(1364–80)

LOUIS I
Duke of Anjou

JOHN
Duke of Berry

Philip the Bold
Duke of Burgundy
+1404

CHARLES VI
(1380–1422)
= Isabella of
Bavaria

Louis
Duke of
Orléans
+ 1407
|
See table 4

Louis II
Duke of Anjou

Bonne = Bertrand VII
Count of Armagnac
|
See table 4

John the Fearless
Duke of Burgundy
+1419

Charles VII = Marie of
(1422–61)   Anjou

René Duke
of Anjou

Philip the Good
Duke of Burgundy
+1467

LOUIS XI
(1461–83)
–
CHARLES VIII
(1483–98)

Isabella
(1)=(2) RICHARD II (1)
Anne of Bohemia

Catherine = HENRY V

(2)=(1) Charles
Duke of Orléans
|
See table 4

HENRY VI = Margaret of Anjou

4. *Orleanist Connections*

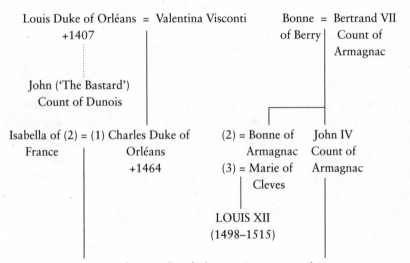

Louis Duke of Orléans = Valentina Visconti   Bonne = Bertrand VII
        +1407   of Berry   Count of
                                                            Armagnac

John ('The Bastard')
  Count of Dunois

Isabella of (2) = (1) Charles Duke of   (2) = Bonne of   John IV
  France   Orléans   Armagnac   Count of
                      +1464   (3) = Marie of   Armagnac
                                                 Cleves

                      LOUIS XII
                      (1498–1515)

        Joan = (1) John II Duke of Alençon (2) = Marie of Armagnac

Notes

The chief source of information 150 years after its publication is Jules Quicherat (ed.), *Procès de condamnation et de réhabilitation de Jeanne d'Arc, dite La Pucelle: publiés pour la première fois d'après les manuscrits de la Bibliothèque royale, suivis de tous les documents historiques qu'on a pu réunir, et accompagnés de notes et d'éclaircissements* (J. Renouard, Paris, 1841–9). Since the end of the royal monarchy the Bibliothèque *royale* has become *nationale*; and other manuscripts have been found elsewhere. Quicherat's volumes treat of: vol. 1, the process of condemnation; vol. 2, the preliminaries to the process of rehabilitation not used in the eventual process, chapters 1–4 of the process; vol. 3, the process continued, chapters 5–9; opinions published in Joan's life; vol. 4, chroniclers and historians of the fifteenth century; vol. 5, contemporary poets, documents, etc.

The first three volumes of Quicherat have been almost replaced by two more editions: Pierre Tisset and Yvonne Lanhers (eds), *Jeanne, d'Arc, Procès de condamnation*, vols 1–3 (C. Klincksieck, Paris, 1960, 1970, 1971). These books deal with the 1431 trial. P. Duparc (ed.), *Procès en nullité de la condamnation*, vols 1–4 (C. Klincksieck, Paris, 1977, 1979, 1983, 1986, 1988). These deal with most of the process Duparc calls a process of nullification, but some of the material in Quicherat is not included.

English translations are available on the Internet and, until I had access to the three editions mentioned above, I had to rely on such translations. Their style is dated and in the case of the process of nullification they conceal the boring way in which the evidence was recorded by trained lawyers; and they omit passages – in the case of d'Aulon a crucial passage that was thought indelicate. I have tried to bring the translations into line with the originals, but it is often hard to change words. If Joan was called '*perniciosa, seditiosa et haeretica*', it is difficult to avoid saying that she was considered 'pernicious, seditious and a (or an) heretic'. For her original French there is no substitute.

For anyone with the time and the requisite languages, the discussions on the documents in Quicherat, Tisset and Lanhers, and Duparc are well worth reading.

Between the First and Second World wars, the leading Johannic scholar, an expert on the whole period of Valois rule, was Pierre Champion. He edited the nullification trial documents, which he called, as was normal then, the rehabilitation trial. He also wrote a specialised study of the fifteenth-century documents for a series called the Bibliothèque du XVe siècle: *Notice des manuscrits du Procès de réhabilitation de Janne d'Arc* (Bibliothèque du XVe siècle, Paris, 1930).

Prologue: the Limits of History

1   For this and what follows, see Pierre Tisset and Yvonne Lanhers (eds), *Jeanne d'Arc, Procès de condamnation*, vol. 1 (C. Klincksieck, Paris, 1960).
2   In the chapter 'The Wicked Womb' of *The Female Eunuch* (Flamingo Harper Collins, London, 2003, pp. 54–6) Germaine Greer discusses the classical and Renaissance theory of hysteria, which influenced early psychoanalysis. For the discussion of possible signs of hysteria in Joan see below.

PART ONE: THE MAID IN LIFE AND DEATH

1: A Prophetess to the Rescue

1   Pierre Tisset and Yvonne Lanhers (eds), *Jeanne, d'Arc, Procès de condamnation*, vol. 1 (C. Klincksieck, Paris, 1960). TLI, pp. 221–2l.
2   Jules Quicherat (ed.), *Procès de condamnation et de réhabilitation de Jeanne d'Arc, dite La Pucelle: publiés pour la première fois d'après les manuscrits de la Bibliothèque royale, suivis de tous les documents historiques qu'on a pu réunir, et accompagnés de notes et éclaircissements*, vol. 5 (J. Renouard, Paris, 1849), pp. 156–9. The text is in German; Quicherat thought it was translated from Latin. A Latin original has been found.
3   P. Duparc (ed.), *Procès en nullité de la condamnation*, vol. 4, p. 472.
4   Quicherat (ed.), *Procès de condamnation*, vol. 4, p. 503. The Inquisitor's name was Johann Nider.
5   Desmond Seward, *The Hundred Years War* (London, Constable, 1996, pp. 6–17).

2: *What Need of the Maid?*

1   Duparc (ed.), *Procès en nullité de la condamnation*, vol. 1, p. 296.

3: *Victory at Orléans and Reims*

1   Duparc (ed.), *Procès en nullité de la condamnation*, vol. 1, p. 318.
2   Quicherat (ed.), *Procès de condamnation*, vol. 4, p. 165.
3   *Ibid.*, vol. 4, p. 12.
4   Duparc (ed.), *Procès en nullité de la condamnation*, vol. 1, p. 385.
5   Quicherat (ed.), *Procès de condamnation*, vol. 5, pp. 287–8.
6   For here and what follows, see *ibid.*, vol. 4.

4: *Defeats and Capture*

1   Quicherat (ed.), *Procès de condamnation*, vol. 5, pp. 96–8.

5: *Coming to Trial*

1   Quicherat (ed.), *Procès de condamnation*, vol. 5, p. 167.

6: *The Preparatory Trial*

1   For here and what follows, see Duparc (ed.), *Procès en nullité de la condamnation*, vol. 1.

7: *The Ordinary Trial*

1   For here and what follows, see Duparc (ed.), *Procès en nullité de la condamnation*, vol. 1.

8: *The Maid's Death*

1   For here and what follows, see Duparc (ed.), *Procès en nullité de la condamnation*, vol. 1.

PART TWO: THE MAID VINDICATED

9: *The King on Trial*

1   This is based on the 1623 Folio text of *Henry V*, Act 4, scene 1, 244–6, 264–75.

10: National Salvation

1   Quicherat (ed.), *Procès de condamnation*, vol. 3, p. 391.

2   *Ibid.*, vol. 4, p. 156.

3   *Ibid.*, vol. 3, p. 392.

4   Duparc (ed.), *Procès en nullité de la condamnation*, vol. 2, p. 208. This quotation comes from a disquisition by Thomas Basin, a contemporary of Joan who was an eminent Church and civil lawyer, Bishop of Lisieux and critical biographer of Charles VII. The context of the quotation is a discussion of Joan's use of male costume, which shows that in order to defend Joan's behaviour a favourable cleric had to have recourse to a careful distinction between the public law of God, which applies to everyone, and the private law of God, which applies to a particular holy individual. This distinction is already present in the theology of the most influential of all medieval theologians, St Thomas Aquinas. See the essay by Jane Marie Pinzino in the collection of essays edited by Ann W. Astell and Bonnie Wheeler, *Joan of Arc and Spirituality* (Basingstoke and New York, Palgrave Macmillan, 2003).

11: The Alliance of 1435

1   As Joan's life on earth moved to its close, in Ghent van Eyck had been finishing off his brother's vision of heaven, *The Adoration of the Lamb*.

2   Duparc (ed.), *Procès en nullité de la condamnation*, vol. 1, p. 388.

13: Voices in Defence

1   For this and following quotations from Christine de Pisan, see Angus J. Kennedy, and Kenneth Varty (eds), *Christine de Pisan, Ditié de Jehanne d'Arc* (Oxford, Oxford University Press, 1977).

15: Witnesses to the Life

1   For this and what follows, see Duparc (ed.), *Procès en nullité de la condamnation*, vol. 1.

16: Witnesses to the Trial

1   For this and what follows, see Quicherat, (ed.), *Procès de condamnation*, vol. 2.

2   For this and what follows, see Duparc (ed.), *Procès en nullité de la condamnation*, vol. 1.

17: *Verdict and Rehabilitation*

1 Duparc (ed.), *Procès en nullité de la condamnation*, vol. 1.
2 François Villon, *Ballade des Dames du Temps Jadis*, in Lucas, St John, *The Oxford Book of French Verse* (Oxford, Clarendon Press, 1908), p. 31.

PART 3: THE CULT OF THE MAID

18: *History, Legend and Myth*

1 See G.B. Shaw, *Saint Joan* (London, Penguin, 2001), preface, pp. 19, 23–4.
2 See www.scuttlebuttsmallchow.com/joanarc.hltm on the subject of Americans and Joan of Arc in the First World War.
3 Louis-Maurice Boutet de Monvel, *Jeanne d'Arc* (Paris, Plon-Nourrit, 1896).

19: *Early Accounts, Partial Histories*

1 For this and what follows, see Quicherat (ed.), *Procès de condamnation*.
2 Daniel Rankin and Claire Quintal (trans.), *The First Biography of Joan of Arc: with the Chronicle Record of a Contemporary Account* (Pittsburgh, University of Pittsburgh, 1964), pp. 54–64.
3 Dominique Goy-Blanquet in *idem* (ed.), *Joan of Arc, a Saint for all Seasons* (Aldershot, Hampshire and Burlington, Vermont, 2003) p. 9.

20: *Reinventing the Maid*

1 Holinshed, in Geoffrey Bullough (ed.), *Narrative and Dramatic Sources of Shakespeare's Plays* (London, Routledge, 1960), vol. 3, p. 75.
2 Hall, in Bullough, *Narrative*, vol. 3, 56.
3 *Ibid.*, p. 57.
4 *Ibid.*, p. 61.
5 Boileau, *Satire III*, in *Oeuvres Poétiques* (Paris, La Veuve Savoye, 1768), vol. 1.
6 Boileau, *Epigramme VIII*, in *Oeuvres Poétiques*, vol. 2.
7 Françoise Michaud-Fréjaville in Goy-Blanquet (ed.), *Joan of Arc, a Saint for all Seasons*, p. 45.

8   Rapin de Thoyras, Histoire d'Angleterre, *Histoire d'Angleterre*, trans. N. Tindal (London, Knapton, 1731), vol. 5, p. 453.

9   *Ibid.*

10   David Hume, *History of England from the Invasion of Julius Caesar to the Accession of Henry VII* (London, A. Millar, 1761) p. 336.

11   *Ibid.*, p. 347.

12   Voltaire, *Henriade*, quoted in Voltaire, *La Pucelle d'Orléans*, in Besterman, Theodore Besterman *et al.* (eds) *Complete Works* (Geneva, Institut et Musée Voltaire, 1970), vol. 7, p. 125.

13   Voltaire, *Abrégé de l'histoire universelle* (better known as the *Essai sur les moeurs*) (London, Jean Nourse, 1754), p. 751.

14   *Ibid.*, p. 752

15   Voltaire, *La Pucelle d'Orléans*, p. 125

16   There is a wonderful evocation of this world in an imaginative and learned account of clerical Angers, not many miles from Orléans, in J. McManners, *French Ecclesiastical Society under the Ancien Régime: a Study of Angers in the Eighteenth Century* (Manchester, Manchester University Press, 1960).

17   The archivist of the Loiret found the texts. The scholar Abbé Boussard copied them.

18   Quicherat, (ed.), *Procès de condamnation*, vol. 5, p. 313. Quicherat did not have access to the full text of the Mystère. It survived only in a manuscript in the Vatican Library, which was printed in the reign of Napoleon III.

19   Richard Wade, *The Companion Guide to the Loire* (London, Collins, 1979), p. 93

20   Jacques Darras in Goy-Blanquet (ed.), *Joan of Arc, a Saint for all Seasons*, p. 105.

21: Reviving the Maid

1   Southey, *Joan of Arc* (Bristol, Cottle and Davis, 1796), Book 3, ll. 355–9, 382–5.

2   *Ibid.*, Book 10, 693–4.

3   *Ibid.*, Book 10, 747–8.

4   Quicherat (ed.), *Procès de condamnation*, vol. 5, p. 244.

5   Laurent Salomé *et al.* (eds), *Jeanne d'Arc, les tableaux de l'histoire, 1820–1920*, p. 15.

6   J. Michelet, *Jeanne d'Arc* (Paris, Hachette, 1925), vol. 1, p. 11.

7   The information on Lingard I owe to Dr Edwin Jones, author of *John Lingard and the Pursuit of Historical Truth* (Sussex Academic Press, Brighton, 2004)

8   Thomas De Quincey, *Works*, vol. 3: Joan of Arc in Reference to M. Michelet's *History of France* (Edinburgh, Adam and Charles Black, 1863), p. 223.

9   Emile Faguet, *Mgr. Dupanloup, un grand evêque* (Paris, Hachette, 1914), pp. 239–40.

22: Holy Patriot

1   D.W. Brogan, *The Development of Modern France* (Hamish Hamilton, London, 1940, rev. edn, 1967), p. 83.

2   Anatole France, *Vie de Jeanne d'Arc* (Paris, Editions Alive, 1999), préfaces, xxxii.

3   *Ibid.*, xxxii.

4   Louis-Maurice Boutet de Monvel, quoted in Salomé *Jeanne d'Arc, les tableaux de l'histoire*, p. 9.

5   Sainte Thérèse of Lisieux, *Histoire d'une âme* (Paris, Editions du Cerf, 1972), p. 75.

6   See Sainte Thérèse of Lisieux, *Théâtre au Carmel* (Bayeux, Editions du Cerf, 1985), pp. 57–83, 117—61.

7   Just before she died, this pious and naïve nun was conned by a charlatan. Léo Taxil pretended that a certain Diana Vaughan had been converted by the prayers of Joan of Arc. Thérèse was allowed to correspond with him and sent him one of Céline's photos. Taxil called a meeting in Paris and in front of a copy of this photo revealed to his audience that he was Diana, that he had not been converted and that he had acted as he had in order to discredit the cult of Joan.

8   These words, put into the mouth of Anatole France by his secretary J.-J. Bousson, are quoted by Nadia Margolis in Goy-Blanquet (ed.), *Joan of Arc, a Saint for all Seasons*, p. 77.

9   Mark Twain, *Personal Recollections of Joan of Arc* (New York, 1997), p. 461.

10   On English artists and Joan see Salomé *et al.*, *Jeanne d'Arc, les tableaux de l'histoire*, pp. 115–27.

11   On Victoria's love of Gounod's setting of Barbier's play, see Marina Warner, *Joan of Arc: the Image of Female Heroism* (University of California, Berkeley, 1981), p. 322, n. 23.

12   Alphonse de Lamartine, *Jeanne d'Arc* (Hachette, London and Boston, 1886).

13   Andrew Lang, *The Maid of France, being the story of the life and death of Jeanne d'Arc*, preface, vi, viii.

14   This account relies on Henry Ansgar Kelly's essay in Bonnie Wheeler

and Charles T. Wood, *Fresh Verdicts on Joan of Arc* (New York and London, Garland, 1996), pp. 205–36.

15 *Ibid.*, p. 236, n. 102.

16 *Ibid*, p. 226.

17 Details on the three miracles, available on the website www.stjoan-center.com, come from a translation of Msgr. Léon Cristiani, *Saint Joan of Arc, Virgin-Soldier* (Boston, Daughters of St Paul, 1977), 154–5.

23: *The Cult of Saint Joan*

1 see www.scuttlebuttsmallchow.com/joanarc.html on the subject of Americans and Joan of Arc in the First World War.

2 G.B. Shaw, *Saint Joan*, preface, p. 25.

3 Dame Felicitas Corrigan, *The Nun, the Infidel and the Superman: the Remarkable Friendships of Dame Laurentia McLachlan with Sydney Cockerell, Bernard Shaw and Others* (London, John Murray, 1985), p. 88.

4 Adrien Dansette, *Histoire Religieuse de la France contemporaine* (Paris, Flammarion, 1965), p. 772.

5 Monseigneur Baudrillart, 'The Saint' from *For Joan of Arc*, London, Sheed and Ward, 1930) p. 111.

6 *Ibid.*, p. 112

7 Louis François Cazamian, *Andrew Lang and the Maid of France* (London, Oxford University Press, 1931), p. 3.

8 Charles Maurras, *Jeanne d'Arc, Louis XIV, Napoléon* (Paris, Flammarion, *c.* 1937), p. 78.

9 *Ibid.*, p. 87.

10 Georges Bernanos, *Jeanne, relapse et sainte* (Paris, Librairie Plon, 1934), pp. 61–8 ff.

24: *Vive La France! Vive Jeanne d'Arc!*

1 Richard Griffiths, *Marshal Pétain* (London, Constable, 1970), p. 161.

2 Jacques Maritain, *Jeanne d'Arc* in Jacques et Raissa Maritain, *Oeuvres Complètes*, vol. 8 (Fribourg, Editions Universaitaires, 1989), p. 695.

3 Charles de Gaulle, *Discours et messages*, vol. 1 (1940–6), p. 12.

4 Robert Brassilach, *Le Procès de Jeanne d'Arc: Pour une meditation sur la Raison de Jeanne d'Arc* (Gallimard, Paris, 1941), p. 5.

25: *St Joan: a Modern Heroine?*

1   Jacques Maritain, from *De l'église du Christ* in *Oeuvres Complètes*
    (Fribourg, Editions Universitaires, 1992), vol. 13. The subject of the
    Catholic revival in France, which involved the cult of Joan and in
    which Maritain was a central figure, requires a book in itself, for
    beside novelists such as Bernanos and Mauriac, poets such as Claudel
    and painters such as Rouault, there were historians of philosophy
    such as Etienne Gilson and Marie-Dominique Chenu and theologians
    such as Yves Congar, Jean Daniélou and Henri de Lubac. Many lived
    to a great age. Robert Bresson, the film director who was born in
    1901, died in 1999; he was the last survivor from a remarkable
    epoch.

2   Jean Anouilh, *L'alouette* (Paris, Folio, 1953), p. 188.

3   The remark is taken from Peter Bogdanovich's interview with Otto
    Preminger in *Who the Devil Made It?* (New York, Alfred A. Knopf,
    1997)

4   Shaw, *Saint Joan*, Preface, p. 23.

5   Wheeler in Wheeler and Wood, *Fresh Verdicts*, xvi.

Bibliography

THE LIFE

DeVries, Kelly, *Joan of Arc: a Military Leader* (Stroud, Sutton, 1999)
Lucie-Smith, Edward, *Joan of Arc* (London, Allen Lane, 1976)
Pernoud, Régine and Clin, Marie-Véronique, *Joan of Arc: Her Story*
   (London, Orion, 2000)
Sackville-West, V., *Saint Joan of Arc: Burned as a Heretic, May 30, 1431,*
   Canonised as a Saint, May 16, 1920 (New York, Doubleday, 1936)
Scott, W.S., *Jeanne d'Arc* (London, Harrap, 1974)

THE FIFTEENTH-CENTURY TRIALS

Kelly, Henry Ansgar, *Inquisitions and Other Trial Procedures in the*
   Medieval West (Aldershot, Ashgate Variorum, c. 2001)
Lightbody, Charles Wayland, *The Judgements of Joan: Joan of Arc, a Study*
   in Cultural History (London, Allen and Unwin, 1961)
Neveux, François, *L'Evêque Pierre Cauchon* (Paris, Denoël, 1987)
Pernoud, Régine, *Jeanne d'Arc per elle-même et par ses temoins* (Paris,
   Editions du Seuil, 1962)
——, *The Retrial of Joan of Arc: the Evidence at the Trial for her*
   Rehabilitation, 1450–1456 (London, Methuen, 1955)
Scott, W.S., *The Trial of Joan of Arc*, with an introduction by Marina
   Warner (London, Arthur James, 1996)
Sullivan, Karen, *The Interrogation of Joan of Arc* (Minnesota,
   Minneapolis, University of Minnesota Press, 1999)

THE MEDIEVAL BACKGROUND

Barber, Malcolm, *The Trial of the Templars* (Cambridge, Cambridge
   University Press, 1978)
Carstens, R.W., *The Medieval Antecedents of Constitutionalism* (New
   York, P. Lang, 1992)

Fraioli, Deborah A., *Joan of Arc: the Early Debate* (Woodbridge, Boydell, 2000)

Hill, Jillian M.L., *The Medieval Debate on Jean de Meung's Roman de la Rose* (Lewiston, Edwin Mellen, 1991)

Huizinga, Johan, *The Waning of the Middle Ages* (London, Penguin, 1968)

Jacob, E.F., *The Fifteenth Century* (Oxford, Oxford University Press, 1961)

Kennedy, Angus J. and Varty, Kenneth (eds), *Christine de Pisan, Ditié de Jehanne d'Arc* (Oxford, Oxford University Press, 1977)

Kieckhefer, Richard, *Magic in the Middle Ages* (Cambridge, Cambridge University Press, 1989)

Little, Roger G., *The Parlement of Poitiers: War, Government and Politics in France, 1418–1436* (London and New Jersey, Humanities Press, 1984)

Lucas, St John, *Oxford Book of French Verse* (Oxford, Clarendon Press, 1908)

Perroy, Edouard, *The Hundred Years War* (London, Eyre and Spottiswoode, 1951)

Rankin, Daniel and Quintal, Claire (trans.), *The First Biography of Joan of Arc: with the Chronicle Record of a Contemporary Account* (Pittsburgh, Pennsylvania, University of Pittsburgh, 1964)

Seward, Desmond, *The Hundred Years War* (London, Constable, 1996)

Vale, M.G.A., *Charles VII* (London, Eyre Methuen, 1974)

Vaughan, Richard, *Philip the Good* (London, Longman, 1970)

——, *John the Fearless* (London, Longman, 1979)

Willard, Charity Cannon, *Christine de Pisan* (New York, Persea, 1984)

THE CULT OF JOAN IN ART, MUSIC AND LITERATURE

Anouilh, Jean, *L'alouette* (Paris, Folio, 1953)

Bauchy, Jacques-Henri, *Une fête pas comme les autres (550 ans de fête de Jeanne d'Arc)*, n.d., n.p.

Boutet, Louis-Maurice, *Jeanne d'Arc* (Paris, Plon-Nourrit, 1896)

Claudel, Paul and Honneger, Arthur, *Jeanne d'Arc au bûcher* (Paris, Editions Salabert, n.d.)

Margolis, Nadia, *Joan of Arc in History, Literature, and Film: a Select, Annotated Bibliography* (New York, Garland, 1990)

Raknem, Ingvald, *Joan of Arc in History, Legend and Literature* (Oslo, Universitetsforlaget, 1971)

Rigolet, Yann, *Jeanne d'Arc, ou l'étonnante pérennité d'un mythe, à Orléans, de 1945 à nos jours*, n.d., n.p. Salomé, Laurent et al., *Jeanne d'Arc, les tableaux de l'histoire, 1820–1920* (Paris, Réunion des Musées Nationaux, 2003)

The Grove Dictionary of Art (Macmillan, London, 1996)

VIEWS OF JOAN: ANGLO-SAXONS AND OTHERS

Brecht, Bertold, *Saint Joan of the Stockyards*, trans. Ralph Manheim (New York, Arcade, 1998)

Bullough, Geoffrey (ed.), *Narrative and Dramatic Sources of Shakespeare's Plays*, vol. 3 (London, Routledge, 1960)

Cazamian, Louis François, *Andrew Lang and The Maid of France* (London, Oxford University Press, 1931)

Corrigan, Felicitas, *The Nun, the Infidel and the Superman: the Remarkable Friendships of Dame Laurentia McLachlan with Sydney Cockerell, Bernard Shaw and Others* (London, John Murray, 1985)

De Quincey, Thomas, *Works*, vol. 3, 'Joan of Arc in Reference to M. Michelet's* History of France' (Edinburgh, Adam and Charles Black, 1863)

Hume, David, *The History of England from the Invasion of Julius Caesar to the Accession of Henry VII* (London, A. Millar, 1761)

Lang, Andrew, *The Maid of France, Being the Story of the Life and Death of Jeanne d'Arc* (London and New York, Longman, Green, and Co., 1908)

Rapin de Thoyras, Paul, *Histoire d'Angleterre*, vol. 5, trans. N. Tindal (London, Knapton, 1731)

Schiller, Friedrich von, *Mary Stuart, Joan of Arc*, trans. Robert David MacDonald (London, Oberon, 1987)

Shakespeare, William, *Comedies, Histories, and Tragedies*, published according to the true original copies (London, printed by Isaac Iaggard and Ed. Blount, 1623)

——, *Henry VI, Part I*, ed. Edward Burns (London, Arden, 2000)

Shaw, Bernard, *Saint Joan* (London, Penguin, 2001)

Southey, Robert, *Joan of Arc* (Bristol, Cottle and Davis, 1796)

Speed, John, *The History of Great Britaine under the Conquests of ye Romans, Saxons, Danes and Normans their Originals, Manners, Habits, Warres, Coines and Scales, with the Successions, Lines, Acts, and Issues of the English Monarchs from Ivlivs Cæsar, to ovr Most Gratious Soueraigne King Iames* (London, William Hall and John Beale, 1611)

Thurston, Herbert, SJ, 'A Rationalized Joan of Arc' in *The Month and Catholic Review*, vol. 112, July 1908, 12–24

——, 'Joan of Arc', in *Catholic Encyclopedia*, vol. 8, 1910 (London and New York, Robert Appleton) (reproduced on www.newadvent.org/cathen/08409c.htm)

Twain, Mark, *Personal Recollections of Joan of Arc* (New York, Edward Mellen, 1997)

THE CULT OF JOAN: FRANCE AND THE CHURCH

Astell, Ann W. and Wheeler, Bonnie (eds), *Joan of Arc and Spirituality* (Basingstoke and New York, Palgrave Macmillan, 2003)

Bancquart, Marie-Claire, *Les Écrivains et l'histoire d'après Maurice Barrès, Léon Bloy, Anatole France, Charles Péguy* (Paris, A.G. Nizet, 1966)

France, Anatole, *Vie de Jeanne d'Arc* (Paris, Editions Alive, 1999)

Bernanos, Georges, *Jeanne, relapse et sainte* (Paris, Librairie Plon, 1934)

Boileau, Nicolas *et al.*, *Chapelain décoiffé: a Battle of Parodies*, ed. Gustave Leopold Van Roosbroeck (New York, Institute of French Studies, 1932)

——, *Oeuvres Poétiques*, vols 1–3 (Paris, La Veuve Savoye, 1768)

Chapelain, Jean, *La pucelle, ou, La France delivrée: poème héroique* (Paris, Augustin Courbé, 1656)

Dansette, Adrien, *Histoire Religieuse de la France contemporaine* (Paris, Flammarion, 1965)

Faguet, Emile, *Mgr. Dupanloup, un grand evêque* (Paris, Hachette, 1914)

Goy-Blanquet, Dominique (ed.), *Joan of Arc, a Saint for All Seasons* (Aldershot, Hampshire and Burlington, Vermont, 2003)

Hales, E.E.Y., *Pio Nono, a Study in European Politics and Religion in the Nineteenth Century* (London, Eyre & Spottiswoode, 1954)

Michelet, J., *Jeanne d'Arc*, vols 1–2 (Paris, Hachette, 1925)

Péguy, Charles, *Oeuvres Poétiques complètes* (Paris, Gallimard, 1975)

Sainte Thérèse, *Théâtre au Carmel: recréations* (Bayeux, Editions du Cerf, 1985)

——, *L'histoire d'une âme* (Paris, Editions du Cerf, 1972)

Tardieu, Marc, *Charles Péguy: biographie* (Paris, F. Bourin, 1993)

Voltaire, *La Pucelle d'Orléans* in Besterman, Theodore Besterman *et al.* (eds) *Complete Works* vol. 7 (Geneva, Institut et Musée Voltaire, 1970)

——, *Abrégé de l'histoire universelle* (better known as the *Essai sur les moeurs*) (London, Jean Nourse, 1754)

JOAN AND THE FRENCH RIGHT

Balladur, Edouard, *Jeanne d'Arc et la France: le mythe du sauveur* (Paris, Fayard, 2003)

Brasillach, Robert, *Le procès de Jeanne d'Arc* (Paris, Gallimard, 1941)

De Gaulle, Charles, *Discours et Messages* vol. 1 (1940–46) (Paris, Plon, 1970)

Foch, Marshal *et al.*, *For Joan of Arc: An Act of Homage from Nine Members of the French Academy* (London, Sheed and Ward, 1930)

Gildea, Robert, *Marianne in Chains* (London, Macmillan, 2002)

——, *The Past in French History* (New Haven and London, Yale University Press, 1994), pp. 152–65

Griffiths, Richard, *Marshal Pétain* (London, Constable, 1970)

Kaplan, Alice, *The Collaborator* (Chicago, Illinois, University of Chicago, 2000)

Maurras, Charles, *Jeanne d'Arc, Louis XIV, Napoléon* (Paris, Flammarion, 1937)

Winnock, Michel, 'Jeanne d'Arc', in *Les lieux de mémoire*, under the direction of Pierre Nora, 3 vols, Les France (Paris, 1992)

SPIRITUALITY AND FEMINISM

Astell, Ann W. and Wheeler, Bonnie (eds) *Joan of Arc and Spirituality* (New York and Basingstoke, Palgrave Macmillian, 2003)

Cristiani, Msgr. Léon, *St Joan of Arc: Virgin-Soldier* (Boston, St Paul's Press, 1977)

Greer, Germaine, *The Female Eunuch* (Flamingo HarperCollins, London, 2003)

Guitton, Jean, *Problème et mystère de Jeanne d'Arc,* in *Oeuvres Complètes*, vol. 6 Oécuménisme (Paris, Desclée de Brouwer, 1986)

Maritain, Jacques et Raissa, *Oeuvres Complètes,* vol. 8 (Fribourg, Editions Universitaires, 1989) and vol. 13 (Fribourg, Editions Universitaires, 1992)

Rearick, Charles, *The French in Love and War: Popular Culture in the Era of the World Wars* (Yale University Press, New Haven and London, 1997)

Warner, Marina, *Joan of Arc: the Image of Female Heroism* (University of California, 1981)

Wheeler, Bonnie and Wood, Charles T. (eds), *Fresh Verdicts on Joan of Arc* (New York and London, Garland, 1996)

JOAN IN PERFORMANCE

Hill, Holly, *Playing Joan* (New York, Theatre Communications Group, 1987)

Morley, Sheridan, *Sybil Thorndike* (London, Weidenfeld and Nicolson, 1977)

FILMS

Some films on Joan of Arc are easy to find, such as those by Victor Fleming and Luc Besson. In England, Carl Dreyer's and Robert Bresson's films can be seen at the British Film Institute. The papal newspaper *Osservatore Romano* included the Dreyer film in its list of the ten greatest religious films, published in 1995 for the centenary of the film industry.

WEBSITES

The following are useful sites for studying Joan of Arc on the Web:
www.archive.joan-of-arc.org (scholarly introduction to source material)
www.fordham.edu/halsall/basis/joanofarc.com (access to 'The Medieval
    Sourcebook')
www.heraldica.org/topics/france/jeannedarc.htm (Joan's coat of arms)
www.jeannedarc.com.fr (house and centre of Joan of Arc, Orléans)
www.orleans.fr (site for city of Orléans)
www.jeanne-darc.com (Joan of Arc Museum, Rouen)
www.scuttlebuttsmallchow.com/joanarc.html (Americans and the cult of
    Joan in the First World War)
www.smu.edu/ijas/index.html (The International Joan of Arc Society)
www.stjoan-center.com (enthusiastic introduction)

Index